Lost Cain

T. Daniel Wright

Lost Cain

T. Daniel Wright

Mockingbird Lane Press

This is a work of fiction. Names, characters, places, and incidents either are the product of the author's imagination or are used fictitiously, and any resemblance to actual persons, living or dead, business establishments, events or locales is entirely coincidental. The publisher does not have any control over and does not assume any responsibility for author or third-party websites or their content.

Mockingbird Lane Press—Maynard, Arkansas

ISBN: 978-1-6341565-4-7

Library of Congress Control Number: 2015934021

0 9 8 7 6 5 4 3 2 1

www.mockingbirdlanepress.com
Cover photograph: T. Daniel Wright
Graphic jacket: Jamie Johnson

Dyersburg,
TN
ARKANSAS
Lost Cain
*Memphis,
* Little Rock

Mississippi County, Arkansas

Table of Contents

For the Kid in the Pew

PART ONE

Prologue

The death of a small town in America isn't like the fiery swallowing of Pompei or the crumbling walls of Jericho. It never happens in an instant. Instead, like a man, a town is born. It grows and thrives on the joys and sorrows of the people who call it home, matures and blossoms as it comes into its own, then slowly begins the descent of age—until one day, like any creature in God's creation, takes a ragged last breath.

Three weeks before the state cut off access to Lost Cain, I went one last time to see the place where I was raised. The paved road had been dug up, leaving a wide berth of freshly tilled and uneven soil mixed with red clay. I parked my car next to the barricades at the end of Main Street, got out and navigated around the upturned mounds of dirt and half-filled puddles to the old abandoned store in the middle of town. The ragged sign that read "VR Dunham's Grocery" still hung on one nail above the entrance, swinging from side to side in the wind. The building looked ready to collapse. I didn't dare go inside but instead looked in through the dirty glass window. *It looked too small to hold all my memories*.

As a child, I had listened for countless hours while the old men in town tossed stories around the big oak table on the porch like a ball, effortlessly handing them off to each other as they drove down the field to score the winning goal. It was a scene that probably played out in hundreds of small towns across the country, but this place was different. Because it was my home.

Though years had passed since I had been there, the sight of the town brought back vividly the voices of all the people who loved me as a child. I couldn't help but hear their particular inflections and tones. As if they were all there with me, together one last time, talking around the big oak table at VR's and telling the story of our lives in Lost Cain.

From here I could look out at the world I had once known: Momma Jewel's house, the old cotton gin by the playground and the tiny courthouse with its simple wooden steps and blue vinyl frame. In the distance the faded white steeple of the Baptist Church peeked out from behind the row of abandoned houses. Next to that church, on a hot August day in 1967, the events that led to the town's demise were set into motion.

The men and children were out early chopping cotton that morning. Working each row with hoes in hand, they gently pierced the ground at the root of each stalk and tore away the weeds with a precision that came from generations of practice. Had they not been so hard at work, they might have noticed the tremors. Noticed that not only the ground beneath their feet, but so much else in their world was about to shift.

A death always begins with a simple act of God. It could be an eruption, a flood, an earthquake or some other catastrophe. But some acts of God are less colossal in scale, although equally divine.

Brucie Lunsford was sitting on her front porch sipping coffee when she felt the first tremor. In the line of trees along the levee, a flock of blackbirds bolted in unison and darted back and forth across the morning sky. Brucie put her hand on her porch railing and waited. A white nightgown billowing in the breeze down by the church caught her eye. It was a girl, heavily pregnant, walking down the road with tiny steps, as if worried the baby might fall out.

Chapter One

For the Sake of Propriety

August 1967

Lola McAllister

My bare feet against the dirt road was the only part of me that felt the least bit cool as I walked past the church toward Brucie's house. It was only six in the morning but the wet heat from the river was already almost more than I could stand.

It'll be hotter than hell by the afternoon. When I got to the house, I grabbed the porch rail and pulled myself up the steps, one at a time.

"Come on in girl," Brucie said. "Has your water broke?"

"Yes, ma'am," I said. Having the baby at Brucie's was what most everyone expected of me and I hadn't given it much thought, but suddenly I felt terrified and it all seemed to set in on me at once. At the top of the steps, I stopped and asked, "Don't you think I ought to go to the hospital after all?"

"I don't believe in hospitals," Brucie said, taking my hand. "Ever person I ever knew that went to one never came out."

Brucie had a shock of steel gray hair that stood straight up on her head. She led me down the hall, through the kitchen and into a back bedroom with yellow flowered wallpaper on the walls.

"Besides," she said, "I birthed all the McAllisters and most everbody else in this town. Where you're born means something. Tells everyone who your people are. Never you mind what advances medical science has made, I take the birth of a Lost Cain citizen over in Blytheville as a personal insult. Now, lie down there. I'll get your momma on the phone."

"Do we have to?" I asked and sat down on the side of the little twin bed.

"I don't relish the thought of Ida Pico in my house either, but she'd skin me alive if I don't call her," Brucie said.

"Please—" I started to say but fell back on the pillow when a pain hit me.

Through the doorway, I caught glimpses of Brucie passing back and forth with pots and pans in her hands. I heard water running and the strike of a match before the puff of the burner on the gas stove. Then the slow turning of the telephone dial, one whirl after another.

"Can't we wait 'til after the baby's here?" I called out.

With the phone cradled on her shoulder, Brucie walked into the room and opened the drawer of the nightstand beside the bed. She took out a small notepad and pen. The long white phone cord stretched out behind her to the kitchen.

"It's long distance down to Frenchman's Bayou," she said. "That'll be a charge."

She put one check on her notepad and walked back

to the doorway. After a couple minutes, from all the way across the room, I heard my mother's tinny voice scream through the receiver, "This baby's come early!"

"There's no need to holler, Ida, I ain't deaf," Brucie said.

Brucie made little checks in her notepad for each minute that passed while she listened to my mother go on about the dangers of a premature birth. There were several while Brucie looked me up and down before she turned away and cupped a hand over the phone. "Now, Ida, she'll be just fine here with that baby," she said.

I felt my face flush. I had snuck away from home and married Dip McAllister in January right before he got sent to Vietnam. My own mother wouldn't talk to me on account of running off like that so I was living with Dip's mother, Momma Jewel, there in Lost Cain. She was always going on about how excited she'd be to hold her ninth grandchild by the time the cotton came up in October. I'd been telling myself that when I came home with a baby in my arms, nobody was gonna waste much time thinking about what month it was. Call it wishful thinking, I guess.

Finally, Brucie hollered into the phone, "Ida Pico, I've birthed many a baby at seven months and not lost one yet." After the loud click on the other end of the line, she looked at me and said, "Not so much as a goodbye. She's a nerve-eater, that one."

You're telling me.

Brucie made another check on her notepad. She thought a second and then made one more. "I always get gypped out of that extra minute," she said. "Your momma's on her way."

"I call her Ida just like Trudy does," I said. "She's been nothing but terrible during all this."

"Fine by me. Whatever you call her, she's on her way," Brucie said. "You want me to call your sister?"

"Just cause I got married at seventeen is no call for a mother to say some of things she's said to me."

"Save your tears, girl," Brucie said, handing me a tissue. The day's not done and you might need 'em. First babies ain't easy. Now, do you want me to call Trudy or not?"

"She's gone to Memphis," I said. "I don't want Ida to come."

"Everbody wants their momma when they're hurting, girl. Trust me," Brucie said and walked out of the room.

I blew my nose and called after her, "Dip's mother loves figuring out whatever notion I get in my head. Momma Jewel's just like that." Brucie didn't answer so I talked a little louder. "Trudy always says Ida could wrestle the joy out of any situation. When Momma Jewel hugs me, she just about pulls me right into her. Ida can't stand it if you hug her. She'll just grab you at the elbows and poke her bony chin on one side, barely even touching. You there, Mrs. Lunsford? Mrs. Lunsford?"

I heard a little ding from the other room as Brucie slammed down the phone before she popped her head back into the door. "Pains gone for now?" she asked.

"Yes, ma'am," I said.

"Figured. Otherwise you wouldn't be talking so much. Now take off that wedding ring and put it on the nightstand. You're liable to swell up like God knows what." She disappeared again and the pain in my stomach tightened.

As if having a baby for the first time wasn't enough. Once Ida shows up, all hell is gonna break loose.

I said the word "hell" in my head all the time since Dip went to Vietnam.

Hot as hell—hell's bells—go to hell—

Language wasn't tolerated in the Pico house. To Ida, even "dang", "shoot", "heck" and "darn" were just substitutes for what you really meant and not to be uttered, ever. She'd always ask us girls, "What would you think if you were visiting someone's home and young ladies were running around cursing like sailors?" Then like always, she'd answer her own question before anyone else had a chance. "You'd think they weren't raised right, is what you'd think and you'd be absolutely correct. No one is ever gonna say Ida Pico didn't raise her three girls right!"

Slipping the wedding ring off my finger I tried my best to stop thinking about my mother. Brucie brought in a cold pan of water and wrung out a wet cloth, then rubbed it over my forehead. It felt so good, I just moaned in appreciation.

One of these days, I swear, I'm gonna say hell right out loud for the world to hear.

Ida Pico

After I hung up the phone, I thought to myself, *it's just like Trudy to be off to Memphis shopping when you really need her. This was all her fault to begin with.*

Those middle ones are trouble, I'll tell you that for a fact. If Trudy hadn't run off at sixteen and married that Leon McAllister, none of this would've been laid on my doorstep at all. Lola wouldn't have even met Leon's little brother, Dip, who I knew was too handsome to come to any good the first time I laid eyes on him. What I'd give to have birthed three plain girls instead of two beauties and Glenda. Thank God for sensible Glenda, my eldest.

If I had it to do all over again, I'd have packed up both Trudy and Lola as soon as they turned thirteen and sent them to live with my Aunt Nema over in Calico Rock. If I'd have known then what I do now, that's exactly what I would have done, no doubt about it.

While I was pacing around my living room, the coffee table leg reached out and bit my toe so hard it made me holler. I'd never noticed it before, but there was a faded path on the carpet between the couch and my console record player that wound all the way around the coffee table and back again. That was another thing I could thank Trudy and Lola for—I'd done worn a worry path on my carpet, and it barely ten years old.

I ran to the shelf in the den, still hopping from that stubbed toe and pulled out two volumes of the World Book Encyclopedia, then took them out to the garage. S-T and P-R were the thickest and usually enough. I had trouble seeing over the steering wheel of almost every car, particularly Pontiacs. I threw the books in the seat and hopped in. My eyes came just above the dash and right below the top of the steering wheel so that I had a little window of visibility so long as I held my head just right.

It's just like Johnny Pico to up and die while we owned a Pontiac. I'll never forgive my husband for that.

Lost Cain was only twenty-three miles north of Frenchman's Bayou as the crow flies, but the direct roads were all gravel. Normally I'd never drive directly, but take the paved highway up to Blytheville and then over to Lost Cain, but today wasn't what you'd call a normal situation. Driving on gravel roads always made me feel poor and common, which is exactly what I always tried to keep my daughters from ever going through. Now two of them were married into a family of cotton ginners and would probably spend their entire lives in that decrepit little town on Island Thirty Seven.

The ladies down here in Frenchman's Bayou never said so, but I knew what they were thinking—that the Pico girls had come down a notch in life. Trudy had run off years ago with a cripple twice her age, and now Lola was married at seventeen with a honeymoon baby. Only Glenda seemed to have made a good match with a policeman down in Memphis who was getting one promotion after another. They'd already bought a big house on the east side of town.

Crime in Memphis must be a booming busines.

It took me near an hour, but I finally turned my car onto the dirt road that ran through the middle of Lost Cain. I heard Lola screaming her head off a full block before I pulled into Brucie Lunsford's driveway. I ran out of the car and into the house as fast as my little feet would take me.

"Lola Jean, you are hollering to wake the dead," I said as soon as I got inside and set down my purse. "Do you think you could keep it down?"

I heard her whimper from another room, "I'll try."

"She's back here, Ida, make yourself to home," Brucie hollered at me from the kitchen. Pains are coming a good distance apart, so it's liable to be evening before the baby comes."

I walked on through the hall of the little bitty house, to the back bedroom turned and saw Lola for the first time in weeks. *She's big as a house.* Even with three fans set up around her, she was soaking with sweat.

"I want Trudy," she said when she saw me, which, I'm not gonna lie, stabbed at me a little.

"Well what you want and what you get's two different things now ain't it?" I said.

"Don't be mean, Momma. It hurts," she said and reached out her hand to me.

Tenderness don't come natural to me, but that don't mean I don't love my girls. I took her hand in mine and put my other one up against her hot face.

"All I've ever wanted from you girls is to do right," I said. "To be happy and do right, but when in doubt do right." *Happiness may or may not follow, but at least you can sleep good at night.*

I sat there beside Lola the rest of the morning while she went in and out of sleep. When Brucie came in with some fresh water, I said to her, "I don't think sleeping's a good sign. This baby's liable to be deformed or God knows what. Just look at Dip's brother."

Brucie just looked me up and down and said, "Ida, why don't you go get some air." She had a bit of a tone to her voice, if you ask me.

"Fine then," I said and walked clean out of the house.

The front porch was one of those ragged, added-on affairs that most of the houses in Lost Cain had, set up on big cement blocks, thicker at the bottom than the top. I kept fanning myself and thinking, *Has anyone in this godforsaken town ever heard of air-conditioning?*

I was about to go back inside when I saw Dip's

mother, Jewel McAllister, waddling down the road toward the house. I bristled. Lola staying with her in Lost Cain was a bit of a sore subject. I had wanted the girl to stay home with me while Dip was in Vietnam, but he insisted she stay with his mother instead. Said he worried about Mrs. McAllister being alone because of her diabetes. I suspected it was because Lola wanted so bad to get away from me.

Dip's mother waved at me and said, "I thought this is where our little girl would be."

"Good morning, Mrs. McAllister," I said.

"Now, you know I don't answer to that."

The woman insisted that everyone call her Momma Jewel, which bothered me no end. I felt ridiculous, at my age, calling a lady anything other than her family name.

"Good morning, Momma Jewel."

"I slept a little later than usual this morning," she said while she lifted one large leg, then another up the steps. "But when I opened Lola's door and saw that water, I knew she must have come on to Brucie's."

As a general rule, I dislike fat people. I consider gluttony to be one of the more serious of the seven deadly sins. I'll admit there was an easiness in Momma Jewel's voice that dared you not to like her and it was hard, at times, not to get taken in by it. However, I've never been one easily deterred by difficult tasks, I'll tell you that. If all that wasn't enough, her cheerfulness about any and everything life brought just told me that there was something untoward about the woman.

I held out my hand and helped her up the porch steps, hoping to God she wouldn't give me one of her hugs. I can't stand to be touched. Just then I heard Lola scream out, "I'm on fire, my God, I'm on fire!" Next thing I knew, the girl was at the screen door.

"God, help me," she said and flung the door open before I had a chance to do a thing. She came storming out and threw herself down on the wooden swing off to the side of the porch. I ran over and nearly slipped on one of the little sweaty tracks her feet left on the concrete.

"Lola Jean! You get back inside that house this minute!" I said and grabbed her by the arm.

"What can I do to help?" Momma Jewel asked.

"Run inside and get me something to cover her up," I said. As soon as Momma Jewel shuffled inside, I turned on Lola. "Girl, if I had the strength I'd drag you back in that house myself. I hope you know how much you're hurting your momma. Lord knows who's going to see you out here. I'm just petrified."

The girl didn't act like she heard a thing. Then Brucie came out the door with a short stool and set it down in front of the swing.

"What's taking that woman so long?" I asked.

Through the front window I spotted an embroidered lace tablecloth on the dining room table so I ran inside and yanked it off like a magician, then ran back to the porch.

"I think I'm going to die," Lola said.

"One more word, Lola, and I swear—"

"Careful with that tablecloth, Ida, my momma made it," Brucie said, then mumbled, "It woulda been polite to ask first."

Me and her's about to go round and round.

I threw the tablecloth over the porch railing beside the swing and saw a few ladies coming down the driveway toward the house. I hollered out loud enough for the world to hear, "This baby's going to die if we don't get Lola in the car and over to the hospital right this very minute!"

I knew that baby hadn't come early. But I'd been around long enough to know that as long as I acted like I didn't know any better, there'd never be another word about it. So as far as public discussion was concerned, this was a premature birth and should be treated as such. One word to the contrary and that child would be labeled a bastard the rest of its days. Every blessed woman in the county would pat my shoulder and nod their heads like they were sorry for me every time the subject came up. And I'd not have that.

The whole morning passed with all of us out on display—Lola sprawled out on the porch swing, Brucie on a little foldout stool between her legs, and me pacing back and forth. Brucie kept sending me inside for this, that or the other. Momma Jewel went home to make some lunch and several ladies from town came by now and then to check the progress and pet Lola with reassuring words. They kept telling her not to worry, that they had plenty of children without being in a hospital and that things always worked themselves out. I let them know right quick that this wasn't just any birth, but a premature one and that if that little baby died out there in those blasted mosquitoes, it wouldn't be any fault of mine.

Around lunchtime, a few of the men in from chopping cotton, made their way in our direction. As soon as I saw them coming, I hopped up and waved my arms to try and shoo them away. A few kept on, but once they figured out what was happening, they perked up their heads, all surprised, and turned away. I imagine they went off to V.R. Dunham's Grocery Store to eat their lunch on the front table and say no telling what about us.

By two o'clock I had dragged out every one of Brucie's TV trays, three potted plants and a hanging macramé table and used them to section off Lola's end of the porch. I'd never been so humiliated in all my born days. I hoped to God nobody could see.

Brucie insisted we open the front window and made me turn up the TV as loud as it would go, so she could hear *As the World Turns*. I finally managed to get Lola so that her back was to the street, but the girl couldn't be talked into going back inside, which I pointed out repeatedly, "Any sane person with an ounce of pride would do."

Mrs. Odell Brinkley

On my way to work at the courthouse, I couldn't help but notice all the ladies gathered around Brucie Lunsford's front porch. My first thought was, *I hope Brucie hasn't passed.* I'd been meaning for years to interview her about the settlement of this area back in the first part of the century—Brucie was a walking, talking history book and I knew her stories would make a nice addition to the library branch I hoped to get us someday.

As I approached the house, I saw Ida Pico scurrying back and forth across the porch in a state of near panic. I heard Peggy Beaufort, a younger girl with peroxide blonde hair, say, "The way people are going on about it, you'd think she was giving birth to the baby Jesus up there.

Well, I'm not afraid to call it what it is—fornication."

"You're just mad cause Dip fell in love with Lola and not you," a girl next to her said.

Naturally a little curious, I stepped around the crowd and onto the yard, careful of my new shoes. I was horrified to see a young pregnant girl on the swing with both her knees in the air. I had been trying for years to get everyone in town to have their children in hospitals. Not to be unkind, but quite frankly, it was so unseemly. *If not for the safety of the child, then at least for the sake of propriety.*

That was when I recognized Lola McAllister, the young girl who had married Dip. I had heard every female in town comment on Lola's speedy progression toward motherhood. Though the custom called for everyone to pretend otherwise in public, it was a thing that was said among two, or at the most, three ladies. Any more than that would be considered idle gossip. Most families in town understood and typically followed suit, should one of their own daughters come due a little earlier than expected.

"I refuse to be a part of this. I'm going home," Peggy said and turned to walk away. Then suddenly from the porch, I heard Brucie call out, "It's crowning!"

Electricity flowed through the onlookers, and I have to say that I was somewhat mesmerized by the thought of a new life coming into the world that very minute. Ida Pico hopped straight up from where she stood, like she might sprout wings and fly away. In spite of myself, I clutched my purse, and leaned forward as I tiptoed across the yard and peeked through the tiny open spaces of the ivory lace tablecloth strung over the rail. Absolutely enthralled, I took one step and then another toward the girl, my new white satin pumps sinking into the freshly turned dirt of the flower garden. Honestly, I tried to pull myself away. But I just couldn't.

Instead, while the wind blew the tablecloth back and forth, I just stood there, my head bobbing around like a fool just to catch a glimpse of something I knew was far beyond my reach. Behind me, the entire group of ladies had gravitated to the front yard and I heard Peggy say, "Would you look at Mrs. Odell Brinkley. If you ask me, just cause the woman's barren is no excuse to act like that."

"Shhh. She'll hear you," another said. "You girls, mind your manners."

I knew the women in town pitied me for having no children. A childless marriage was a mystery they could never quite figure out. It would be one thing if I were too odd or homely to get a man, like Dorinda Wilson, who lived alone on the outskirts of town. Dorinda was sufficiently odd and homely as to be considered above pity. However, a married woman of a certain age without children was something unfathomable to them. I glanced back in their direction and the ladies all shook their heads and gave each other sympathetic nods as they brought their hands to their chests.

"Hmph," Peggy said, lowering her voice slightly, but not nearly enough that I couldn't hear quite plainly. "Governess of all things beautiful in Lost Cain—that's how they introduced her at the Baptist Young Women's meeting last week. Just look at her now, standing between two rose bushes with her pillbox hat squeezed up against the rail while that Lola Pico—I refuse to call her

McAllister—is groaning on the porch like a cat in heat."

Manners or not, I decided I was going to give that young girl a piece of my mind and steadied myself on the porch railing. When I turned to face her, I saw she had grabbed the girl next to her and was walking down the driveway. They hadn't taken two steps before both fell to the ground. Around them, the other ladies held on to each other and leaned against the cars as the earth shook.

"It's an earthquake," Peggy screamed.

I felt the ground beneath me begin to buckle and tried to straighten up. Just then Lola reached through the railing and grabbed me by the hand. My feet sank further into the soft ground and she pulled my arm through the rails of the porch, pressing my face against the lace tablecloth. I tried to steady myself until the quake passed, but Lola had a steel grip on my hand. Above us, the boards crackled and then a railing snapped. I felt myself pulled halfway through and heard screaming. Down between Lola's legs, I saw tiny hands thrashing and a fat, bloody face, hollering like the dickens.

I was so overwhelmed I felt paralyzed as Brucie lifted the child into the air. It was a boy. My heart leapt with so much excitement that I feared it would burst.

Trudy McAllister

I was having myself a good old time, tapping my press-on magenta fingernails against the dash in time with the radio as I drove into town. I had spent the day shopping with my sister, Glenda, down in Memphis and then treated myself to a trip to the beauty parlor on my way home. That earthquake hadn't slowed me down a bit.

I just hopped over that shifting road in my little red Impala like I'd done it all my life. I was so excited to tell Leon that I might have actually seen Elvis on the side of the road in a black limousine with a flat tire on Summer Avenue that I didn't even notice the crowd across from the church until I had plumb passed it by.

In my rear view mirror, I caught a glimpse of my mother on Brucie Lunsford's front porch and did a double take. *What on earth is Ida doing at Brucies? This is just going to ruin my Elvis sighting.* Well, my possible Elvis sighting, but it was still a good story. Then it hit me—*Lola! It must be time for the baby.*

I slammed on the brakes and jumped out of the car. I was already a good ten feet away before I realized I had forgot to put the damn thing in park. I looked back. *Oh hell, it'll hit something sooner or later.*

As I came up on Brucie's, I noticed Mrs. Odell Brinkley, head to toe in white, hunched over a rose bush by the front steps like she was about to be guillotined. One arm was just swinging back and forth in the air. On the other side of the rails on the front porch, Ida was running back and forth holding a screaming baby, rocking it up and down in her arms. About ten or so ladies stood in the front yard on their tiptoes like they was watching one of those outdoor hippie theater productions that they do over in Eureka Springs.

"He's not going to make it. He's not going to make it," Ida said.

"Let me see," I said, taking the baby. I fell in love with the little booger on the spot.

"You're so ugly, you're just adorable," I said to my brand spanking new nephew. "Just as fat as you can be.

Would you look at that Ida?" I squeezed his big cheeks between my thumb and finger.

"That baby is liable to be dead by dark if we don't get him over to Blytheville this minute," Ida hollered, both her fingers stuck up in the air while she stalked around in a tiny circle. "Am I the only one in this whole godforsaken place that can see we got ourselves a life and death situation here? You give that baby back to me right now!"

"Ida, stop getting yourself worked up. You're gonna hurt somebody," I said.

"Don't you speak that way to your momma, missy." Her hands snapped all around the baby while I maneuvered him away.

"Ida, snap out of it!" I said.

Then she finally had the conniption fit I knew she'd been nursing all day, stomping her tiny feet and moving around in a tight circle, hands in the air. I'd seen her do it my whole life. Normally, I had more patience, but I was beginning to think she might knock that baby plumb out of my hands.

"You ain't no doctor," she screamed at me, swinging her arms straight up and down by her sides. "If you think I'm gonna sit around here and do nothing, then you got another think coming. This baby's come early and we—"

Finally, I had heard about all I could stand. I shifted the baby to one arm and did something I'd dreamed about since I was twelve. I reared back and slapped her right smack across the face.

"Momma," I said, quiet but dead serious. "This baby's eight pounds if he's an ounce. He's gonna be just fine. Now quit making a spectacle."

A few seconds passed while Ida stood there with her

mouth open wide. Then all at once she elbowed her way through the ladies, and stormed past her car without so much as a glance back.

"I'm too hot, Trudy," I heard Lola moan from the swing. I walked over and handed her the baby, then yanked the lace cloth from the railing.

I threw it over her and said, "Good Lord girl, cover your business," then turned to face the ladies in the yard. "All right now, I'd say it's time we all got home for supper. He'll just turn into another piss-poor excuse for a man." They all smiled because they knew I was right.

Down the road toward the levee, I spotted my red Impala up against a tree in May Prevost's front yard, the engine still running. Just beyond that a tiny trail of dust floated through the air behind Ida who was pecking her way down Main Street with her scrawny little arms swinging like mechanical ratchets on the wheels of a fast moving train.

"Ida Pico has got a condition," I said to Brucie who was too polite to say anything but didn't disagree either. Right then, the baby stopped screaming, and I could have swore I saw him nod his little head in agreement.

Mrs. Odell Brinkley

I had managed to wriggle through the porch railing and slide up on the swing next to Lola, who, once she was handed the baby, finally released my hand. My eyes didn't leave him for a second. I sat there next to her the whole time, while the other women came by to look. He was so beautiful.

Before I knew it, everyone had gone and only Trudy

and I remained on the porch with Lola and the baby. There was an uncomfortable silence.

How I must look, I thought to myself and reached into my purse for my compact while they both cooed over the baby.

My lipstick was smudged all up one side of my face and when I turned, I could see the faint imprint of the lace cloth handiwork embedded in the skin of my other cheek. I reached for my hat, only to find it not there.

"I think it's over yonder," Trudy said, pointing to the flower garden with a kind wink.

"Thank you, Trudy," I said, standing up. "I ought to be on my way home. Odell will be wondering where I am." I smiled at Lola and put my hand on the baby's fat cheek, then bent over and kissed his smooth forehead, trying my best not to cry.

"Well, I appreciate you being here for my baby sister," Trudy said.

"Of course," I said and made my way, barefooted, down the steps to fish my hat out of the rose bushes in front of the porch. It took me two tries and I cut my finger on a thorn, but I finally got it. Then, with as much grace as I could muster given the circumstances, I discreetly dug one foot around the flower bed until I found my shoes.

While there may have been a mean spirited soul or two in town that did the math and held accounts, Lost Cain, as a whole, was a pretty forgiving place. After Lola decided to name the baby Cain, in honor of the town, people became even more attached to him. Not a day went by that Momma Jewel's doorbell didn't ring a half dozen times. I know I went by every other afternoon to help give him a bottle. I even saw Ida Pico driving through town at regular intervals, her head just over the steering wheel, halfway smiling.

For years afterward, people would talk of the day the earth shook in 1967 and Cain McAllister came screaming into the world on Brucie Lunsford's front porch. All claimed to have been there at some point during the birth, whether they actually were or not. Leaving out all but the most pleasant of the details, the town created a gauzy myth that made people wonder if this boy wasn't meant for something. I wondered as much myself.

Chapter Two

No Comfort at All

February, 1968

Mrs. Odell Brinkley

It was one of those days that made it hard to imagine anything bad happening in the world. Unusually warm and sunny for February, everyone in town seemed to think up reasons to get out of doors. From my desk at the courthouse where I volunteered every afternoon, I could hear the faint shrieks of children from the playground across the street. On the radio in the mayor's office, Loretta Lynn crooned "you ain't woman enough to take my man," and I sang right along, thumping papers into alignment with the beat of the music before stapling and stacking precise piles along the front of my desk.

Across the street on the front porch of the McAllister house, I could see Lola in a rocking chair, giving Cain his bottle. My afternoon visits with Cain had filled a part of me I didn't realize was so empty. Lola would always greet me at the door with a pretty smile and say, "Looky here, Cain, Miss B's come to see you." I never would have imagined it before that day on Brucie Lunsford's front porch, but I'd grown quite attached to them both.

For so long I had been only Mrs. Odell Brinkley, barren wife of the successful auctioneer, President of the Lost Cain Homemaker Club, Member of the Daughters of the Confederacy, and proprietress of the only local residence on the Mississippi County Christmas Home Holiday Tour. Mrs. Odell Brinkley was held up as something to be admired. An exquisite wax figure perpetually on display for the town's befuddlement at its life-like qualities. But something about witnessing Cain's birth had changed me. Now, for the first time since I was a girl, I felt like anything could happen. It was wonderful, but also dangerous and unsure.

Pushing those thoughts from my mind, I concentrated instead on the plans and petitions to get Main Street paved. They were signed by every resident, all three hundred and fifty seven, and ready to be sent to the Highway Commission in Little Rock. The earthquake in August had breached the levee in two places and almost cost us the cotton crop, so it was by no means assured we would make the deadline for signatures. However, I was determined to make my mark on this town.

Just as I placed the last copy face down on the desk, I noticed a stranger's car coming from the west. I bent my head and looked over my reading glasses. The car pulled into the McAllister driveway and two uniformed men got out; one short and robust, the other tall and distinguished, both handsome, from what I could tell from a distance.

Something immediately sank inside me. I bit my lip and watched as the men approached Lola and Cain, the shorter man reaching out for the baby's fist once they reached the porch. I rose from my seat, but stopped before taking a step.

This is a family matter. It's not my place to intrude.

My throat tightened.

If Momma Jewel doesn't come out in thirty seconds, then I'll go to her, I told myself as I started counting out loud.

At eleven, the radio host gave an update and then introduced a new Conway Twitty song. At twenty-one, the shorter soldier took Cain from Lola's arms. At twenty-three, Lola's knees buckled and the other soldier guided her back to the chair. At twenty-six, Lola screamed. By twenty-eight, I had my hand on the door and at thirty, I saw Trudy McAllister, pink clip-rollers in her dark red hair, come running down the street.

Someone must have called. Of course, that's what I should have done; I should have called Trudy immediately.

I kept my hand on the door and watched Lola run to her sister and bury her head in Trudy's breast. They both fell to their knees in the front yard. On the front porch behind the screen door, Momma Jewel's thick shadow stood perfectly still.

The tall soldier went to Trudy and Lola and took each by the arm and led them back to the house, while the one holding Cain followed them inside. The screen door closed with a loud slap. I stood there with one hand still on the glass door of the courthouse and heard only the sounds of the children playing next to the peaceful house. *How deceptive looks can be.*

After a few moments, the McAllister door opened again and Momma Jewel, carrying little Cain, walked out, one leg pulling the other, sat down, and rocked the baby in her arms.

My hand fell from the door handle. I walked back to my desk, sat down and wept.

Lola McAllister

I sat on the couch while the soldiers talked to Trudy. No matter how hard I tried, I couldn't understand a single word they said. Nothing made any sense. They kept talking and talking, but all I could think of was Dip.

It never dawned on me that I might love Dip McAllister until one day four months before our wedding. He was picking up loads of cotton to deliver to the gin when he stopped by my house and asked if I wanted to come along. If Ida had been home, she'd have never let me go.

"Sure smells funny in here," I said when I got into his truck. Dip's face turned a little red and I realized it was his cologne.

"You want a smoke?" he asked.

Ida was sure to notice the smell on my clothes, but I could tell her that Dip and the men at the gin were smoking. *I'm going to catch it for even coming, so why not?* "Sure," I said.

When Dip tapped the pack and offered me one, I took it like it was something I did all the time. Dip was the only boy who never seemed nervous or fidgety around me, but I noticed his hands shaking when he lit the cigarette.

"Thanks," I said, real proud of myself that I didn't even cough. We drove along in silence until Dip pulled over to the side of the dirt road.

"I gotta stomp the cotton before I get the last load,"

he said. “It’s too bad you’re wearing a dress or you could come up with me like we did when we were kids.”

I threw the cigarette out the window and said, “I don’t see how a dress gets in the way of walking on top of a load of cotton.” I took my time getting out and at the back of the trailer, told him, “You first.”

“You betcha,” Dip said as he hopped up the side, and threw himself over headfirst into the cotton. Then he poked his fingers through the green wire mesh and smiled at me.

“Your turn.”

“Go to the other side,” I said. I kicked off my shoes and gathered my dress in my hands just above my knees. At the top, I sat on the ridge and put one leg over, then the other.

“Jump in, the water’s fine,” Dip said and threw fists full of cotton into the air. I jumped down feet first. When we were kids, all the cotton was picked by hand and playing in the trailer was as soft and light as jumping on a cloud. Now the combines did the work, but the bits of stalk and bud made the cotton coarse to the touch.

For a few minutes we walked in circles around the middle of the trailer. Dip smiled and sped up. I ran faster and faster, giggling, while he came after me until we both fell exhausted on top of the cotton. Dip pulled me close to him and kissed me. It wasn’t my first kiss, but it was my first romantic kiss and I was surprised at how much I didn’t want him to stop.

From that moment on, I could think of nothing but Dip McAllister. Despite anything Ida said, I saw Dip every day. If Ida forbid it, I snuck out of the house. If Ida locked me in my room, I snuck out the window. If Ida nailed my windows shut, Dip climbed the tree outside and waved to me goodnight. By Christmas, we were engaged.

When the soldiers got up to leave, one of them took my hand and for just a moment, I don't know why, I thought he was Dip. I jumped up and hugged him tight until Trudy pulled me away.

"Thank y'all for coming," Trudy said.

Then everything went dark and in the darkness, the soldier's words appeared and rearranged themselves in an order I could finally understand.

Missing In Action. No hope for recovering the body. Take comfort in knowing that whatever had come of Dip, it came quickly.

I take no comfort in that at all, was all I could think as I fell to the floor. *Not one little bit.*

Mrs. Odell Brinkley

I'm proud to say that Lost Cain gathered around the McAllisters, as any town should. The women poured into the house with covered dishes and good intentions while the men held vigil at V.R. Dunham's Grocery store across the street.

Throughout the afternoon, the house filled with far-flung relatives and loved ones. Not being family, I had hoped that I waited an appropriate amount of time before I stopped by. I desperately wanted to hold little Cain, but realized that getting to a baby in a house filled with upset women was a hopeless task. Now and then I caught a glimpse of Ida Pico's jet-black hair as she bobbed through the mourners, collecting dishes and cups almost as soon as they were set down. After a half hour, I finally managed to wrangle Cain away from Eupha Lovelady, a notorious baby hog. Cain nestled in and gave me the grin that had gotten me through many a bad day the past six months.

I didn't think I missed having children. Odell had a severe case of the mumps when he was seven, and his family, who sharecropped out at Number Nine, had never seen a doctor in their entire lives. Odell rallied at the last moment and lived, but his ability to have children didn't.

I often asked myself, *Would I have married him if I'd known?*

We could have adopted. Odell would've agreed. But knowing him like I did, I knew he wasn't the type of man who could ever love a child not his own. Forced to pick cotton from the time he was three, Odell knew nothing but poverty and hunger all his early life. His father pushed the children mercilessly and all had come close to death more than once from disease, heat exhaustion or malnutrition.

Odell ran away at the age of fourteen and since then, had made something of himself, but there were some scars only a wife could see. He never lost the feeling of guilt for leaving his siblings behind, three of whom died before turning twelve.

We had every material thing one could want, but many days I wondered what my life would be like had I married the man I truly loved.

Leon McAllister

We was all sittin' around the store telling stories about my baby brother, Dip, that afternoon after we got the news. I'd have rather been with Trudy, but she was with all the ladies. Something about bad news always seems to get men and women running in opposite directions.

They was all congregated over at Momma's house while me and the rest of the men come here to the store. I owned a little place in the middle of town called V.R. Dunham's Grocery. Had since 1953 when I bought it with some money I made playing cards down in Memphis. The rusty sign with the old man's name that sold it to me still hung outside. I figured I had better use for my money than a new sign. I was always a practical man when it come to gambling and business.

V.R.'s was the appointed gathering place for all the men in Lost Cain on occasion of election, public trial, coon tournament, marital discord, lunar launch and most of all—death. Men started coming by as soon as they heard the news 'bout Dip.

We was all talking it over when a farmer from way past the levee walked in. He was one of those old country people that only come to town every month or so.

"Whatta you think are the chances for a good crop this year, V.R.?" he asked me.

"Fair to middlin'", I said. No sense in correcting him, he'd just forget it by next time. The whole time we was talking, he kept calling me V.R. After he left, one of the younger fellas asked me, "Leon, how come you don't up and tell him your name ain't V.R?"

"Let me give you a little lesson here, son. You listening?" I asked as I straightened out the dirty one-dollar bills and stuffed the money in the register. "Now you remember this. Any man who's giving me money—well, that's just about the rightest man on earth, in my opinion."

The old fellas laughed and the young one said, "You something else, Leon McAllister, something else, altogether."

"Been called a lot worse," I said as I pulled myself off my stool with the bar that hung down over the counter and slid across, then climbed down the other side. The young fella got that look on his face that people who ain't used to me get.

Yes, sir. Been called a hell'uva lot worse.

"People used to call me all sorts a things when I was a kid," I told him. "Never bothered me. I'd just tear into 'em and before long they learned that one word to me and they were in for a fight. Nothing worse than getting an ass whoppin' from a kid with no legs."

I was born with unformed feet, tiny stumps for legs, and a balled hand with no fingers on the end of my left arm. My right one's as normal as any man's, though, stronger than most. They never knew what caused it. Most likely some medicine Momma took for her circulation when she was pregnant.

"Don't you ever"—the young fella started to ask, then stopped hisself.

I let him stew a little bit. It's a trick I did to get me by. People come across a man with no legs, they get a little out of sorts. It's part pity and part wonder, I think, but whatever it is, it puts 'em ill at ease. I figured out a long time ago that it made folks vulnerable to whatever I asked for, so I usually just asked for whatever I wanted. People always said I had a way with people, but that's all it was. My deformities never seemed to stop me from living a pretty good life. Learned to use the heels of my hands to walk when I was just a baby, and they said I got places no other child my age could.

"It's all I ever know'd," I told him. "I like to tell folks God got embarrassed by the mix up and figured the only way He could make up for my gnarled stumps was to make me lucky in cards and love."

"Don't seem fair to me," the fella said.

"Fair?" I said. "Hell, I'm married to the prettiest woman you could ask for, and before her, I did my share of this and that. The doctors all told Momma I'd never live past four or five, but here I am on the backside of forty and doing just—"

Then it hit me again about Dip. Barely twenty years old and gone. I'd raised Dip like he was my own when our Daddy died and now his own son was gonna to have to grow up without a father. My whole life, people was always asking me how come, given my condition, I never thought life was unfair.

Thinking about Dip, it struck me, *Before now, I never had call to.*

Peggy Leggett

The way everybody was just doting on Lola made my stomach turn. There I was standing in the doorway of the kitchen with a green bean casserole my mother sent over, and nary a soul had asked me if I was okay. Me and Dip were born just four days apart and had spent our whole lives growing up together. Probably would've gotten married if Lola hadn't come along and stole him away.

Belle Lanscomb waved at me from across the room. *Good Lord, what has she done to her hair?* It looked like she had a bird's nest on top of her head.

"Can you believe it Peggy? Our Dip's gone," she said with her mouth full.

"He wasn't your Dip, he was mine," I said.

"Was not. That one time you told him that you loved him in 9th grade gym, he just pretended not to hear you," Belle said. "Tell the truth, you only married Bud Leggett 'cause he looks a little like Dip, didn't you? Course Bud's not near as handsome as Dip. But he's got those sideburns like him—"

Lola's momma, Ida Pico walked between us with a stack of plates. "Somebody bring me those glasses," she said. "They'll need to be washed. Stop dawdling."

"I brought something," I said.

"More green bean casserole, how nice," Ida said as she set down the plates.

I was about to tell her how sorry I was when Theda Crawford barreled through the kitchen door with a plate full of fried chicken.

"Well, if it ain't the newlywed," Theda said to me. "Let me see that ring."

I still had the casserole in my hands so I poked out my finger. I had just got married to Bud Leggett over Christmas and so what if it was a little because he reminded me of Dip?

Theda looked over at my hand, squinted her eyes and said, "Now someone tell me where I can set this chicken down."

"Theda Crawford," Belle whispered to me, "must get up every morning and fry a chicken just in case someone dies." That was probably true. Theda was infamous for having a chicken at people's front door before a body was even cold.

Ida came back through the doorway with a pitcher of tea and said to me, "You gonna stand there all day, girl, or give me some room to work in this tiny kitchen?" She said it more like an order than a question. I plopped the casserole down on the counter and ran out the kitchen door. Out on the stoop, I started to cry.

I heard Belle say from inside, "I guess the honeymoon's over."

Ida said, "You're one to talk, Belle Lanscomb, I don't see a ring on your finger. Remember, a girl's got to be married before she's twenty, or people'll think she's spoiled goods."

Wiping the tears away, I pulled a cigarette out of my purse and lit it. *I'd'a wore Dip down eventually, if it hadn't been for that Lola Pico.*

Trudy McAllister

I was plumb worried about my baby sister. She wouldn't eat a thing and hadn't said a word all afternoon. The ladies were all trying their dead-level best to get something out of her, but Lola just sat there on the couch, rocking back and forth. I'd have felt better if she cried or hollered or something. Anything but that silence. Toward the end of the day, I snuck her off and walked her over to the store to see if that might help. Outside the door, I could hear the men laughing, but they all hushed as soon as we came in.

"Don't pay us no mind," I said. "The ladies across the street mean well, but all that crying is taking a toll." I led Lola to a seat over in the corner. As we passed, the men's eyes fell to the floor, one after the other like a line of soldiers drawing down their swords at the sight of her grief.

"Ya'll go on with your stories," I said. "I didn't come over here for more of the same. What kinda coke you want Lola?"

She just sat there like she didn't hear me. Leon got back to his story while I grabbed an orange Shasta out of the cooler and popped the lid on the opener fastened to the side. I stuck a straw in like I always did for Lola when she was a little girl. I had to bend down and guide her hand to the bottle. Then I sat in the chair with Leon and put my arm around him while he went on.

"Even before he could talk," Leon said. "Dip was always struck with me not having any legs to speak of. He didn't think I was pitiful at all. He'd try to copy the way I walk."

Leon started to laugh at the thought and could barely go on.

"He was only two years old, but he'd cross his legs Indian style and use his hands to move around, just like I do. At first it was right funny. But after awhile, Momma started getting worried he wasn't going to learn to walk like the other kids. Every time I'd come up from Memphis, I'd try to coax him into standing up straight. What was it I'd get for him down there anyway, Trudy? You remember me saying?"

"Chicken bones," I said.

"That's it! Those little butterscotch candies they put in the tin box. I'd say, now come on boy, get up and walk straight and I'll give you a chicken bone. He'd just look at me, stick out his tongue and scoot on across the floor. Did that till he was four or five, I think. Dangdest thing."

"That's how your Daddy got to calling him Dip," someone said.

"Is it? I never thought to ask, to tell you the truth," Leon said.

"Well, I guess Troy passed not long after he started calling the boy that, so maybe he never told you."

It went quiet in the room. I never could stand a room full of people and no one talking, so I reached over and put my hand on Lola's shoulder.

"Lola, did you ever know why they called him Dip?" I asked.

She shook her head without looking up.

The old man went on, saying to Leon, "Well, your daddy always said the way Dip's little head would bob up and back imitating Leon, reminded him of the first mechanical carnival ride he ever saw. Called The Big Dipper. So he took to calling him Dip."

"I'll be damned," Leon said, and squeezed my hand. "I gone my whole life and didn't know that about my own flesh and blood." He hugged me closer and said, "Eventually, Dip straightened up on his own, but I could tell when he'd copy me in other ways sometimes. It always made me proud." The men all pretended not to notice the tears coming up in the corner of Leon's eyes. I kissed him on the forehead and let my lips linger against his skin long enough to wipe his face with my hand.

Whenever a lull came up in the ceremony at V.R.'s, and make no mistake that's what it was, somebody else would kick in with a new story. Dip was a trickster and well thought of by everybody who ever knew him. There was the time he and Leon got arrested for stealing watermelons out of Les Inman's field or a joke Dip had played on an old teacher. After a while, like it usually did at times like that, came stories of other days and other people, lost and gone.

I had hoped the men and their talk might give Lola some strength, but nothing seemed to help. Once I got her settled in for the night, I took Cain from his crib and went out on Momma Jewel's porch to have a good cry of my own.

Across the railroad tracks, I could still see the light from the store and the stark shadows cast from inside. Like most of their kind, the men of Lost Cain grieved only through laughter.

Sitting there on the quiet of the front porch with the baby in my arms, I could hear them well into the night, and it comforted me.

Chapter Three

Bits and Pieces

1973

Lola McAllister

Cain grew up hearing stories about his father. I made sure of that. Everyone in town pitched in. They did such a good job, that I worried he thought of Dip as a swashbuckling hero or colorful jokester in a bedtime story. It terrified me that when Cain realized Dip was an actual person—a lost father who could never be replaced—that all those stories he'd been told would make it worse.

I walked into the den to find Cain, now all of six-years-old, sitting in front of the television as he did most every morning before school. Before I could scold him, he looked up at me, smiled and said, "You're so pretty, Momma."

Keep in mind, I was wearing an old pair of flannel pajamas under an untied yellow robe and still had toilet paper wrapped around my hair from the night before.

This boy sure has my number.

"Is that what you're wearing to school?" I asked.

Popeye was getting pulverized by Bluto on the TV set, so Cain was too busy waiting for the can of spinach to pay any attention whatsoever to me. I walked over to the television and turned the volume down.

"Did you hear me?"

"Yes, ma'am." Cain said, still straining to see the cartoon.

I took a gander at his latest outfit—it was a pair of red checkered plaid pants, red tennis shoes, a faded yellow tee shirt with the words Bad Company emblazoned across the front in metallic letters, and a belt almost as wide as it was long. Every morning I laid out sensible pants and shirts on his bed, and every morning, without a word he put them back and chose for himself.

"Where did you even get that shirt?" I asked.

"It's one of Billy Ray's. I found it over at Momma Jewel's," he said.

Billy Ray was Leon's ten-year-old son from his third marriage. He lived in Paragould with his mother, but stayed over at Leon and Trudy's every weekend. Billy Ray showed nothing but intense dislike for Cain, yet Cain followed him around like they were connected by some invisible cord. Cain had trouble making friends at school and I wondered if it was because he was the only boy in first grade without a father.

I made another attempt to wrestle his attention from the TV set and asked, "Do you even know who Bad Company is?"

"I just like the letters," he said, tracing the silver letters on his shirt.

"Fine," I said. I'd learned the hard way that there was no use arguing when it came to Cain and one of his outfits. “I’ll be at work when you get out of school, so you head straight to Momma Jewel’s house, you hear?”

Keeping his eyes glued to the television, he just nodded his head while Popeye stuffed Bluto into a barrel and tossed him over the side of Niagara Falls.

Our refrigerator was going out, so I had taken a job at the shoe factory in Blytheville to earn enough money to buy a new one. Once I made enough to replace it, I’d quit. I didn’t mind the work. It kept me busy.

I’d had several suitors after Dip was declared MIA, but I was so numb and overwhelmed that I had no interest at all. Ida pestered me nonstop and after a time, even Momma Jewel began to encourage me to find a good husband and father for Cain. Finally, I gave in and started to date someone about a year after Dip was killed. His name was Bill Austin, a sweet natured man around thirty who owned a farm not far from town. We dated for another year before he asked me to marry him.

I didn’t love Bill anything like I loved Dip, but I liked him a lot. It seemed a reasonable amount of time had passed, and everyone approved, so I accepted his proposal. In the foyer of the church just before the wedding, I nearly backed out, but Ida told me that to go on grieving over Dip forever was nothing but pure selfishness on my part and reflected poorly on her.

So at nineteen, a widow and the mother of a two-year-old, I settled in, and got ready to experience married life for the first time. Three weeks after our wedding, Bill Austin drowned in the Mississippi when his fishing boat capsized, and I determined never to marry again.

Bill didn’t leave me much after he drowned, but he did have life insurance. I still needed to work when big expenses popped up, but otherwise I could stay home and take care of Cain. I'd sold our farm to the neighbors and bought a nice little house on Pecan Street in Lost Cain behind the Methodist Church.

I kept the money the Army gave me when Dip died in a separate account for Cain, so that he could go to college someday and, I hoped and prayed, never to war.

Mrs. Odell Brinkley

The lady at the State office had asked me to send a few pictures while they considered whether or not Lost Cain would qualify for the money to have Main Street paved. So I stopped my car, grabbed my Polaroid from the seat beside me and snapped a picture of the road into town that passed in front of Lost Cain Baptist Church, a plain brick building with a high white steeple.

What little attractiveness the initial building possessed had been dragged down by a two story wooden addition built at a perpendicular angle to the back of the main sanctuary. Last year, a Methodist on the city council called it an eyesore at a meeting, so the offended Baptists overcompensated by painting the whole thing a brilliant white. The newer half of the building seemed at an odd angle to the older section and always gave the impression that one held up the other by a thin agreement.

In contrast, the Methodist Church on the other end of town was an elegant, weathered stone building about half the size of its Baptist counterpart. Where the Baptist building was plain and practical, the Methodists chose quaint and decorative. It was a pattern common in towns across the South—Methodists being the first land owners and Baptists, the poorer migrant workers who came to work clearing the land and stayed to plant once cotton had recovered after the Civil War, or as some still referred to it, The War of Northern Aggression.

I always liked to say that Lost Cain was bordered on each end of town by God. The two congregations had carried on a subtle feud for as long as anyone could remember. The town's population was equally divided as well, with the Baptists slightly ahead and the odd Pentecostal here or there. Though it wouldn't happen today, there was a time when a Pentecost would be run out of town on a rail. Pew jumpers, as they were called back in my day, were thought to have a destabilizing effect on a community, given their emotional and undisciplined faith.

Whenever I saw news reports on the divided city of Jerusalem in the Middle East, it always struck me how the world was basically just the same, but simply differed on the matter of scale.

On my way back into town I stopped at V. R's to get gas and when I backed up to the new pumps, I felt a jolt. *Goodness, I've done it again*. Sure enough, when I got out and looked at my bumper, the scratch was deep and pronounced.

Leon had put a new semi-circle of concrete around the new gas pumps at the store and my car seemed drawn to it like a magnet. It didn't help that the gas pumps were at the lowest point in the little gulley that made up the parking lot. I'd never tell anyone this, but I found V.R. Dunham's Grocery Store to be one of the least attractive buildings in Lost Cain. It was a large older wooden home that had been hollowed out on the inside to make room for a few small aisles and counters. Trudy kept the place tidy, but the building was so old, it couldn't help but look dirty.

For years, I had harbored a secret desire that it burn to the ground, so perhaps we could put up something nice. If the building had some history, that would be different. I'd sooner tear down the Taj Mahal than a shack with some history. The only thing V.R.'s could brag about was that someone was once shot in the parking lot during a fight between two loggers around the turn of the century when the land here was first cleared. Before I got back into my car, I grabbed my camera on the spur of the moment and snapped a picture of V.R.'s. As I waved the little photo back and forth in the air, I looked at the building more closely. I suppose it could be argued that though it certainly had no real beauty to it, the building did have character.

Trudy came out from the store and said, "I told Leon that concrete was too high."

"No, it was my own fault. I've done it a dozen times," I said and stepped in front of my bumper so Trudy wouldn't see the scratch and feel responsible.

"It's that slope coming down from the railroad tracks," Trudy said. "How bad is it?"

"You can't see a thing," I said and reached into my pocketbook and handed her a crisp five dollar bill.

"Was that you I saw at church on Sunday?" she asked.

"Guilty as charged," I said. "I had to drop something off."

The previous week, after teaching my Sunday school class at First Methodist, I dashed down the street to Lost

Cain Baptist just so that I could hide a Hot Wheel in the pew where Cain sat with Momma Jewel each week, then sprinted back to the Methodist church just in time for services and slid into the pew next to Odell. He looked over at me, breathless and wiping at my forehead and made an off-color joke about sweating in church that doesn't bear repeating. Odell had ranted daily about the gas money I spent on trips to Jonesboro to stock up on Hot Wheels, all so I could give them, one by one, to Cain.

Trudy took the money and said, "I thought maybe you converted. Now wouldn't that be some gossip for the Eastern Star meeting. The one and only Mrs. Odell Brinkley becoming a Baptist."

"Odell would shoot me," I said.

"Wonder what it is that sets churches to bicker like they do?" Trudy asked.

"In this case I can tell you exactly. I found it in the minutes of an old book they've got at the courthouse," I said. "It was all on account of the town's name. The Baptists wanted it to stay Island Thirty Seven and the Methodists forced Lost Cain in a close vote."

"I'm glad the Methodists won that one," Trudy said.

"I agree. Ever since, though, the town council has to have three Baptists and three Methodists. It's in the bylaws."

"Lord help us if they get in a tie," Trudy said.

"That's what the Mayor's for. This year we've got a Methodist and next the Baptists take over," I said.

"The things people find to fuss over," Trudy said. "Don't tell anyone, but the preacher at church always says the Methodists are just this side of communists, but that we oughta be polite just the same."

"Our minister calls Baptists dumb as rocks," I smiled and whispered, "and just as charming."

Trudy put her arm on my shoulder while she laughed. We had never spent much time together, Trudy and I. Her laugh was infectious.

"Oh, I'll have to tell Leon that one, he'll love it. I try every Sunday to get him to come with me, but he just brags on being the most famous backslider in town. Says if he came to church, the roof might fall in. You got time to come in for some coffee?" Trudy asked.

There was always a pang of jealousy I still felt around Trudy, even after all these years. I wanted to say yes, but didn't.

"No, I figure I better get going. I have to get these pictures in the mail to the Highway commission," I said. "Here, I took one of the store."

"Well, we sure do appreciate all the work you're doing to get us a paved road," Trudy said and took the picture from me.

"Y'all are liable to get lots of new business with a proper road," I said.

"Leon'll be tickled," Trudy said and went back inside the store.

All during the day, I couldn't stop thinking about the walls people put up between each other in life. Trudy and I could have been the best of friends, yet this history would always be between us.

Cain McAllister

"I'm here and I'm playing on the porch," I yelled through the screen door to Momma Jewel after school.

"No reason to holler," Momma Jewel said from the chair she always had pulled close to the television while she watched *Search for Tomorrow*. Momma Jewel had spells where her eyes didn't work how they're supposed to.

"There's nobody to play with, can I go to the store?" I asked.

"You just got here, now stop interrupting my stories," she said.

I went to the old tin box by the door filled with leftover toys from my cousins who were all grown up. Momma Jewel always told me that if I had been born ten years earlier I'd be so overrun with cousins that I'd be sick to death of them. I didn't think so. I thought it would be nice to have someone around.

On top of the old toys I found a gift, wrapped in blue paper. I snatched it up and knew what it was even before I saw the note attached.

"For Sugar Cain, From Miss B," I read out loud.

I had taught myself to read watching Sesame Street before I started to school. Momma always talked about how surprised she was one day when I read from the menu at Dog-n-Suds when I was just four.

I tore the paper off the box and gave a big wave in the direction of the courthouse, where I knew Miss B would be watching. Her giving me Hot Wheels was a little game we played. The car was a Red Baron and had a little scooped silver roof over a red buggy. I ripped it out of the box and rolled it across the porch to see how it would go. The ones that went straight and smooth were my favorites. This one curved to the left, but I liked it anyway.

"I got a new car," I called out to Momma Jewel.

"Miss B sure is sweet to you, now ain't she," Momma Jewel said.

"You wanna see?" I asked.

"After my story, now shush."

"But I'm bored."

"Cain Joseph, quit pestering me."

I knew that if someone on *Search for Tomorrow* started crying that Momma Jewel would let me do anything, so I sat down by the door and waited. Sure enough, after about ten minutes, I saw her reach for a Kleenex from the embroidered box that my Momma made for her last year.

"Hey, Momma Jewel, you got any peanuts?" I asked through the screen.

Momma Jewel never had peanuts. She hated nuts of all kinds. When she took a bite into Christmas fudge that had pecans hidden inside, she'd holler and wail. She said it was like eating beetles. Momma Jewel always talked about how food felt, not how it tasted. She didn't eat raisins because she said it was like having spider eggs in her mouth. I'd never tasted spider eggs, so I just took her word for it and never touched raisins myself.

"No, child, you know I don't like peanuts. Now hush."

I waited just long enough for her to start back watching the show.

"Do you think I could run to V.R.'s and get me some?" I asked.

"Go on," Momma Jewel said, waving her hand toward the porch. "Go on."

I took off running before she had a chance to change her mind. *It's a good thing somebody on Search for Tomorrow cries pretty much every day.*

When I got to the store, I hopped up on the concrete circle by the gas pumps and walked around it like a tightrope before I went inside. Uncle Leon was sitting in his chair ringing up sales on the cash register.

"Hey Squirt," he said and threw me a piece of penny bubblegum.

Aunt Trudy called out from behind the meat icebox that was filled with slabs of bacon, ham and thick tubes of bologna. "I was wondering how long it'd take you to get here."

"I got a new car, Aunt Trudy," I said.

"Miss B's going to spoil you rotten. Sit down, I'll make you a baloney sandwich," she said to me. She looked over at Uncle Leon and said, "I'm just happy I don't have to call her Mrs. Odell Brinkley anymore, every time I pass her on the street."

Uncle Leon said, "Yeah, Sadie's got less of a stick up her ass lately, though it's still there considerable."

"Leon," Aunt Trudy said, "Lola is gonna kill me if you teach this boy any more cuss words, so you cut that out."

She grabbed a tube of bologna and went over to the meat slicer. I stood by the icebox and watched the shiny round blade as it started to turn really fast.

"Don't you even think about stepping back here, ever. This thing could take your little fingers off like that," Aunt Trudy said, snapping her fingers while her other hand worked the tube across the spinning blade.

"I know, you tell me that all the time," I said. "There was a man at church named PeeWee Whittingham who got one of his fingers cut off at the cotton gin last year. Preacher said that it was a good thing he was born with six fingers and that it just goes to show you that the Lord knows what He's doing."

"Who told you that story?" Aunt Trudy asked.

"Uncle Leon," I said.

She shot Uncle Leon a look and grabbed two slices of white bread and poured ketchup on one side.

"It's the God's honest truth, Trudy," Uncle Leon said. "Just ask PeeWee to show you his scar next time you see him, right Cain?"

"Yes, ma'am," I said.

"You get you a coke and go out to the porch to eat," she said. "And stop listening to everything your Uncle Leon tells you."

I ran to the counter cooler along the other side of the store and pulled out a bottle of Coke. "Make sure you pick up that bottle cap," Aunt Trudy said. I snapped the bottle open and caught the bent bottle cap in my hand. When Aunt Trudy handed me the sandwich, I asked her, "Aunt Trudy, is Uncle Leon black?"

Uncle Leon threw his hands up in the air and said, "I swear to God, he didn't get that one from me."

"Why on God's green earth would you ask that?" Aunt Trudy asked me.

"Well, Mammy Pico says he's a perfect heathern. And at Sunday school they say all the heatherns live in Africa," I said.

Uncle Leon laughed out loud. "I told ya! You can't blame that one on me."

"Cain, the word is heathen, not heathern, and it's not a very nice word," Aunt Trudy said. "But no, your Uncle Leon is not black."

"Why do you live in a trailer?" I asked.

"Now Cain McAllister, go eat your sandwich and let me get some work done," Aunt Trudy said. Then she slammed the door of the icebox and said to Uncle Leon, "Lola has got to stop leaving this boy alone with Ida."

Outside, I sat at the big oak table against the wall and took two big bites out of my sandwich. A truck pulled into the parking lot and a man got out and went inside without talking. Through the window, I watched him go to the magazine rack by the front door.

The rack had three sections, each a couple feet high. At the bottom were comic books and movie magazines with glossy covers of famous people that I could look at as long as I didn't wrinkle the pages or spill anything on them. In the middle row was the farmer's almanac and car magazines that I didn't like because they got my hands dirty. At the very top were magazines covered by a thick plank of wood. I tried to get on a stool once and pull the plank forward, but Aunt Trudy had a fit. Nobody ever lifted that board when Aunt Trudy was working.

The man inside put his head down, and looked around before he reached for the top shelf. He grabbed one of the magazines without even looking at it and went over to Uncle Leon by the cash register. Aunt Trudy headed out from behind the meat counter real fast. The man mumbled something, then walked out of the store, empty handed with Aunt Trudy right behind him.

"You ought to be ashamed of yourself, Buck Hart," she said.

"Well, Trudy what y'all selling them for then?" the man said, walking fast back to his truck.

"That's Leon's doing, not mine," she said. "I go to Sunday school with your wife."

He got into his truck and said, "Aw, Trudy, I'm sorry."

"Tell Leona I'll see her on Sunday," Aunt Trudy said, like she wasn't mad anymore, and then closed the door.

The man started his truck and said, "Shit." Then he spun out his tires in the loose gravel as he pulled away. I stuffed the rest of the sandwich into my mouth and washed it down with the last of my Coke. I could hear Aunt Trudy and Uncle Leon arguing before I went back inside, but when I opened the door, it got quiet.

"You ready to go to work?" Aunt Trudy asked.

"Yes, ma'am."

"Take that bottle out back, then sort the rest and I'll give you an Orange Pushup if you do a good job."

I went to the small room on the back porch where I came every other day to sort bottles. I knew I'd get an Orange Pushup whether I did a good job or not, but I was still careful not to bust any.

Trudy McAllister

When I heard the back door shut and knew Cain was gone, I threw my apron down on the counter and said to Leon, "This discussion ain't over."

"Now, Trudy," he said, but I just ignored him and walked out the front door. I was just about to our trailer next door when I heard two honks and turned around to see Ida Pico's Pontiac approaching.

This is just not gonna be my day.

"Have you seen your sister's house lately?" Ida asked through the open window before the car came to a full stop. "I went over there to hang some paper in her bathroom and let me tell you, it's a pig sty. Lola's the only person I know who can set out to clean a room and leave it dirtier than when she started."

"Afternoon, Ida," I said barely getting a word in edgewise before she hopped out of her car, never pausing for a breath.

She was parked on the slope and had to put both her hands on the door and push with her whole body to get the thing closed.

"I just can't abide a dirty house so I end up cleaning a full hour before I even got around to the wallpaper. Then Lola gets home from work and ain't there ten minutes before she says she's got to go to church. Who goes to church on a Tuesday, I'd like to know?" Ida asked.

"She's got the bazaar this weekend to raise money for the Annie Armstrong missionary fund," I said.

"Well, if you ask me that girl's taken too much to church. All things in moderation," Ida said and shook her head. "Baptists. Another thing I have your father to thank for."

Daddy had talked Ida into raising us girls in the Baptist church years ago, insisting on the 'fire insurance' in case the Baptists were right about hell. By the time he died, Glenda and me were married and Lola refused to change to Presbyterian like Ida wanted.

"When I think of how many god-awful backward sermons I've sat through for the sake of my family," Ida said.

"Is that all you stopped by for, Ida? To gripe about Lola going to church and keeping a messy house?" I asked.

"Yes, it is. I'd think you'd be more concerned you're sister's living like white trash, but I guess I shouldn't be surprised," Ida said.

"Ida, you can't get to me like you do Lola, so you might as well give up," I said. "Bad mouth this trailer all you want, but someday I plan on seeing Europe, come hell or high water."

"Leon offered to build you a house two years ago," Ida said. "Lola told me, so don't act like he didn't. Why on earth you'd want to live like this when you got the money to do better, I'll never know. Don't you ever want more for yourself, girl?"

"Some days, yes, I'd like better," I said. "But it's more important to me to see some of this world than it is to live in a three bedroom house."

"Seeing the Eiffel Tower ain't gonna bring back your daddy," Ida said.

Every now and then, even with me, Ida could land a punch.

"You may be right about that, but it don't mean it won't make me feel good to see all those places he talked about when he came back."

"That war changed him. Why you'd want anything to do with Europe is beyond me," Ida said.

"I'm sure it is," I said right back.

"I swear, nobody but you and Johnny Pico could ever try me so," she said.

Though she'd never do it on purpose, Ida had just made my day. It tickled me to be in the company of Daddy as one of the few people in the world who could, "try Ida Pico so."

"You girls think I favor Glenda just because she's got that big spread down in Memphis, but that ain't so. All I've ever wanted for you girls—"

I finished the sentence for her. "Was to be happy and do right. I know. I hear it in my sleep, you say it so much."

She looked at me, a little wounded.

"Ida, you need to let Lola be, is all. It's hard for her being on her own," I said. "Church helps lighten her load."

Huffing in disgust, she got back into her car. Before she left, she stuck her head out the window and said, "I'll tell you the same thing I told your sister. Every day she stays an unmarried mother grieves Jesus so much that no amount of fundraising is going to help."

Her Pontiac swerved off down the road and I wondered to myself what Paris was like that time of year.

Cain McAllister

When I finished with the bottles, I went back to the front porch and sat with my knees up to my chest against the wall underneath the oak table while I ate my Orange Pushup. I liked to sit there so I could listen to the old men who came in every day to sit, drink Cokes and talk about the world. Under the table, no one could really see me unless they were looking.

By the time I finished my push-up, several of them had drifted in after work and sat around the table. I used the hollow plastic straw to shoot tiny spitballs onto Sam Lee's black shoes. Sam Lee was a really old farmer who came to V.R.'s every single day. Uncle Leon used to tell me all the time that Sam Lee was the most opinionated man in Lost Cain, but then Aunt Trudy would always say, "Look who's talking, Leon."

"At my age," Sam Lee said to one of the other old men, "I got every right, even a goddamn responsibility, to have my say on whatever I please."

"That don't mean we got a responsibility to listen to it," someone said.

"Then hit the damn road," Sam Lee said and spit tobacco juice into his empty Coke bottle. "We just put that damn Skylab up in February, now we gotta shoot up a load of astronauts to make repairs. Shit. If that don't got USSR written all over it I don't know what does," he said, and pounded the table above me with his fist.

They had already talked about Richard Nixon, Patty Hearst and now it was the Russians. According to Sam Lee, the Rooskies were behind everything wrong in the world. World famine. The Russians. Nuclear Arms. The Russians. Flat tires. The Russians.

"I can't wait 'til we fight those commie bastards," he said.

"Leave it to Richard Nixon to put a lab up in space, not so we could do experiments, but repairs," someone said.

"Don't bring him up again," Sam Lee said.

Sam Lee hated Nixon on account of the Vietnam War. Vietnam was a daily subject for the men at V.R.'s. I heard Uncle Leon say once that Sam Lee had supported going into Vietnam, and preached about it every day. "Now, ten years later, here he stands in the exact same spot cussing the people who took his advice," Uncle Leon had said.

"It was bad enough when Dip McAllister was killed in the Tet Offensive and that was six years ago now," Sam Lee said.

Hearing Daddy's name, I smiled, and wondered which story they would tell. I knew them all by heart.

"Things were bad then and ain't never got better. Trying to make it sound like that Tet thing was a victory for us. Shit. Tell that to Lola McAllister. You know they send home bits and pieces of Dip as they run across them over there. Sometimes an ear, then maybe a foot or a toe. Hell, ever time she goes to the mailbox there's no telling what she gets."

I had never thought to ask how my daddy had died. I only knew that he was doing something heroic and brave for his country.

"Bits and pieces of Dip McAllister will be coming for years before those bastards admit we never shoulda gone there in the first place," Sam Lee said.

As he got up, he kicked the table and his Coke bottle tipped over. Once he was gone one of the other men said, "I don't like him talking that way about Dip. It's not respectful."

"Do they really ship over body pieces as they find them?" another asked.

"That's just Sam Lee being dramatic. He don't mean nothing."

Tobacco juice dripped through a crack in the table onto my shoulder while I sat there and cried.

Leon McAllister

After the fellas cleared out and went home, I come out to make sure Cain was okay. Soon as I opened the door, I saw him, arms swinging, running down the street toward home.

Maybe I shoulda come out here and stopped Sam Lee when I heard what he was saying about Dip. I tried to tell myself that the sooner Cain got a thick skin when it come to his daddy, the better off the boy'd be.

A place inside me said different. Thick skin can't stop a knife that cuts deep.

Chapter Four

Communist China

August 1975

Cain McAllister

The the first day of school was the most dangerous of the year for a third grader in Lost Cain and I climbed onto the bus keeping that in mind. Everyone knew that Bobby Lee Brewster, a fourth grader who was supposed to be in the sixth, would pick a new victim every year from the third graders who had graduated to riding the bus at the same time as the older kids.

The men at the store called the Brewsters the meanest kids north of Hell. They lived on a farm up by Huffman on the Missouri state line. There was Bobby Lee, and his older brother, who I heard almost died once because he drank shoe polish out of an old bottle thinking it was whiskey. And a little sister, Terry Lynn, a skinny girl with an unusually long face who was in the same grade as me. Not many people in Lost Cain had much money, but the Brewsters were what Momma Jewel called "poor in spirit." She told me that she'd known his grandpa and that Bobby Lee came by his meanness just as natural as he did his blue eyes.

When I got on the bus I looked over all the empty seats. I had watched *Mutual of Omaha's Wild Kingdom* on Saturday and remembered that Marlon Perkins had said that the safest place to be was in the middle of the herd, so I picked one behind a fat girl toward the middle of the bus.

Hoping the girl was fat enough that it might keep Bobby Lee from even noticing I was there, I slipped into the seat. I guess I wasn't the only one with that idea, because a short boy who got on the bus at the next stop came straight to my seat and let out a groan when he saw it was taken.

"Let me in," he said to me.

I slid over next to the window, figuring that way, there'd still be someone between me and the open African savannahs. At least that's how Marlon Perkins would have put it. The boy frowned and took the seat across the aisle instead. I moved back over behind the fat girl.

"I'm Frankie Copeland," he said. "I'm in the fifth grade even though I don't look it."

"My name's Cain."

"I know that. Just like the town," Frankie said, both of us keeping an eye on the front of the bus. "This your first time?" he asked.

I nodded.

"There's eight more stops before the Brewsters," Frankie said. "Any kid that gets on after them is like one of those little ducks you shoot from a booth at the County Fair."

Each morning, the bus went from Lost Cain to all over north Mississippi County before coming back to where it had started three blocks from my house. Momma tried to convince me to walk but I was determined to ride the bus. I had heard Uncle Leon tell Aunt Trudy at the store that Momma was making me too soft. Aunt Trudy told him, “You lose two people like that and see if you don’t hold tight to what you love.” Aunt Trudy always had a way of saying things that meant the conversation was over.

Across the aisle, Frankie pulled an orange out of a brown paper bag and started to peel it. He stacked his orange peels in his lap while the bus rattled down the gravel road. “What you all dressed up for?” he asked.

I had on a pair of black leather shoes, brown checkered bellbottom pants that Momma Jewel had made for me last Easter, an acrylic mist gray shirt with a big collar, and a shark tooth necklace.

“I’m going to woo Miss Caroline,” I said. “That’s what my Uncle Leon calls it. I put on some Brute and everything. It belonged to my dead stepdaddy who drowned in the river before I could remember him.”

Frankie leaned over and smelled. Then he took his orange, threw it out the window and started to eat the leftover peels out of his lap like it was nothing special.

“I’m going to be in her room,” I said.

All during second grade, I had watched Miss Caroline from the playground during recess. Whenever she came outside, she’d take a bright scarf from her purse and put it over her hair, then tie it under her chin like one of the ladies from the Channel Three late movies I watched with Momma Jewel on Friday nights. The scarf would flutter behind her head like a kaleidoscope when she walked. She was the prettiest lady in Lost Cain

Elementary, maybe the world.

The bus came to a stop and Frankie stopped eating his orange peels long enough to count on his fingers. “Three more,” he said. “I’ll give you my other orange if you trade seats.”

I shook my head and Frankie got a look on his face like he was doing a really hard math problem.

“All right then, scoot over by the window,” he said.

“You was smart to sit here,” he whispered and pointed at the fat girl in front of us. “Next to Becky Atwood is the safest spot on the bus.”

“How come?” I asked.

“Over the summer, Becky walloped Terry Lynn Brewster upside the head for saying that Becky’s little brother, Scott, died ‘cause Becky sat on him.”

“Did he?” I asked.

“No, he fell off a horse and broke his neck,” Frankie said. “Terry Lynn went and told and Bobby Lee and he waited for Becky outside her house and pounced on her as soon as she come out. Becky almost beat the tar out of Bobby Lee. Ever since then, the Brewsters won’t have nothing to do with Becky Atwood.”

After a few more stops, the bus pulled up to the Brewster’s house. Terry Lynn came on first and looked over the seats with her long homely face. At first she gave Becky a sour look but then Terry Lynn gave her a big ugly smile. She strolled over and sat down next to Becky.

“That sure is a pretty dress you got on Becky,” Terry Lynn said.

I sank down in my seat and looked at Frankie who was staring straight ahead as Bobby Lee passed us by.

I wonder if this is what it feels like in Communist

China?

Somewhere behind me I heard loud thumps and whimpers. I didn't look, but figured Bobby Lee must have been back there, thumping someone's ears.

"All those pretty colors and flowers. I bet it cost your momma something," Terry Lynn said. Her lips slid up her crooked front teeth and her tongue pushed through the space between.

"My daddy bought it for me," Becky said.

"Well, then your daddy must be shopping at the Salvation Army, cause that's one of my momma's old dresses she gave to the poor," Terry Lynn said. Then she turned her head and said loud enough so that everyone on the bus could hear, "Becky Atwood's so fat and poor, she has to wear people's trash!"

Even from behind, I could see that Becky tensed up and I waited for her to hit Terry Lynn, who looked a little nervous herself, but didn't back off.

"I remember the last time my momma wore that thing," Terry Lynn said, still loud enough for everyone to hear. "She was feeding the chickens and got some poop on it and said it wasn't good enough for white folks to wear."

Becky's big shoulders started to shake as she cried. Terry Lynn just smiled that big ugly smile. It made me so mad I couldn't see straight.

"Terry Lynn Brewster, you look just like a possum!" I stood up and screamed before I knew what I was doing. As soon as I said it, I sat straight back down and put my hand over my mouth. I looked over to Frankie, but he was already gone. I saw two legs disappearing under the seat beside me. Then the hair on the back of my head stood up straight and I perked my head up like a gazelle while I tried to figure out where to run.

If it hadn't been for the thick Mead Trapper Keeper notebook I begged Momma to buy me at Sterling's Dime Store in Paragould, Bobby Lee might have killed me instantly. He was only on top of me a second or two before the bus driver lifted him into the air, carried him all the way to the front of the bus, and planted him in the front seat without saying so much as a word.

I grabbed the cold frame of the seat and lifted myself up from the floor.

The rest of the way to school, Bobby Lee sat, facing backwards, and stared at me. About the time the bus got to the end of our route, he slowly smiled. I looked away as the Utly boys came on the bus. Last summer the police had arrested them all for going around claiming to be collecting for the Humbolt's house fire, but actually taking the money and spending it at V.R.s. Uncle Leon was the one that tipped the sheriff off. He said anytime an Utly had spending money, something suspicious was going on.

When the bus got to the front of the school building, Bobby Lee jumped up from his seat and ran down the steps. I looked out the window but couldn't see him anywhere. On my way to class, I weaved in and out of the crowd and tried to blend in with the other children. Just as I got to my new classroom and went toward the door, I felt someone grab my shirt and pull me back into the crowd. Bobby Lee pushed me down to the ground. At first I tried to use my Trapper Keeper as a weapon but then figured it was best to treat it like a bear attack and play dead. I saw that on Wild Kingdom too.

"Tickle him, Terry Lynn!" Bobby Lee screamed.

Terry Lynn joined her brother and the two poked at

my sides so hard that I was laughing and crying at the same time. A crowd gathered around us and started cheering the Brewsters on. I was laughing so hard, that even the teacher who passed by didn't stop to help. The Brewsters kept at me and at first I didn't realize what I had done, until I felt something wet all over.

Dang that extra glass of Tang this morning! I swore I was going to punch Buzz Aldrin in the face if I ever saw him. Getting little boys to drink more Tang than a small body could possibly hold under extreme conditions.

Once it started, I couldn't stop. I peed like I never had before.

"Oooh! He peed in his pants!" Terry Lynn shrieked, then jumped up and ran away with her arms in the air, shaking her hands.

"Pee Pants! Pee Pants!" Bobby Lee howled as he got up.

I just laid there on the ground for what seemed like six years, then felt a hand on my shoulder and looked up. It was Miss Caroline. Beautiful Miss Caroline. She lifted me gently by the arms. "Let's go get you cleaned up, young man," she said and took my hand.

I had planned to woo her. First impressions are everything. Uncle Leon told me that all the time. Miss Caroline's first impression of me would always smell like Tang, pee and Brute.

For that, someday, I'm gonna make Bobby Lee Brewster pay.

Chapter Five

Arrowheads

Cain McAllister

From my window by the porch, I watched as Momma Jewel climbed the steps to our house with a shoebox under her arm. Once she got up the steps she took a second to catch her breath, then came through the door without knocking. Momma Jewel hardly ever left her house so I knew something was going on.

"Cain, Lola," she called out. "I got something to show you. Hurry."

I ran down the hall and peeked around the corner. "What did you bring me?" I asked.

"Cain, mind your manners," Momma called out from the kitchen.

Momma Jewel said, "Come see," and set the shoebox down on the table in the living room. She lifted the lid and took out a wad of tissue paper and unfolded it.

"Look what I found behind a row of hat boxes in my bathroom closet. Your daddy must have put it there before he left for Vietnam." Inside was a small arrowhead the size of a half dollar.

"Your daddy used to scour the county for arrowheads

when he was your age," Momma Jewel said.

When I reached into the box, I felt dozens more. Momma came in from the kitchen and I smiled up at her. "Look what Momma Jewel found," I said. One by one, I unwrapped them and spread the arrowheads on the carpet while they watched. In the bottom of the box I found a stack of faded white notebook paper. Across the center of the top page was written, "The Official Collection of Dip McAllister's Arrowheads."

On the papers were traced outlines drawn in pencil with a date and location written to the side in large block letters. I looked up and smiled at Momma again and I read the first one out loud.

"June 13, 1949, Found by Dip McAllister in Mr. Speck's field."

Momma Jewel sniffled and Momma put her hand up to her mouth. I took out each arrowhead and set it against the outlines on the pages until I found a perfect fit for them all. I turned over the last page of paper and there was one last empty outline left.

"September 4, 1952, Found by Daddy at Barfield Point," I read.

"I imagine that's the one Dip always kept with him," Momma Jewel said.

"Do you think maybe he took it with him to Vietnam?" I asked.

"I reckon he did. It was the last one he found with his Daddy, your Grandpa Troy. He always kept it in his front shirt pocket," she said, looking to Momma. "For luck, he always told me."

Momma got up and ran out of the room. I traced the empty outline and Momma Jewel put her hand on my shoulder. "I reckon he did," she said again.

At school the next day, I took one of the arrowheads out of my pocket and went to the front of the empty classroom where Miss Caroline was sitting at her desk reading a Photoplay magazine.

"Want to see my arrowhead?" I asked.

"Don't you want to go play outside, Cain?" Miss Caroline asked.

Out the window I saw Bobby Lee Brewster push a smaller boy down then take a red kickball away from him and throw it at one of the girls by the swings, knocking a bag of potato chips out of her hands.

"Do I have to?" I asked.

Miss Caroline took the arrowhead from me and rubbed it between her fingers. She smiled as she handed it back to me and reached over to the record player beside her desk. She winked and my favorite song, *Rocketman* started to play. I went back to my desk and watched the children outside through the window.

Nobody will ever want to play with PeePants McAllister.

When Miss Caroline had found me that first morning of school, she let me use the teacher's bathroom to clean up. The way she acted, you'd think some kid was tickled until he peed in his pants every day at Lost Cain Elementary.

"You put these on sweetie," she said, handing me a pair of green sweatpants that I cinched up around my chest. Then she took me to my house and put her arm around my shoulder before she rang the doorbell.

"Cain Joseph McAllister, what have you done?" Momma said when she opened the door. When I started crying she said, "What is it, Baby?"

"It's so good to see you again, Lola," Miss Caroline said. "Cain here was sweet enough to agree to go with me to Blytheville for a milkshake at McDonald's, if that's okay with you?"

"Okay," Momma said slowly.

I ran past her to my room and changed clothes. When I walked back into the living room, Momma wiped at her eyes and walked over to kneel down beside me.

"I'm so jealous," she said. "A milkshake in the middle of the day." She hugged me hard.

On the way to McDonald's, Miss Caroline rolled down the windows and turned the radio up as loud as it would go. "Don't go telling anybody about this little trip," she said. "It'll just be our secret."

She took off her scarf and let the wind blow through her hair as we drove down the road and I thought about how Uncle Leon would have been proud of me. I set out to woo her that morning and there we were on our first date. Whenever the other kids teased me, that's the part of the day that I thought about instead.

The bell rang to end recess and everyone ran back inside to take their seats. Miss Caroline lifted the needle off the record player and said, "Now if everyone will quiet down and get to work on your projects for the science fair, we can keep listening to the music."

I put my arrowhead back in my pocket and thought about the one Daddy took with him, laying somewhere in a field in a country far away.

Lola McAllister

I had tried to take a little time for myself while Mrs. Brinkley kept Cain entertained out on the front porch, but I couldn't sit still. I had meant to do some cleaning or maybe take a bath but found myself back in the living room looking through the curtain as Mrs. Brinkley talked and Cain listened in rapt attention

"They say that northeast Arkansas boasted the largest concentrated Indian population north of the Mayans," Mrs. Brinkley said, turning one of Dip's arrowheads in her hand. "Out on Chickasawba mound, I've heard tell that the Spanish explorer Hernando DeSoto himself was asked by a Chief to pray to DeSoto's God for rain in 1541. Later, when the Chief refused his demand for two hundred men, DeSoto wiped out the entire population!"

Cain let out a little gasp and she went on about the Indians who lived all over Island Thirty Seven years before.

Since Cain's trouble at school, I couldn't seem to get a hold of myself. For the first few weeks I made up reasons to go over to Momma Jewel's every day during the morning, lunch and afternoon recesses. I'd sit in her kitchen that looked out onto the playground and watch. Momma Jewel pretended not to know why I was there, and acted pleased to have the company, but I could tell she knew. Cain usually walked over to the far side of the playground and played quietly by himself. The few days the other children did approach, I would watch, my stomach in knots, while Cain fended them off. I couldn't hear the words, but imagined the worst. Some days I stood there at the window and cried the whole time.

The people in Lost Cain had always treated Cain like he was special. Whenever we walked into the gymnasium during a basketball game, it was like a giant spotlight was turned on and someone would holler, “Look there. It’s little Cain McAllister.” My face always flushed, remembering how, after Cain was born, people would count the months Dip had been gone in their heads, thinking I didn’t notice.

“My how he’s growing!” Someone else would say. They’d pinch his cheeks or tussle his hair, like you would a turquoise rabbit’s foot you won at the Mid South Fair. Like he was Lost Cain’s own little good luck charm. As if some tragedy might befall the whole town if they didn’t pay their respects.

After a while Cain asked if we could not go to the ball games anymore. I didn’t mind. I only went because I hoped he might hit it off with some of the children there, away from school. But the children of Lost Cain seemed to have gotten together and decided that as much as their parents paid Cain special attention, they’d all try to ignore him just as thoroughly. Then when the teasing started at school, it was almost more than I could bear.

It must be so strange for him. To drift between a world where he’s constantly adored and another where he’s consistently ridiculed. I heard Cain’s laughter from the porch and realized I had been pacing in a circle around the room. *I swear I’m gonna turn into Ida Pico if I don’t watch it.* That thought sat me down immediately and I pulled the curtain back as Mrs. Brinkley finished her story.

“In some places out by Barfield Point,” she said to

Cain. "You can still find bits of pottery and shanks of bones sticking out of the bank as the river cuts through. And DeSoto—well, he died two hundred miles downstream the next year from a fever. They just threw his body in the river to float above all the bones of his earlier victims. All the way from where we sit right here, clear down to the Gulf of Mexico, nothing but bones."

Spooked, Cain looked around as if a ghost might appear at any moment and I smiled, seeing a bit of his daddy in the look.

"I bet you didn't know you lived in all that history, now did you?" Mrs. Brinkley said.

I let the curtain fall and looked around the room. I had decorated this living room with the intention that it be a place of my own to come in and enjoy, but I hardly ever set foot in it.

"Don't make no sense to let the biggest room in the whole house go to waste," Cain always told me.

"Everybody's got to have a sitting room," I'd say. "Otherwise it won't feel like a home. This room's for company. You keep your bee-hind in that nice den back there, you hear me?"

It was the only room in the house anyone could call fancy. In the center of the wall facing the window was a white linen couch that I had re-covered last year down in Memphis. There were doilies and linen tablecloths covering every square inch of the antique tables I inherited from Aunt Nema over in Calico Rock. A big Oriental rug covered most of the floor.

Little knickknacks were scattered about. Things I picked up here and there when I went shopping with Trudy down in Memphis. A tiny gun that was really a cigarette lighter. A fat Chinese man whose arms held coins, like a scale. A jeweled ring box with large blue, green and red stones all over the outside cover.

I sat down on the plush couch and decided for a few moments at least to do nothing in particular. I picked up each little doodad, looked at it and then carefully put it back in its place.

I tried not to think about anything at all but simply enjoy the prettiness of the room. Then came the memories, as they always did when I was alone and quiet. I thought back to the day Dip left me for Vietnam. How I placed my class ring in his hand as we stood outside the Greyhound bus station in Blytheville. "So you'll have something of mine with you always," I said before he kissed me. "Now you give me something of yours," I said as the bus pulled up beside us.

A tear swelled up and hung on my eyelash as I heard Mrs. Brinkley saying her goodbyes to Cain on the porch outside. Next to me, on the table by my nice white linen sofa, inside the jeweled box that I never opened, set the arrowhead Dip left behind with me that day.

Along with all the luck he had left in the world.

Chapter Six

A Cake in the Oven

1977

Cain McAllister

I sat on the edge of the drained baptismal pool in front of the empty church and wondered if I was going to hell. In my hand was a little pamphlet I'd found in the foyer that showed cartoon pictures of people hung by their feet while flames licked at their hands and backs, taking off little bits of skin while they screamed in agonizing pain. Printed in bold letters on the back, it said that all had fallen short of the glory of God.

The Sunday before, we had gotten a new preacher at church named Brother Neil who looked a little like Han Solo. All during his fiery sermon, Brother Neil stormed from one side of the stage to the other, shouting the dangers of eternal damnation. Afterward, he stood in front of the church as the congregation started singing the invitational hymn, *Softly and Tenderly*, Jesus is calling.

Fourteen verses later, Jesus wasn't calling so softly or tenderly anymore, so I decided to get saved. I was old enough and figured a new preacher was as good a reason as any to get it done. I was walking down the aisle and practicing what I'd say to Brother Neil when one of the deacons pulled me to a seat on the front pew. While he started leading me in prayer, the congregation sang another verse and someone whispered, "Yes, Jesus," from the choir. I kept looking to see if Brother Neil was going to come talk to me, but he stood in front, swaying back and forth, his eyes closed and both hands in the air, one holding a big Bible. The deacon next to me kept asking questions I couldn't hear and by the time the singing was over and he finished praying, I wasn't sure if I was saved or not.

That's why I had come back to church. To nail it down one way or the other. I leaned back and lay down with my feet still in the empty baptismal pool. The sunlight through the stained glass ran across my face, and made me see flecks of blue and yellow and orange. I squinted to make little rainbows in my eyes. A voice from the back of the church startled me.

"Cain Joseph McAllister, you get your feet out of the Lord's Baptistery before I cut them off, you hear me?" Momma said. Momma's voice felt right at home at church. Silky and drawn out, but all business.

"Is Brother Neil gonna baptize me today?" I asked.

"Don't be silly Cain, nobody gets baptized on a Friday afternoon. Now come down here," she said.

"But what if I get run over by a freight train, before Sunday? Would I go to hell?" I asked.

"Of course not. You sound like one of those crazy Church of Christers, down at the levee. Now you be good when Brother Neil comes to talk to you. None of that silly talk. You're almost eleven-years-old now, practically grown." She licked her fingers and ran them over the cow lick on the back of my head.

"Yes, ma'am."

"And don't you ask him too many questions, you hear?"

"Yes, ma'am."

She walked away and then turned back before she closed the door. "I'm real proud of you, Cain."

Once I was alone in the sanctuary again, I ran back up to the baptismal pool and sat down on the edge. I couldn't have ever gotten this close if there was water in it. Anytime I thought about going under water, even if it was just in the bathtub, I got this sick feeling in my stomach. Sometimes I threw up. Sometimes I passed out.

It all started when Gary Edrington asked me to spend the night at his house when I was in the second grade. We walked the two miles out of town to where Gary lived, just on this side of Big Slough Ditch. When we got to his house, Gary and me decided to build a raft by tying a few logs together and putting a flat piece of cardboard over them. I had seen this in the movie *Swiss Family Robinson* that Aunt Trudy took me to see over at the Capital Theater in Paragould the year before. Of course, the Robinsons had wood instead of cardboard, but I figured it would work pretty much the same.

We put some food in a Styrofoam cooler and floated about ten feet out. For a few minutes everything seemed to be going all right, then Gary reached for some Twinkies and the whole thing turned right over, sending us both into the water. As I fell over I grabbed onto the little white cooler, but it broke into pieces in my hands. Before I knew it, I couldn't breathe. Everything started going black and quiet. I don't remember anything specific, only a feeling.

Like I was being pushed down so hard that it was squeezing the breath out of me. Momma said that Mr. Edrington spent ten minutes trying to get me to breathe when he pulled me out of the creek after Gary ran in to get him.

All I remember afterward is waking up with Mr. Edrington leaning over me, and Gary sitting next to him eating one of those Twinkies. Right after they got me up, I saw Momma and Mrs. Edrington come running down the levee. Mrs. Edrington grabbed Gary so hard the Twinkie flew out of his hands, back into the creek. She told him to pull down his pants as she pulled the twigs and leaves from a switch she yanked off a nearby chinaberry tree. Gary did just what she said and she started to hit him. Little red whelps came up and Momma turned my head away, still holding me tight. I couldn't see but I could hear Gary yelp as his mother kept hitting him.

Gary didn't come to school the next two days. When he finally did come back, he told me that he wished I'd have drowned. I told him that if he wasn't so fat we probably wouldn't of fell over in the first place. Ever since then though, I don't get anywhere near water if I can help it.

For a little bit, I thought about what it would feel like to be a preacher and then climbed over the railing in front of the baptistery so I could stand behind the pulpit and imagine it. I loved church. It was the one place in the world where I knew exactly where I stood. I was a no-good, dirty, rotten sinner who's better than anybody else on earth. At least that seemed to be the gist of it.

"Brothers and Sisters! I am here to tell you!" I hollered out at the empty church, my voice echoed back and it made me feel strong.

"The time has come for you to stop your evil shenanigans," I turned and faced the wooden cross above the baptistery and stretched out my arms like Jesus. "Turn from your sinful ways and come seek the forgiveness of the LOOORRRDDD!" I tried to draw out the word like Brother Neil did in his sermon. When I turned back I saw Brother Neil standing by the last row, smiling. I ducked down behind the pulpit.

"So, looks like we got ourselves a future preacher here," he said.

I stood up and said, "I'm real sorry—"

"Don't be silly," he said. "We are going to need all the preachers we can get, the direction this world's heading. Why don't you come around here, so we can talk?"

He put one hand on my shoulder and led me to a seat on the first pew. "Your momma tells me that you want to get baptized. Is that true?"

"Yes, sir."

"Do you know what it means to get baptized, Son?"

"It means I don't wanna go to Hell," I said.

Brother Neil looked at me like I had said something funny. "Yes, it does mean that, but it has to mean more," he said.

Thinking back on the pictures in the pamphlet of the people being tortured, I wasn't sure what more it could mean. It's all the information I figured was needed. It's not a place I wanted to go. And not going there was one good dunk away. No matter how much I hated the thought of going under water.

"Have you accepted the Lord Jesus Christ as your personal Savior?" Brother Neil asked.

Now I was getting confused. I'd sat through hundreds of puppet shows, thousands of hymns, and countless Bible stories, all telling me that Jesus Christ **was** my personal Lord and Savior. I wasn't under the impression that it was up for debate. Brother Neil might as well've asked if I accepted the sun coming up every morning. It's a fact, whether you accept it or not. Then I started thinking that if Brother Neil didn't know what that meant, how could I be sure he even knew how to baptize a person the right way, anyway? All I needed was to get to the Pearly Gates up yonder and be told that I had an invalid baptism. It happened to Momma Jewel the other day at the DMV over in Blytheville. They said her license was invalid and had expired in 1961. Who's to say Heaven didn't work the same as the DMV?

"Do you know what that means?" Brother Neil asked. "To accept Jesus Christ as your personal Lord and Savior?"

"Maybe I need to think this over some more," I finally got out. *Who'd a thought getting saved would be so complicated?*

"I think that's a good idea," Brother Neil said. "It's the most important decision you'll ever make."

"Tell me something I don't already know," I said and pulled the little pamphlet out of my pocket, waving it in the air. "I've seen the pictures!"

"Why don't you think it over and we can talk more about it later," he said. "You know, I've got a boy about your age. He always hates it when we move to a new town where he doesn't know anyone. I think the two of you might hit it off all right. Why don't you come by for supper tonight, and I can introduce you?"

Brother Neil walked me out through the foyer and opened the door.

"You just come by our house around six o'clock," he said and closed the door. Alone on the church steps, I began to think over the possibilities. School was already out for the summer, so nobody would know to get to the new kid and tell him that I was Pee Pants McAllister.

Maybe I could have a best friend.

All of a sudden, Hell didn't seem that important anymore.

Trudy McAllister

There wasn't a soul in the store on a Friday afternoon and I could finally get a little organizing done. I had sent Leon and Billy Ray over to Momma Jewel's to work on setting her down some walking stones through her front yard. She'd been after Leon about those things for as long as I could remember. Besides, I needed the place to myself to get any real work done. There's nothing like men underfoot to get in the way of real progress, that was my motto.

No sooner did I get everything laid out to make new aisle labels, but Peggy Leggett ran through the door like her dress was on fire. I'd never liked that girl one ounce. Face so flat you could serve supper on it. I made my way up to the counter while Peggy stood there, shifting to one foot, then the other, just a huffing, like it took me an hour.

"I got a cake in the oven," she said, as if that made up for treating me like hired help. I got her regular order ready.

"So what do you think of our new preacher, Trudy?"

she asked.

"Too soon to tell, I guess. But he seems a good sort," I said.

It drove Peggy nuts when someone didn't ask her opinion about something so I made sure not to, just out of spite. She'd always been downright rude to Lola, and if you were mean to my baby sister, you'd better believe I noticed.

"Well, I'm just pleased as punch," she said. "Brother Ben was older than God. I didn't think he'd ever retire! It feels so good to have someone in the pulpit us young folks can relate to."

"Uh, huh," I said, trying to show as little interest as humanly possible. Sadly, Peggy rarely needed encouragement to keep a conversation going.

"I've had nothing but good reports from my contacts down in Mississippi. They say he left a church three times as big as ours on nothing but the calling of the Holy Spirit."

Now, I'm not above idle gossip now and then, but not with the likes of Peggy Leggett. I handed her the bag and said, "The Lord works in mysterious ways, I guess," and left it at that. Peggy went on a full ten minutes more. Finally, I left her standing there and went back to work on my labels. Wouldn't you know it, the woman followed me down the dog food aisle and stood there yakking on while I worked. She went on, barely taking time for a breath between sentences.

A cake in the oven my ass.

Cain McAllister

As I came up on Momma Jewel's house, Uncle Leon and my cousin, Billy Ray were working in front of Momma Jewel's house. Billy Ray was sixteen and for some reason, hated me more than anything else on earth. I never could figure out why. I never did anything to him except get Aunt Trudy to make him play with me when he came to visit.

Billy Ray picked up a big slate stone and moaned to Uncle Leon, "Cain don't never have to do nothing around here, Daddy. Hell, this ain't even my house."

Uncle Leon was out of his wheelchair and it always surprised me how fast he got around without it. He didn't say anything to Billy Ray, but just kept on working. Uncle Leon could ignore a person like nobody's business.

"It ain't fair," Billy Ray said.

"It ain't fair!" I hollered back at him as I went into the house. "I can't even lift one of those things, how do you figure I'm gonna help?"

"Go on in, Cain, and leave us be," Uncle Leon said. I went inside and decided to turn around and stick my tongue out at Billy Ray through the screen door. That was when he flipped me the finger.

"Momma Jewel! Momma Jewel! Billy Ray just gave me the finger!" I screamed into the house. I turned back to the screen door and hollered out, "You're going to Hell for that Billy Ray! You're gonna go straight to Hell, do not pass Go, do not collect two hundred dollars!"

Momma Jewel came in from the kitchen wearing an apron with patches of flour peppered on the front, carrying a big wooden spoon in her hand.

"What did you say young man?" she asked me.

"Billy Ray gave me the finger, Momma Jewel!" I said with shock and excitement. I had seen people give the finger before, but this was the first time it was done straight at me. I felt a little honored, like I had just won a Cub Scout award or something. Momma Jewel walked over to the screen door and gave Billy Ray one of her looks.

"Billy Ray, you come on up here," she said. Billy Ray let one of the big stones drop and walked up the steps staring at me like murder. I moved back a step and touched Momma Jewel's apron like it was going to protect me. Billy Ray got to the door and stood there.

"Don't make me talk to you through that screen door," Momma Jewel said. Billy Ray walked in.

"Yes, ma'am," he said.

"Did you give Cain the finger, Billy Ray McAllister?" she asked, pointing her spoon at him.

"No, ma'am, I sure didn't, Momma Jewel," Billy Ray said, just as plain as if it was the truth.

I gasped.

He's lying to Momma Jewel!

I didn't even know it was possible. If there were any doubts left as to Billy Ray's eternal destination, they were gone then. Not that I had many to begin with.

"You did too!" I yelled.

Momma Jewel looked at Billy Ray. He shook his head. She turned to me and lifted up her chin and raised her eyebrows. I was just looking at that wooden spoon.

"Cain, did you or did you not see your cousin givin' you the finger?" she asked.

I hesitated.

That was all it took. "I thought I did," I said, knowing full well that I did.

"Well, did you or didn't you?" Momma Jewel said.

"I don't know," I said.

"Well, next time, I suggest you be sure. Now, Billy Ray, go help your daddy lay my walkin' path. Heaven knows I've waited five years for that thing and if it don't get done now, I'll be tracking through the mud every time it rains for the next five." Momma Jewel turned and walked back to the kitchen, leaving Billy Ray and me alone in the hall.

I looked at Billy Ray with astonishment and a certain amount of respect. He slapped me upside the head and walked out the screen door. Halfway down the path, he turned around and gave me not one, but two fingers as he walked backwards. For a second it dawned on me that maybe there was such a thing as sin without punishment. I hadn't considered it before. *Did I really need to get saved after all?* If not, then I could follow through on all those evil and sordid schemes of revenge I'd planned for Bobby Lee Brewster the past three years but was too afraid to try.

Before I got too far into my new life of sinful freedom, Billy Ray, still giving me the fingers, tripped and fell back, splitting his head open on one of the large stones in the yard. I guess he had tested the waters for me and paid the price.

Momma and Aunt Trudy ran over after Momma Jewel called and they all piled into Aunt Trudy's station wagon, Momma driving, Uncle Leon in the passenger side and Aunt Trudy in the back, holding Billy Ray while he hollered. Momma Jewel and me walked up to the car just as they were about to leave and I leaned in.

"I don't see what they're gonna sew him up for since it's obvious that this is God's punishment for his evil ways and he is heading straight down the path to Hell," I said.

Uncle Leon laughed and Momma Jewel cracked me on the head with her wooden spoon. "Stop talkin' so much 'bout Hell," she said.

The station wagon pulled out while I rubbed the sore spot on my head. Billy Ray screamed so loud as they drove away that I couldn't help but think of that little square pamphlet from the church about people being tortured and wondered if that was the way it would sound.

Mrs. Odell Brinkley

Momma Jewel called me up on the phone and asked me to take a look in on Cain that afternoon while everyone was at the hospital. Odell was gone to another auction over in Dyersburg so I had just been sitting at home all by my lonesome and was happy to have something to do.

When there was no answer at the door, I walked on in. Lola didn't have much, but I always admired the way she put together a room. I found Cain completely decked out in his Sunday best, sitting straight and still on the couch in the living room with a copy of Southern Lifestyles laying open in his lap. He looked up at me and beamed.

"Beauty fascinates me," he said, pointing to a picture of a mansion in Shreveport with lush green landscaping and a porch running half way around the house like a big hoop skirt. The things he'd say out of the blue were always my favorites.

"Now, does it?" I asked and sat down next to him on the sofa. I pulled him into the crook of my arm and together, we slowly turned the pages of one magazine after another. We strolled through the streets and homes of Tupelo. Past the old courthouses and town squares with tree lined streets in Yazoo City, Charleston, South Carolina, Franklin, Tennessee, and Vicksburg, Mississippi.

"Who's your best friend, Miss B?" Cain asked.

"Well, Sugar, I've got lots of friends," I said, trying to think of who I would call a best friend. I don't expect I'd had once since I was a girl.

"Don't you want a best one, though?" he asked. "I sure do."

"I've got Odell," I said and hoped he wouldn't pursue the idea further. *The harsh reality of marriage is nothing to inflict upon a child.*

Instead, he continued to flip the pages. Every now and then we ran across a town in Arkansas—a restored plantation in Monticello or a beautiful vista in Eureka Springs.

"That's right here in Arkansas," Cain said hopping a little where he sat. "Miss B, do you think we could ever get them to put Lost Cain in their magazine?"

"I don't know about that, Cain," I said.

The stone cold truth was that Lost Cain looked nothing like the places in the pages of Southern Lifestyles. There were no magnolia trees lining a cobblestoned Main Street. No elegant old homes or manicured gardens. No gazebos in front of picturesque lakes with ducks and geese.

Some would have considered it generous to call this part of Arkansas plain. The land itself was farmland. Flat for as far as the eye could see. Fields followed by fields, ending up in even more fields. Row after row, a tree here or there, a river or creek ever so often. Though I'd always seen it as beautiful, I imagine it drove some people crazy to be able to see that far.

I'd only been to the mountains once, on a trip to the Rockies with Odell ten years before. I remembered how the distant snow-capped mountains were so stunning that I could scarcely believe I wasn't looking at a postcard. They seemed too beautiful to be real. After a few days, however, I couldn't help but feel claustrophobic. These great things towering above me everywhere I turned. The delta had spoiled me that way, I guess. The comfort of being able to see exactly what's coming.

"Lost Cain ain't pretty enough, is it?" Cain said.

"*Isn't* pretty enough," I corrected before I realized what I was saying. I could feel his little spirit deflate and did my best to correct myself as well.

"Lost Cain has its own kind of beauty, Cain." I said. "Come fall, I'll take you out when the cotton is good for the picking. We'll walk out the back door of my house and go stand way out in the middle of the fields. White as far as you can see. Just like a new snow that shakes and shimmers at every breeze." Scripture talks about the faith of a child being needed to enter God's kingdom. When I saw the way Cain trusted that what I told him was true, the words took root inside me in a way they never had before.

"I've never seen snow in person," he said. "But that

sounds pretty."

"You just wait until October," I continued. "I'll take you out and show you real beauty. Just as pretty a picture as you'd see anywhere else on earth."

"Do you think we could write that in a letter to the magazine, about the cotton, and ask them to come take our picture?" he asked.

I hadn't thought of it before, but I couldn't think of a single reason why not. I certainly believed there was more than one kind of beauty.

"Why don't we do exactly that, young man," I said.

Cain simply curled closer, content in my arms. Before long I felt him drift off to sleep and for a moment, like catching sight of some remote peak on a far-off unexplored mountaintop, I glimpsed motherhood.

From a distance, that was true, but real nonetheless.

Cain McAllister

When it came time for supper, I ran all the way to the preacher's house. I got to the door and was breathing so hard I couldn't even knock. I felt a sharp pain in my side and bent over so it'd ease up.

"Who are you?" someone said from the driveway.

It was a blonde headed boy with a basketball in his hands. He was a little shorter than me, but before I could tell how much, he took the basketball and put it on the ground, then sat on top of it.

"I'm Cain McAllister. Who are you?"

"Mark McElroy," he said while he rocked back and forth on the ball. "You the kid that's coming for supper? What you all dressed up for?"

I didn't have all my breath back yet, so I just nodded my head.

"I heard Daddy telling Mom about you. He said you was awkward. What's that mean exactly?"

"Heck if I know," I said, though I really did. I just didn't want Mark McElroy to think I was awkward. *I thought preachers weren't supposed to say anything bad about anybody.*

Mark stood and picked up the basketball. "Wanna play?"

"Sure!" I said, and ran over under the goal nailed to the end of the carport. I hated basketball, but that was something else Mark McElroy didn't need to know.

Chapter Seven

Died and Gone to Heaven

Mrs. Odell Brinkley

I set up my tape recorder on Brucie Lunsford's front porch and waved for Cain and Mark as they passed to come join us. I was finally getting around to interviewing Brucie about her life here growing up in Lost Cain. Brucie's family was among the very first settlers who came in the late 1890's when the entire area was still nothing but a swamp.

"You boys come on up here and sit a spell with me and Mrs. Lunsford," I said.

They did as they were told, though I didn't doubt they'd rather have been on their way. The two boys had become inseparable over the summer. Every morning, without fail, Cain waved to me as he passed the courthouse on his way to the small parsonage beside the church. He and Mark then headed off toward the river and weren't seen again until well into the afternoon, usually loaded down with fish, turtles or even now and then, a snake they'd trapped in a bucket.

"I want you young men to know a little bit about where you live. Especially since you," I said to Mark, "are new to our little community."

"Yes, ma'am," he said.

"Somebody get the door," Brucie called out from behind the screen and Mark jumped up to open it for her. She handed out glasses to each of us before she settled down on the porch swing.

"Thank you," Mark said.

Preacher's children were notoriously bad behaved and Mark had quite the reputation in town before he had ever opened his mouth. However, I'd seen nothing but a sweet, confident, gentleness in Mark. Quite the charmer, I'd say.

"You were born on this swing right here, Cain McAllister," Brucie said as if Cain might never have heard of it before.

"Yes, ma'am, I know," Cain said.

"Really?" Mark asked.

"Land of Goshen, you should have seen all the goings on that day!" Brucie said. "Second to the last birthing I ever did here, God willing. I reckon it don't hurt none for the girls to go off to the doctor," she said in my direction, "though nine times out of ten it's just another excuse to spend money, if you ask me."

"Mrs. Lunsford is going to give us a little history of Big Slough Ditch today," I said.

At this the boys perked up. I knew that was where they headed every morning, even though they weren't supposed to. *It'll do them good to hear a little of its history.*

"Big Slough Ditch," Brucie said, "was once a deadly offshoot of the Mississippi called the Devil's Spur."

The boys shared a surprised look.

"The Devil's Spur would lure newcomers or little boys trying to get out of the heat into its shallow water," Brucie said. "What they didn't know was that because of the New Madrid Quake, that spur was a full fifteen feet below the rest of the Mississippi. Once you got in up to your waist, a current might drag you straight to the bottom, just like if a tiger'd got hold of your foot."

"Did that one feel bigger than the earthquake when I was born?" Cain asked.

"Well, I wasn't here child, for crying out loud!" Brucie said. "That was back in 1812."

The New Madrid earthquake was a series of quakes for two years that rocked the entire Mississippi Delta from Minnesota to New Orleans. It was centered just north of Lost Cain about thirty miles and said to have been the largest earthquake in North American history. The fault line ran right beneath Lost Cain down to Memphis.

"Did it kill more people than the one in San Francisco?" Mark asked.

"Couldn't tell you," Brucie said. "Wasn't nobody here but the Indians back then. But I will say, the Mississippi river run backwards for three full days, that much is written down."

"It did not," Mark said.

"Now, don't sass," I said to him, but Brucie waved her hand in our direction.

"I like a kid with a little sass," she said, then pointed her finger at Mark. "You just go on over to Reelfoot Lake in Tennessee and you'll see. Whole thing made by the river running backwards and then finding its way back home again."

A half hour later the boys still listened intently while

Brucie went on about the stories her father had told her about setting out for the wilds of Arkansas from their home in Virginia. When I realized the tape recorder wasn't working, I cried out so suddenly they all jumped.

"I forgot to punch record!" I screamed, so upset I thought I might cry. "Such a wonderful conversation, gone. Oh no!"

Brucie chimed in, "Now, don't you worry none, I'll tell it again before long. Hell, I got nothing but time these days."

At this the boys giggled, which seemed to tickle Brucie and she said, "Bet you never heard an old lady cuss before, have you? Cussing's probably the only good thing about getting old. You stop giving a damn."

"I'm so sorry I didn't get all this on tape," I said. "It was a wonderful talk."

"Give you an excuse to come back," Brucie said. "But my hips startin' in, so that best be it for today."

"All right then, another time," I said.

Cain and Mark both looked at me with pleading eyes. "Yes, you boys can go on," I said. They both jumped up and took off running toward the river.

"Don't you boys forget," Brucie called after them. "The last little boy that went swimming in that ditch turned up three weeks later down in Vicksburg."

"Brucie, I didn't know about a boy drowning here," I said.

"Well, that ain't exactly the truth," she said. "But, I'm trying to knock into these young'uns thick fool heads that the river's a dangerous thing. I lost a little brother to Devil's Spur seventy some odd years ago."

Brucie went inside and I sat down on the swing

trying to recall some of the details of the conversation so that I'd remember to ask about them the next time I came. She had described the Mississippi as a gentle, but dangerous giant. An accurate portrayal, in my estimation. It always struck me how the waters lapped against the shore on the far side of the levee with small tender flutters.

Running below were undercurrents with enough strength to sink a barge the size of Memphis, but on the surface the water was so untroubled and serene, it looked to be standing still.

Lola McAllister

I had pulled down every picture in the house and started scrubbing all the walls just to have something to do. Now that Cain had a friend to keep him busy, I had all this time on my hands. Ida nearly fell out when she walked in to find me with the pictures scattered all around me. She took a long look at the walls and then back at me.

"What?" I asked. "You're always saying how dirty this place is."

Ida usually spent her entire visit straightening and dusting my house, so I foolishly thought for a moment that she'd be pleased.

"Lola Jean, you are starting to worry me," Ida said. "Reminds me of my Aunt Clara. A spinster, just like you're liable to be. When she turned thirty-five, she took to plucking out her eyebrows and eating wallpaper before they finally carted her off to a funny farm down in Memphis. It's not natural for a young woman to be single."

"I've been married twice," I reminded her.

"Don't count," she said, swatting away my two dead husbands like she would a house fly. I made up a reason to sneak off to the kitchen to take a nerve pill—something I did every time Ida came to visit. When I came back into the room, she was going over a spot I missed on the wall with a rag she must have brought with her.

Once the pill started kicking in, I got a little brave while we were hanging pictures and asked, "Why don't you get married again, Ida? After all, it's not natural for a woman to be single."

"I said a *young* woman," Ida snapped, "And you watch that tone with me, missy."

As always, one look from Ida and I felt fifteen.

I settled in for the lecture I knew was coming, which, of course, came quickly.

"Me, get married," she said. "What call does a woman over sixty with money in the bank got to get married? And while we're on the subject, what call does one under thirty got not to? It'd be different if you were past your prime and didn't need help with your son. Who's going to show that boy how to be a man? You think you, your sister, Dip's mother, that Mrs. Brinkley—all these women babying Cain is going to do him any favors in this world? If not for me that boy wouldn't have a firm hand in his life—"

I wish to God I'd just kept my mouth shut. If I should have learned anything by then, it was that Ida Pico knew where to aim for the kill.

"He's got Leon," I said.

"Good Lord, don't get me started on the cripple," Ida

said. "The man gambles, divorced, unchurched, drinks—need I go on?"

The front door opened and Cain called out, "I picked you some flowers, Momma, come see!"

"We're in here, Sweetie," I said from the living room.

Cain bounded in, holding a mess of bright, yellow daffodils in his hand, the dirt still dangling off the stems.

"They're beautiful, Sweetie," I said, giving him a hug.

Ida just shook her head and said, "Dirt all over the carpet. Get those things to the kitchen Cain." Cain took the flowers and scampered out. Ida shot me a look before calling out to the kitchen, "Then come back in here and give your Mammy Pico some sugar."

He came back in and gave Ida a peck on the cheek. "Momma, can I spend the night at Mark's?" he asked.

"Cain, you've stayed at Mark's two nights in a row," I said.

"But his mom said it was okay."

Normally this was where I would've given in, but Ida was staring me down, so I said, "You can play the rest of the afternoon, but then you're coming home, you hear me?"

"Yes, ma'am," Cain said looking at me like I had just shot his dog.

"Now, thank you for my flowers, and you go on out and play." After he left, I looked over at Ida and asked, "You happy now?"

"A firm hand—" Ida said looking all smug and content, sitting straight up in the corner chair like a queen.

For weeks afterward, I fretted over what she had said about it being selfish of me to keep Cain from having a father just because I didn't want to marry. Cain seemed happy, but I worried things with Mark might change once school started. Children could be so cruel. Mark was in the sixth grade, a year ahead of Cain. My fear was that once he got around boys his own age, he'd ignore Cain, or worse yet, join in the teasing. That would break my baby's heart.

After the first week of school, I went by Momma Jewel's during lunch recess and spotted Cain's third grade teacher, Caroline Oxford, still just pretty as ever. I called her over and we talked through the chain link fence separating Momma Jewel's and the playground. She told me that on the first day of school, Mark made sure to include Cain in every activity during recess.

"Oh, the boys resisted a little at first," she said. "But pretty soon they learned that calling Cain "Pee Pants" wasn't a good idea if Mark McElroy was anywhere nearby."

"I'm relieved," I said. "I was awful worried Mark might change once school got started."

"I've never seen anyone quite like Mark," Caroline said. "He doesn't have to threaten the other boys to get them around to his way of thinking. He just gives them a disappointed look and they just take it on themselves to make it up to him. Sheer force of personality, I think. There are some people like that."

"Cain's father was like that," I said, forgetting the unwritten rule of young widows to not call attention to their 'condition,' as Ida had put it in one of her lectures. That night I slept better knowing that Cain had someone to protect him at school, but still, *I'd do anything in the world to stop thinking about Dip McAllister.*

Cain McAllister

Just about every day after school, Mark and me would walk along the banks of Big Slough Ditch with a rake we borrowed from Uncle Leon. Every few feet we'd toss the rake out and pull in crawdads and turtles. We threw the turtles back and put all the crawdads in a big white bucket. Then we took the bucket out to the big pond behind Old Lady Lindly's house and used the crawdad tails as bait.

"Did you know that Old Lady Lindly has the only two-story house in all of Lost Cain?" I asked Mark. "And only one foot to boot," I added. "Literally. She's just got one foot."

Mark wasn't listening and ripped off one of the tails from a crawdad in the bucket and threw it into the pond, the claws still snapping.

"The trick is to take your time and grab them right on the body behind the pinchers," Mark said. "Here, try one."

Every time I ever tried it I got pinched, so I ignored him and kept on with my story, "They say her husband went crazy one night and tried to kill her with an ax! After he cut off her foot, she managed to take the ax away from him and then chopped him into eleven pieces!"

"How come eleven?" Mark asked.

"Don't know," I said to Mark. "The police let her off 'cause she was only defending herself, and, after all, he did cut off her foot. But everyone says she was never the same after that night. Always keeps an ax by the front door." We both looked at the door of the house, then laughed and he took off running and I followed after him.

When we got far enough away we fell on the ground laughing.

The truth was that Mrs. Lindly got sugar diabetes after her husband died and they had to cut off her foot. But I heard Sam Lee say once at the store that it was the obligation of a storyteller to liven things up for his audience. He said it wasn't really lying when you were doing them a favor by making things more interesting than the truth, and I agreed. Besides, I really had seen an ax by Mrs. Linley's front door once when I went there with Momma when she was delivering food to the homebound for church.

"I hope Daddy don't get another preaching job anytime soon," Mark said. "I like it here."

"Do you think you might move?" I asked.

"Nah, not for a while. Daddy never gets called by the Lord until after a couple years," he said. "Guess what I heard Daddy say was happening to Bobby Lee?" Mark asked.

Mark and me talked every day about how I was gonna get revenge on Bobby Lee. That first time we had met at the beginning of the summer, he asked me to sleep over after we finished supper. We stayed up the whole night playing Pong and I told him all about being called Pee Pants McAllister and how Bobby Lee and the kids at school had teased me ever since. Mark didn't act like it bothered him a bit.

"I'll help you get back at him," he said. Being a preacher's kid, Mark had been forced to listen to an ungodly number of sermons, so he showed me lots of interesting torture ideas in the book of Deuteronomy from the Bible underneath his bed.

Bobby Lee didn't go out of his way to pick on me anymore at school, but I could always tell that he was there watching me, seeing if he could ever find me alone. Since Mark and me became friends we were always together, so Bobby Lee got all the other kids to start teasing Belinda Mason and Frankie Hudson after someone found them in the clump of trees behind the playground touching each other "down there."

"What about Bobby Lee?" I asked Mark.

"Daddy says all the teachers had a meeting one day and told the principal that she had to get him out of elementary school whether he could read or not," Mark said. "Daddy said Bobby Lee was so big they were worried he was gonna kill some first grader, so they're shipping him off to Junior High next week."

Mark and me lay there on the grass, looking up at the empty sky. *It's like I'd died and gone to heaven.*

PART TWO

Chapter Eight

The Call of Nature

Summer 1979

Mrs. Odell Brinkley

By all accounts, the trip to the annual Southern Baptist Convention had been the success that Brother Neil had wanted. I wasn't even a Baptist, myself, but there I sat with practically the entire population of Lost Cain, crammed onto a borrowed school bus for the ride home from St. Louis. Odell, at Brother Neil's urging, had signed us up for the trip, then backed out at the last minute. Apparently church membership wasn't a factor, as hundreds of conservative churches across the south bussed in anyone who would come, and managed to win back the presidency from the so-called liberals of the denomination.

I, myself, wasn't sure what I thought of the whole experience. The tone of the meetings was angry and the services more pessimistic than I would have liked for a religious conference. It seemed to me that the Gospel should be about hope and redemption. From everything the speakers had to say, you'd assume the communists were going to take control any second and start burning Bibles and indoctrinating children. The world didn't seem as bad as all that to me. But then, lately I had begun to question my own faith, so perhaps I wasn't the best judge.

Brother Neil stood up at the front of the bus and said, "I hope you all take this experience and let it speak to your hearts and ignite a fire that will touch this great land. Ministers who don't really believe the Bible have infiltrated our churches and set up ultra-liberal seminaries where students are taught to question things like whether Adam and Eve actually existed, if you can imagine that!"

He rocked back and forth with the bus as we rolled down the highway.

"The thought keeps me up at night. A whole generation being corrupted, led down a path that leads nowhere but to death and damnation."

Brucie Lunsford said to the young girl next to her rather loudly, "I don't know what I think about getting a sermon on a bus," but Brother Neil continued, unfazed.

"If the folks who don't believe in the infallible, inerrant Word of God wasn't enough, there are the homosexual and feminist radicals that have almost passed the Equal Rights Amendment. This country is at a crossroads and I hope you will all feel the call," he said just as the bus hit a pothole and knocked his head against the steel bar running from floor to ceiling.

"The only call I feel is the call of nature," Brucie said. "We gonna swing by that truckstop over in Sikeston?"

"Yes, Mrs. Lunsford, we can," Brother Neil said as he rubbed his head with his hand before he sat back down.

I almost felt sorry for him. For a full year he had

preached fire and brimstone from the Lost Cain pulpit, with little to no effect. My opinion was that he didn't know his audience. Maybe the good people of Meridian, Pascagoula or Hattiesburg found his fiery sermons to be a shock to the system, but the people around here had known nothing but threats of damnation and hellfire for as long as they could remember.

These were the descendents of old time rural planters who migrated together and stayed put. Most every family in town had been in the same spot for five generations or more. Because of that, there were none of the social shenanigans or showing off like you saw in city churches where people came and went. Nor was there any raising of hands or playing loud music like the hill churches over in the Ozarks. Lost Cain was friendly, but stoically delta serious when it came to their preaching. They expected nothing but fire and brimstone and had grown pretty numb to it.

Trudy got up from the seat across the aisle and moved next to me. "It's colder than a witch's titty in a brass bra on this bus," she whispered. "Just can't seem to get warm these days. How's your garden growing, Sadie?"

"Pardon?" I asked.

"Just an expression. You doin' all right? You don't seem yourself lately," she said.

"Oh, I'm fine. It's just been a long time since I've taken a trip is all. I'm sorry Lola couldn't make it. I know you enjoy her company. Is she feeling any better?"

"Got Ida Pico running around in her head is all," Trudy said.

A few silent moments passed as Trudy clicked her long, pink fingernails against each other and appeared to be thinking before she continued.

"I've always figured we're all put on this earth to learn something from each other. Like God kinda throws people in your life for a reason. Ida, in her own strange way, taught me how to be my own person. And Leon, well he teaches me to laugh. And little Cain..." Trudy took my hand and with a slight tremor in her voice said, "Oh, what did we do before Cain?"

She squeezed my hand and for some reason I had to fight the urge to cry.

Shaking her head, she said, "What Ida and Lola have to teach each other must be something big."

I put my other hand over hers. I could tell that she was concerned about her sister. Lola was constantly moving from one project to another, almost furious in her need to stay busy. She'd spend weeks learning to macramé until she had the house filled with hanging owls or horses, then switching to embroidery, before moving on to something else.

"I'll run by and visit with Lola tomorrow," I told Trudy. "See if I can't get her out of the house."

"I'd appreciate that," Trudy said before she went back to her seat.

For the rest of the trip, I sat silently watching the lines on the highway pass the tires and felt like Jacob wrestling with God's angel. Locked in a battle no one could see.

"I will not let thee go, except thou bless me," I whispered so softly it was barely a sound. I hadn't missed a church service in twenty-seven years, but I knew my heart. I'd broken the most sacred commandment a woman could. I had committed adultery in that heart.

Brother Neil

God had called me to Lost Cain for a reason. The trip had confirmed to me that I was in the center of the Lord's perfect will for my life. The services were inspiring. Anita Bryant was the keynote speaker and Jerry Falwell, though not a Southern Baptist himself, had come in for the closing prayer meeting. His new organization, "The Moral Majority" was exactly what America needed. This retaking of the leadership in the denomination was proof that there were more of us than there were of them.

It's time to bring this country back to God. The bus rolled down the highway I prayed for God to reveal to me how I could better do my part. There hadn't been much response to my previous talk, so I decided on a new approach after we loaded back on at the truck stop. As soon as all were settled in their seats, I stood and said, "As a sign of our devotion, I'd like us all to spend the rest of the ride in silent prayer."

I stood for a few moments until finally everyone bowed their heads. All except the young girl sitting next to Brucie Lunsford. She stared straight ahead, unwilling to close her eyes, but I waited her out. Finally, she bowed her head as well and then I sat down.

I had met with the girl's father the previous day. His marriage was in serious trouble, much of it caused by the child's rebelliousness, and he had decided to send her to spend the summer with her grandmother in Lost Cain in the hopes that he could restore his marriage. That afternoon when we had picked her up from her parents, there was a tension in the air as they had all said their awkward goodbyes.

"Keep an eye on Macy," the father told me as we shook hands. "Don't let her out of your sight until you get there or she's liable to run off."

A wayward child is a living, breathing testament to the rebellious spirit in us all that must be tamed. Every morning I asked for God's strength and guidance, lest they all, including my own boy, fall prey to the wickedness of this world.

Macy Hollister

You can make me bow my head, but you sure as hell can't make me pray. The preacher stared me down until I finally closed my eyes. I was glad to be leaving St. Louis. I hated it there. I didn't know if I'd stay at my Grandma's or just take off again, but one thing was for sure. I was never going back home.

There was a cold draft coming from a cracked window by the seat in front of me. I reached over to push it shut and caught one of the men from across the aisle sneaking a look at me. I hadn't worn a bra on purpose 'cause I wanted to piss off my mother one last time before she sent me away.

I may have ugly feet, but I've got great tits.

With my arm up to the window, I could feel them sway as the bus rocked, and I pretended not to notice the man looking. Men looking never bothered me. When my parents took me to meet the preacher underneath the new Arch downtown, his eyes went straight to my chest when he shook my father's hand. I could see my mother squirm and that made everything worth it. I was only fifteen, but

I knew a lot about men. That's why they were sending me south.

The old lady next to me started snoring, so I got up and headed to the back of the bus. Every single person I passed had their heads bowed and eyes shut.

Suckers.

It's not that I wouldn't have liked to pray sometimes, but I knew it didn't do any good.

Cain McAllister

I hated that Macy Hollister the second I laid eyes on her. I was sitting in the back with Mark playing rock, paper, scissors when I saw her coming our way. Mark won, so I held out my forearm and he licked his first two fingers and swatted me hard. As soon as Macy walked past us, Mark wanted to stop.

"That's for kids," he whispered, pulling away. I puffed up and sat back in my seat. I didn't think she was all that pretty. She had hair the color of Mamma Jewel's pie crusts and freckles across her forehead. Mark nudged me when she passed. Macy turned sideways as if to give us a better look at her big stupid knockers.

"I'm gonna go see what I can find out," Mark said.

"I can tell you everything you need to know. I heard her grandma, Mrs. Hollister, talking with my Aunt Trudy at the store. Macy hates her momma and Mrs. Hollister says it's cause the girl's just like her."

Mark wasn't looking at me at all.

'Hey!" I nudged him. "For someone who wants to find out all there is to know, you sure ain't listening."

"I want to find out from her, stupid. I'll be back in a

minute," he said, as if he called his best friend stupid every day in the world.

Ninety seven minutes later—I was keeping time on the digital watch I got for Christmas—I was still sitting all alone while Mark talked to Macy three rows behind. Once it got dark I snuck a look. All I could see were the outlines of two sets of knees peeking over the edge of the seat. Miss B was a couple rows behind them, so I knew Macy couldn't be showing Mark a boob or anything, like Karen Murphy did last year on that very bus.

Ever so often I'd hear Mark laugh. It was the one he used when he was trying to talk someone into something. Macy never laughed, but I imagined she was smiling at Mark the way all the girls smiled at Mark. I'd liked to have got up and went back there, but I decided to stay put and hate Macy Hollister from right where I sat.

Chapter Nine

Promise?

Cain McAllister

Mark wasn't at our usual place. For the past year, every Sunday morning we had met at Momma Jewel's front gate and walked to Sunday school together.

"Where's Mark this morning?" Momma Jewel asked.

I just shrugged my shoulders.

"I'm sure you'll see him in Sunday school. You gonna come sit with me during services?" she asked.

"Yes, ma'am," I said. Momma Jewel put her thick arm around my shoulder and leaned on me as we walked. When she was nine, Momma Jewel cut her leg on a field plow left in some tall cotton while she was looking for her daddy. It got so infected she almost died. In the middle of her left calf was a deep crevice that folded the skin all the way to the bone, so I always made sure to walk on that side.

"Does it still hurt?" I asked.

"Nah, it don't hurt, but that leg ain't been worth much since," she said.

When we got to church, she reached into her purse and pulled out two sticks of Juicy Fruit gum, and said,

"Now you make sure you share with Mark."

I put them in my shirt pocket and went down the hall to my Sunday school class expecting to find Mark, but he wasn't there either. All through Mrs. Thompson's lesson on brotherly love, I kept watching for him at the door and didn't raise my hand once, even though I knew all the answers like I always did. Then I noticed part of a verse she quoted from First John about anyone who hated his brother not entering the Kingdom of Heaven.

"And we must always remember that everyone is our brothers and sisters," Mrs. Thompson said.

I shot my hand up in the air. Mrs. Thompson pulled the glasses that hung from a gold chain around her neck up to her face, holding them out in front of her like a pirate with a telescope.

"Yes, Cain, what is it?" she asked.

"I don't have any brothers," I said.

"No you don't, Cain, but, for example, everyone in this room is your brother and sister in Christ. You must love them all."

Scanning the room, I gave it some thought. Gayla Mason once told on me for cutting in the lunch line, Billy Penter had a hairlip and I didn't like Jeannie Tabor very much. With Mark gone, I didn't see that there was much of anyone to love in the whole room. But I didn't hate them either, so I figured it'd be okay.

"So we have to love everybody that's a Christian?" I asked.

"No, sweetie, we have to love everybody. Especially those that don't yet know the Lord," Mrs. Thompson said and let her glasses fall down and rest between her breasts, which usually meant that she wanted me to stop asking questions. I thought of the one person that I truly hated and shot my hand back in the air.

"What is it now, Cain?" she asked.

"But I can't love everybody!" I said a little louder than I meant to.

"Don't be silly, of course you can. Now let's finish—"

"Who in here loves Bobby Lee Brewster, raise your hand?" I called out to the other kids in the class.

"Now Cain McAllister," Mrs. Thompson said. "This is not something we talk about in Sunday school." I could tell by the way she said it, that she knew I had a point. I bet she'd taught all the Brewsters at one time or another.

"I hate those Brewsters!" I hollered.

"You don't hate anyone, Cain. You just don't like them," she said. "We can love someone without really liking them."

That don't make a lick of sense to me. "No ma'am, I hate their ever-loving guts," I said.

"Well," Mrs. Thompson said and waved her hand. "I guess you just won't make it to heaven then now will you, young man?" Then she closed her Bible as if to say that was that.

I knew she couldn't see without her glasses up, so I stuck my tongue out at her. The other kids all laughed.

"What's so funny?" she asked.

Before Gayla Mason could tell on me, I decided to bolt. I ran down to the end of the narrow hallway and grabbed the wall as I rounded the corner. I crashed right into Mark and we both fell to the ground.

"Who you running from, Cain?" Mark asked as he got up, dusting off his slacks.

"Mrs. Thompson told me I'm going to hell!" I

hollered from the floor with my arms spread wide, "Me!"

Mark laughed.

Two arms lifted me up from the ground and a soft voice from behind said, "Hell's just something they use to scare you into doing what they want." I knew it was that Macy Hollister before I even turned around.

She had on a long white dress, bunched up in the middle and nothing but a tube top and spaghetti straps above that. I tried not to notice her boobs, but they were mashed together in the tube top that had a scrunchy fabric that wasn't smooth or even. I was pretty sure I could see where her nipples were underneath.

Mark was blushing and pushing down his hair and that's when it hit me that he and Macy had been walking together! For all I knew they were holding hands the whole time I waited by the gate at Momma Jewel's. Kissing while I was being sent to hell by the Sunday school teacher.

"What do you know about it, anyway," I said, pushing Macy's arms away from me. "My Mammy Pico says most Yankees ain't even Christians."

Macy just smiled and said, "I guess I'll see you in hell then. You want some Doublemint?" She offered me a stick of gum straight from the package.

"No thanks," I said. "I got my own."

Reaching into my pocket, I pulled out the two sticks of Juicy Fruit, and offered one to Mark just as Macy swung her arm over to him.

Mark just stood there a second and then took the Doublemint from Macy.

"Fine then," I said. I unwrapped both sticks of Juicy Fruit, shoved them into my mouth and threw the wrappers on the ground before I walked away.

Mark ran after me.

"You wanna come sit with Macy and me?" he asked.

"I promised Momma Jewel, I'd sit with her," I said.

"Okay," he said, without even offering to stay. He just went straight back over to Macy and her big boobs.

During the service, I shot dirty looks in their direction, but couldn't get Mark's attention long enough for him to notice. They sang my favorite song, *There's Power in the Blood*, during the offertory, but I couldn't enjoy it a bit.

During the chorus, I kept looking over at Mark and Macy who were writing notes and giggling together. Ed Hannon, the old man who sat behind Momma Jewel kept spitting on me every time he sang out the word power. There is power, power, wonder working power, in the blood, in the blood, of the lamb, of the lamb. There is power. Power. Wonder working power in the precious blood of the lamb.

There sure is a lot of powers in that song. I wiped the back of my neck with my shirt. I had planned on sneaking out during the sermon to get the gum wrappers I left in the hallway so I could make little trophies and cars out of the silver linings like I always did with Mark. But Brother Neil's sermon surprised me. It was interesting.

Brother Neil was always a little interesting because he ranted and hollered, but today he was talking about mighty horsemen riding down to earth and beasts with seven heads smiting the world, and I couldn't help but listen. A few of the men murmured "Amen" when he started talking about the rapture.

Instead of angry, like usual, Brother Neil sounded

excited while he preached. When the choir started the invitational hymn, I felt like I should go forward and inched toward the end of the pew. Before I could take a step, one person, then another, then three others left their seats and walked down the aisle to Brother Neil's waiting arms.

Staying put, I decided I'd at least try not to hate Bobby Lee Brewster. Macy Hollister was another story.

That night during Training Union, which, if you ask me is just another way of saying Sunday school at night, Mark asked me to practice doing the puppets with him. I was still mad because he ditched me for Macy that morning, but I liked doing puppets so I went over by the stage and stood next to it.

Mark and me put on puppet shows for the little kids in "Children's Church" sometimes. The shows were pretty much just someone punching "play" on a taped song about being happy all the time and us moving the mouths of the puppets in time with the music. It wasn't as easy as it looked. If we didn't practice we'd get tired and let their little puppet heads sag until they just about disappeared behind the stage before one of the leaders would whisper for us to perk up.

"You want to spend the night tonight?" Mark asked.

"I'm still mad at you," I said.

Mark held up the Barnabas puppet with bright yellow hair and moved it so that it mouthed the words while he said, "Come on, Cain, Mark said he was sorry. Won't you be a good Christian and forgive him?" He bobbed Barnabas' head up and down while he waited for the answer.

I never stayed mad at Mark very long so we spent the rest of Training Union making Barnabas whack the Apostle Paul on the head over and over. By the time we went into the sanctuary for the Sunday night service, everything was back to normal until Macy walked in and sat down on the other side of Mark without even saying hi to me.

"You must get tired of listening to your daddy preaching all the time," Macy said to Mark. "I've only been here a week, and I know I am."

"Ain't nobody keeping you here," I said.

"Yes, there is," Macy said. Just then her grandmother walked by and said to Macy, "Macy Lynn, you put that sweater on. No girl over thirteen should have bare shoulders in church."

Macy shook her sweater out in front of her and held it out for Mark to hold, which he did with a big stupid grin on his face while she put one arm in and then the other.

"Does he always get that worked up in his sermons?" she asked Mark.

"Daddy's preaching is like a play," Mark said. "Sunday morning, evening and Wednesday night performances. He's not like that at home."

During the hymns, I drew little pictures of planes with "USA" written across them, dropping bombs on tiny houses, all in a row, with a big sign that read, "Welcome to the USSR." I poked Mark during the announcements and showed him my picture. He looked at it a second and then rolled his eyes at Macy, who smiled back at him and nodded her head.

"Brothers and Sisters, I'm glad you're here," Brother Neil said from the pulpit. "The renewal of the church must start with the faithful. Right here in this sanctuary are the seeds and the last hope for all humanity." He stepped out from behind the pulpit and down the little stairs that led from the stage.

I looked around at the crowd of people gathered in the church. Most of them were really old and I wondered if maybe humanity didn't have much hope after all.

"They say that the only way for revival to begin is with one heart at a time," Brother Neil said as he walked over and stood in front of the center aisle. "Instead of a sermon, tonight we're all going to pray that revival comes to Lost Cain. Bow your heads with me."

We never started Sunday night this way so I looked over at Mark but he just shrugged his shoulders and bowed his head, still writing a note to Macy on one of the bulletins from the morning service. Around the sanctuary, every head in the congregation was bowed and every eye closed. For a long time, we all just sat there in silence.

After about twenty minutes it felt to me like the quiet might flow out from the pews and seep into the cracks of the walls and ceiling and make the whole building come crashing down on us. It felt like I imagined it would if maybe the Russians were finally coming. For all I knew they might have already dropped the bombs. I pictured them in mid-air right above our heads, ready to crash down at any moment. A chill went up my spine and Brother Neil finally spoke.

"These are your faithful, my Lord. These are the believers who thirst after you with all that is within them."

All of a sudden Brother Neil fell down to his knees at the front of the church. "Hear our prayers, O Lord," he cried out. "Send us revival. I want all of you to take this time to entreat the Lord to bring revival to our community."

For the longest time he didn't move. I watched him there in the front of the church, his head drawn down, one arm folded into the other that rested on his forehead. Then I closed my eyes and started praying too, asking for God to send us a revival. I didn't even really know what a revival was, but I begged God for one all the same. When the tears started to run down my cheeks, I wiped them away so Mark wouldn't see.

Later at Mark's house, while we lay in bed, I kept thinking about the service and the invitation at church that morning. I couldn't fall asleep so I got out of bed to get some water. It felt strange to be walking around someone else's house in my underwear. Down the hall, there was a light on in Brother Neil's study so I walked down and looked into the room.

A big picture of Jesus in the Garden of Gethsemane hung on the wall. Brother Neil was sitting in a chair turned toward it, his feet on the desk, leaning back with his eyes closed. He had on a pair of checkered boxer shorts, and there was a Bible lying open in his lap. The dark hair on his chest puffed up like cotton candy, but on his shoulder, there was a small patch all to itself, like an island surrounded by the rest of his white skin.

I took a step into the room. Brother Neil was completely still, but I couldn't tell if he was asleep or praying. I took a few more steps and tried to see where the Bible on his lap was open to. The chapter was Revelations, the pages were littered with scribbled words and underlined passages.

Then Brother Neil opened his eyes, making me jump back a little.

"Hey Cain, what are you doing up?" he asked.

For some reason, I didn't want him to know I was wide wake, so I rubbed my eyes. "I was just getting a drink of water," I said.

"It's awful late," Brother Neil said.

"Are you studying?" I asked.

"A little. Here and there."

"I prayed before I went to bed tonight," I said. "For a revival."

"So did I Cain," he said and smiled at me. He reached across to put his hand on my shoulder, and said again, "So did I."

"Brother Neil, what is a revival anyway? I mean I been to revivals before over at the tent in Blytheville, but I never heard of one that was in a church."

Brother Neil always seemed so much nicer at home than when he was preaching or else I wouldn't have asked. He smiled again.

"Well, Cain," he said, "A revival in the church means that every single person in the congregation rededicates their lives to Jesus. They feel his spirit every day and every moment."

"Does that mean they try better to do what's right?" I asked.

"When you let Jesus be in charge," Brother Neil said, "doing what's right is the easiest thing in the world."

I got the same scared feeling again that I'd had earlier at church. Something empty and alone.

"Brother Neil, you remember that time we talked in the church about me getting saved?" I asked.

"Yes, I do," he said.

"This morning I almost came down front, but after all those other people did, I didn't want to. And tonight, when we all prayed. I did too. Not just asking for God to bless everybody, but I really prayed, like I couldn't breathe if I didn't."

"I'm glad, Cain."

"I think I want to get saved," I said.

Without another word, Brother Neil straightened up in his chair and took my hand then led me to the small couch beside the desk.

"Are you ready to accept Jesus Christ as your personal Lord and Savior?" Brother Neil asked.

Tears welled up in my eyes and I nodded my head. It was like when I heard them say at the store that they were sending Daddy home in parts. Something I couldn't stop heaved up from inside me.

"Then let's pray," he said and Brother Neil closed his eyes but kept his face straight ahead. He took both of my hands in his and I looked at him while he prayed. I had watched Brother Neil before, but always out of the corner of my eye, afraid he'd see me looking. His face was peaceful and smooth, like Jesus in the picture that hung on the wall above us.

"Lord, we ask you to come to us in this very important moment in Cain's life. Cain, do you acknowledge that God is the creator of all things, including yourself?"

"Yes," I said.

"Do you confess that you have sinned and fallen short of the glory of God?"

I tried to think of the sins I had committed. I took

two dollars from Momma's purse the week before when she wasn't looking. I peeked at one of the magazines behind the wooden board at the store. I hated Bobby Lee Brewster. That had to be a sin.

"Yes," I said.

"While we were yet sinners, Christ died for us. Offering a path to salvation for all who confess that Jesus Christ is Lord. For whosoever calls upon the Lord shall be saved."

Tightening my grip on Brother Neil's hands I started to cry again. He moved over to the couch beside me and put one arm around my shoulders.

"Repeat this prayer after me," he said. Which I did, word for word, crying the whole time.

At the end of the prayer, Brother Neil said Amen and I looked up at him. He pulled me in and hugged me. I could feel the thick hair on his chest moving up and down against my face with every breath, then remembered I was in my underwear and felt embarrassed.

"I think it's probably time you got back to bed and get some sleep," Brother Neil said as he stood up. He bent over and kissed me on the top of the head. I didn't feel embarrassed after that, just happy.

"Yes, sir," I said and went to the door. "Brother Neil, does this really mean that I'm saved?" I asked.

"Yes, it does," he said.

I ran down the hallway, shuffling my feet in little steps to be quiet and climbed back into bed with Mark.

"Where the heck you been?" he rolled over and asked.

"I was just getting some water," I said.

We both lay there for a minute and then Mark asked,

"Cain?"

"Yeah?"

"Do you think Macy likes me?" he asked.

"Oh, shut up!" I said.

"What?"

"She's fifteen and you're thirteen!" I said and then hit him on the shoulder.

"So? That don't mean nothing," Mark said and tried to push me off the bed with his foot.

"Stop it," I said, laughing and pushing back with my own feet. Then we started a kick battle underneath the covers.

"Boys," Mark's mother said, standing at the door. "You two stop playing and get to sleep right this minute."

"Yes, ma'am," Mark said. Mrs. McElroy stood in the doorway another minute while we straightened up in bed and tried to lay still. Mark pinched me under the covers, and I hollered.

"Shhhh," Mrs. McElroy reminded us, then disappeared from the frame of the door.

"Ow," I said under my breath. "That's not fair. I was just minding your mom."

Mark didn't say anything but pushed me a little and then rolled over to face the other direction.

"Mark, are we always going to be best friends?" I asked.

"Sure," he said.

"Promise?" I asked.

"Promise," he said.

Before long, Mark fell back to sleep and I lay in the bed listening to him breathe. My eyes kept drifting shut, but I didn't want the feeling to end so I tried to stay awake for as long as I could.

Chapter Ten

They Just Get Stupid

Cain McAllister

I hadn't said anything to Mark that whole week about getting saved. Macy had been tagging along on just about everything we'd done ever since. Every Tuesday, Mark and me went fishing out to Big Slough Ditch. Macy didn't "do" fishing so instead I was stuck sitting there on Momma Jewel's porch listening to Macy talk about her grandmother's house.

"It's like an abandoned wax museum overrun with vines," she said.

"Wow," Mark said. All Mark ever said to anything Macy said was wow.

My cousin Billy Ray drove up in his 1972 silver Camaro and revved his engine when he stopped the car right before he cut it off. He always did that, like when a person coughs so someone else in the room will notice them.

"Cool car," Macy said.

"He got it in March, and now he won't let anyone call him Billy Ray anymore. We have to call him Billy," I said.

Billy got out of the car, shook his stringy hair, walked back to the trunk and pulled out a bag of groceries for Momma Jewel. His hair was down to his shoulders and he always wore a cap with KISS in big letters across the front.

"Billy worships KISS," I said. "Aunt Trudy tried to talk him into cutting his hair, but finally gave up on the condition that Billy would sign a contract saying he wouldn't start smoking dope."

When he came up the steps, I could tell the second Billy spotted Macy on the swing. He moved his eyes in the opposite direction, pretending not to notice her at all.

"Hey dorks," Billy said. "Cain, I think your momma needs you to come roll her hair."

"Shut up," I said.

"Good comeback," he said and flicked his fingers out at me. "Face."

"They told us in Sunday school that KISS stands for Knights In Satan's Service," I said.

Billy made a sign with his first and last fingers and bared his teeth like a dog.

"Who's the chick?" he asked, barely looking in Macy's direction.

Macy said, "I'm the chick, who's the dick?"

Mark and me both laughed at that one. I could tell it bothered Billy a little too. When he went inside, Mark turned to me and asked, "Maybe we could talk Billy into taking us to the bridge?"

"Yeah, like that's gonna happen," I said.

"What bridge?" Macy asked.

"They're building a new bridge over the river, up in Missouri." Mark said. "I hear it's really cool. You can walk right up to where they got the concrete bases poured."

"It sure sounds better than sitting around on this porch all day," Macy said.

"We could have been fishing," I said, but no one answered. "Anyway, there's no way Billy'll take us. Even if he wasn't a Knight In Satan's Service, you have to go on a gravel road to get there. He washes that car every single day."

"Then it won't matter if it gets a little dusty," Macy said smiling.

It turned out that Billy didn't take all that much convincing after all. A few words from Macy and the four of us were in the car, headed up the back roads toward Missouri, with both windows down and the radio blaring. Mark and me were stuffed into the small backseat. I was sitting directly behind Billy, who had his seat pushed back as far as it would go so he could lean back and look cool up front. I couldn't even fit my feet in the space left, so my knees were up to my chest.

Macy was in the passenger seat, fiddling with the radio with her right hand, so that her shoulders were turned to Billy. Billy couldn't seem to make up his mind if he wanted to watch the road or Macy's chest.

It's a good thing I got saved last week. The car swerved down the road and Macy pulled a few eight tracks out of the glove compartment.

"I'm getting a cassette player put in just as soon as I save up some money," Billy said, "It's gonna smoke."

I had never seen Billy try to be charming before. I was a little disgusted, but less intimidated.

"Is KISS all you got?" Macy asked.

"There's nothing else," Billy said, like the disciple that he was.

The speakers right behind our heads vibrated and sounded like they might blow up when Macy popped an eight track into the stereo. Mark and me plugged our ears and Macy punched the button for track four.

"I hate your cousin," Mark said.

"What?" I asked.

"I hate your cousin," he screamed each word. "Hate. Your. Cousin."

"It was your idea," I yelled back.

We drove the rest of the way with both hands over our ears. Once or twice, I saw Billy yell something to Macy and her yell something back, but I couldn't hear any of it. I watched the empty fields go by, each separate row coming into focus for a tiny second before the next one would take its place. Four times, Billy swerved into the gravel and swung the car back to the road. He took one curve so fast that Mark tumbled into me.

"Slow down," I yelled at Billy. "You trying to kill us or something?"

Macy and Billy didn't hear a thing. I yelled again. Macy reached over and turned the volume down.

"Did you say something?" she said to me, still yelling a little.

"I was telling Evil Knievel there to slow down," I said. "He's going to flip this thing and kill us all."

Billy took both hands off the steering wheel, put one arm out the open window and the other across the car, and yelled, "If I go, let it be in a blaze of glory!"

Macy laughed and I looked toward Mark and put my finger down my throat.

Once we got to the river, Billy pulled the car up as close as he could get to the enormous concrete poles and skidded to a stop.

"Thank God," I said from the backseat.

"I got you here, didn't I?" Billy said.

"Hurry up and let me out of here, I said and pushed against the driver's seat. "I'm getting claustrophobic."

"Watch it, dipshit, and don't break my seat or I'll throw you in the river and you can drown just like your stepdad," he said.

"Your stepdad drowned in the river?" Macy asked, putting her hand on my shoulder.

I pulled away.

"It was before I could remember. Now let me out of here Billy Ray or I'm gonna start kicking this seat as hard as I can."

It was one of the few things that I could do to bother him because I knew how much he hated being called Billy Ray.

"Billy Ray," Macy laughed, "why ain't that so southern of you."

We all walked over to where the green steel beams tilted out about a third of the way over the river toward Tennessee on the other side. The Mississippi was almost a mile wide and though the concrete supports looked enormous up close, the frame of the bridge barely stood out against the river and the bluffs on the other side.

"Wow, this thing is going to be huge," Macy said.

"I hear that all the time," Billy said.

"Yeah," Mark said, "going to be huge, maybe, but it's so small now."

"I say we leave the two little turds here," Billy said to Macy.

"Hey, those turds are my friends," Macy said and put

her arms around both Mark and me, giving us a squeeze. "Let's get a closer look."

I couldn't understand why Macy wanted to be our friend. Now that she knew Billy, I wondered if maybe she'd abandon Mark and me and start running around with the older kids. I hoped so. She'd only been here a couple weeks and already Mark was flipped for her. She was all he talked about.

Being that close to the river always made me nervous, so they walked closer to the bank, but I stayed back. They climbed up the levee wall to where the steel beam went out about fifty yards.

"I bet you're too chicken to climb out there, Cain," Billy yelled back at me.

"Or too smart," I said and started to climb the steep hill of the levee.

"That's what I thought," Billy said as he pulled himself up and climbed on top of the girder. He planted his feet, one in front of the other and stretched his arms out like he was on a surf board.

"I bet you're too scared to walk out past the concrete and over the river," Macy said and winked at me.

"Just watch," Billy said and started to slowly walk across.

As he got further away, Macy said to both of us, "Boys get stupid around fourteen. It would be hilarious if it weren't so sad."

Just then Billy looked back and waved his arms in the air. Macy waved too and said under her breath, "You stupid dipshit." Mark and me smiled, especially when Billy yelled, "Right on," and waved back at Macy.

She put her arms around us both and said, "Don't

ever try to impress a girl. If risking your life to walk a beam over the most dangerous river in the world impresses any girl, then she's not worth having."

I still didn't like Macy one little bit, but that made some sense.

"I don't really blame Billy," she went on. "He doesn't know that I'm too smart for him. Some stupid girl might actually think that's something." She took a deep breath and said, "And they'd live stupidly ever after."

About that time, Billy finally got a little sense himself and sat down on the beam, inching out past the concrete pillar, about forty feet over the shallow banks of the river.

"This is where I act like I'm scared and beg him to come down," Macy said.

Instead she hollered, "Keep going Billy Ray, keep going!" I couldn't help but giggle. At first, the way Macy said everything always sounded mean to me. But the more I was around her, it seemed like it was more wounded than mean. Like a hurt cat hissing at you when you tried to pick it up.

"What?" Billy yelled. "You want me to come back?"

Macy gave us a look and threw her arms up, "Yes, come on back," she said, then said "dipshit" again under her breath. Billy, looking all proud, inched back down the beam toward us.

"About fourteen," Macy said. "They just get stupid."

Chapter Eleven

Baa Baa Black Sheep

Cain McAllister

Every Sunday, Macy's grandmother would drag her along for a walk through the cemetery. It creeped Macy out, so she persuaded Mark and me to go with them. Well, it'd be closer to the truth to say that she persuaded Mark and once I figured out he was going with or without me, I said okay. After church, him and me went over and Mrs. Hollister sat us down in the living room while they got ready.

Mrs. Hollister had a thing for grapes. They were everywhere you looked. There were plastic grapes, pictures of grapes, grape fabric and grape wallpaper. Plastic vines and bunches poured off the top of all the cabinets in her kitchen and living room.

"It's like being in a jungle," I said to Mark. "Surrounded by rampaging grapes."

"Look at this," Mark said, pointing to a picture of a family with three kids. "There's a little piece of duct tape over the lady's face."

"That's weird," I said.

Other than the duct tape, it looked like a typical

family. Tacked to the wallpapered paneling were dozens of pictures of the various Hollister families. Momma Jewel had told me that there were seven Hollister children but none who still lived in Lost Cain, which was unusual since people around there didn't move much. The only way you'd know any of the Hollisters even existed at all was on those walls and the number of cars parked outside on Christmas Eve. Mark and me started looking around the room and there were lots of pictures with one or two of the faces covered with perfectly cut pieces of gray duct tape.

"Look," I said, "there's hardly a picture in this place without somebody covered up like that."

"You think they died or something?" Mark asked.

I was looking at the outline of a woman in a yellow sundress, standing with a man and two young boys outside the entrance to Dogpatch, USA when Macy walked in. Mark turned toward her before she made a sound. It was like he could telepathically sense her breasts entering the room. Every time Mark saw Macy he had to take a second to adjust to their presence, like a person coming out of the sunshine into a really dark room. I figured if Mark had tried to talk too soon in the same room as Macy's breasts, nothing but gibberish would've come out.

It's not like I hadn't been around boobs enough. One or two of the girls at Lost Cain Elementary had them already. Gayla Mason was already out of her training bra and into an A cup. At least that's what I had heard her tell Shelly Wallace in the lunch line. The women at church all had them, some enormous.

But there was an electricity that came into the room

with Macy and her breasts. They seemed dangerous for some reason. Like they were undetonated mortar shells left lying around after a war that could blow your leg off at any moment. Since the summer had started, all Mark talked about were breasts. He noticed every pair in the world.

Finally able to speak, Mark asked, "What's with the duct tape, Macy?"

"Divorce," she said.

"Divorce?" I asked.

"All her kids and grandkids keep getting divorced. After the first few, Grandma said she was tired of taking down perfectly good pictures just 'cause somebody got divorced." She pointed to the portrait of the family at Dogpatch. There was a square picture of a blonde woman taped to the upper right corner.

"That's Uncle Frankie and this woman," Macy said, pointing to the duct tape. "Was Aunt Louise. Then they got divorced and Uncle Frankie married Aunt Sarah." Macy pointed to the woman in the corner. "Believe me, it's not the strangest thing Grandma does."

Looking around at the grape infested room, I didn't doubt her for a second.

"Look at this," she said and pulled a large photo album from under the table by the couch, and sat down. Macy opened the album toward the middle and Mark and me sat down on either side of her. The pages were covered with black and white pictures of an ancient old man, white as a ghost, laid out in a coffin.

"Holy crap," Mark said.

"That's Grandma's grandpa," Macy said, "He died in 1927." She flipped through the rest of the album.

There were black and white, then color Polaroid's of body after body, all dressed up—the women's hair poofed out in spidery webs and the men's plastered against their pale skin.

"Somebody gave her the picture of her Grandpa when she was a little girl and she's taken one of every person in the family that's died ever since," Macy said.

On one page was a black and white picture of a young girl, dressed in a frilly dress with her hair in little ringlets around her shoulders.

"I think the young ones are the creepiest," Macy said.

"Why would anyone take pictures of dead people?" Mark asked.

"Beats me," Macy said.

"I think it's kind of interesting," I said.

Macy looked at me and said, "You would."

Before I could think of something smart to say back to her, Mrs. Hollister, a short old lady shaped like a square, the same distance across as she was tall, came in and grabbed the photo album away from Macy.

"I'm glad y'all are getting in the spirit of things," she said and put the album back underneath the table. "Now, I don't mind you boys coming along with us to the cemetery but I don't want no cutting up. It's a place to be quiet and respectful."

Both us said, "Yes, ma'am."

Mrs. Hollister took a black and white polka dot scarf out of the pocket of a coat hanging by the door and wrapped it around her head, tying a double knot under her thick chin.

"Let's get going," she said.

Macy, Mark and me all followed her out the door to

the blue Chevy Nova in the driveway. Macy got in the front seat while Mark and I got in the back. Mrs. Hollister started the car and slowly pulled out of the driveway.

As we drove down the road out of town, Mark nudged me to look at the outline of Macy's body against the light from the windshield, but I just shook my head at him. Macy reached over to turn on the radio, but Mrs. Hollister slapped her hand away.

"No music, young lady," she said, "Have some respect for the dead."

"Jeesh, Grandma, we're not even there yet," Macy said, "How far is this place anyway?"

"Hey, Cain can tell us about the graveyard," Mark said, "He knows stuff about everything here."

"That would be nice, Cain," Mrs. Hollister said.

"There used to be a Pentecost church next to the cemetery," I started off. It burned down during a service when the entire congregation was speaking in tongues and a candle tipped over and caught the pulpit on fire.

"I remember that fire," Mrs. Hollister said.

"They was either all so "in the spirit" that no one noticed, or, like Sam Lee says it, no one wanted to be the first to come out of it, lest the person in the next pew think they were faking."

"Sounds like something Sam Lee would say," Mrs. Hollister said.

Macy Hollister

He's such a little know it all. Cain told another story about the graveyard where my grandpa was buried. I'll admit it was slightly less boring than everything else in this town—something about the graveyard being the only high ground by the river because of the earthquake and how every time they buried people other places, the graves kept popping up during floods.

"How did you learn all that, Cain McAllister?" Grandma asked.

"I don't know," Cain said. "I just picked it up, I guess."

"Cain remembers everything," Mark said, leaning over the front seat with his head between them. "Before I got to town, Cain didn't have a best friend for five years. All he did was sit up at V.R.'s and listen to those old men talking. Can you imagine listening to Sam Lee for five years?"

"I certainly can't," Grandma said.

I pushed Mark's head back from the seat. "Why didn't you have any friends for five years?" I asked Cain. *As if I didn't know, you little smart ass.*

"'Cause Bobby Lee Brewster tickled him til he peed in his pants," Mark said.

Cain hit Mark in the arm really hard.

"Ow," Mark screamed.

"You poor thing," I said to Cain, giggling a little.

"But we're going to get him back one of these days," Mark said. "We got it all planned"—then Cain hit him again.

"Revenge always helps," I said.

"Hush that talk," Grandma said as she turned the car off the road and parked next to a rotting old church that tilted a little to one side. There was a graveyard behind it with a line of big trees that went all the way around.

"They built that one after the other burnt down," Cain said, pointing at the old church. I could tell he was trying to change the subject.

"Who cares," I said. "Let's talk about how you're going to get revenge on, what was his name?"

"Bobby Lee Brewster," Mark blurted out.

"It's the first thing all summer that hasn't bored me to tears," I said.

"Sam Lee aside," Grandma said and pulled herself out of the car, then reached back inside to grab her purse. "I can tell you the world would be a better place if everyone was so bored all they had to do was sit around and listen to old people."

"Yes, Grandma," I said and opened the car door.

"Don't 'yes, Grandma' me, young lady," she said. "It's the truth."

As we walked behind the old church and through the gate, Grandma reminded us, "Be respectful." She went straight to the far side and the three of us waited toward the front. There was a batch of pale yellow jonquils growing by the gate so I bent down and picked one.

"Over there's where Grandpa's buried," I said.

"I'm sorry," Mark said, trying to be sympathetic.

"Don't matter none to me," I said, twirling the flower in my hand. "He died before I was born, so I never met him." I put the stem behind my ear while we walked between the rows of weathered stones with names and dates so worn down that we could barely make out what was written.

"This one says 1892, I think," Cain said. "Don't you wonder what life was like back then?"

"I sure don't," I said.

"Me neither," Mark said. Cain just looked at him with disgust. I could tell Mark was just agreeing with me. Boys did that a lot. I could've said the sky was pink and Mark would have just stared at my tits and said, "Yep, it sure is." But not Cain.

"Brother Neil says when the rapture comes that all the Christians will go straight up to heaven and the ones already in their graves will rise up to join them in the air," Cain said.

"Brother Neil's full of shit," I said. Cain always jerked a little whenever I cussed. I thought it was funny, so I made sure I cussed around him a lot.

"You can't go around saying stuff like that all the time, Macy, you don't know what's gonna happen," Cain said.

"I do know that—" I stopped to read one of the stones. "Maybelle Hardy, who died on May 17, 1905, ain't gonna pop up out of this grave and start sailing to heaven, that's for sure."

"You don't know near as much as you think you do," Cain said.

"Think about it, Cain," I said, stopping to do the math with my fingers, "Her body's been in the ground for seventy three years. It's all decomposed and full of maggots by now."

"Well, all things are possible through God," Cain said. "Why do you even go to church if you don't believe none of it?"

"'Cause they make me, that's why! You think I'd sit there listening to Mark's daddy holler and strut if I had a choice?" I threw up my hands and walked away.

Mark immediately followed me and Cain stayed a few steps behind us while we kept walking. After a few minutes, I turned back and said to Cain, "Sorry I yelled."

"Ain't you even worried about where you'll go when you die?" he asked.

"Who's got time for that? I'm more worried about what I'm going to do between now and then," I said.

"I got saved last Sunday night," Cain said more to Mark than to me.

"No you didn't," Mark said. "I was there. You never went up."

"Not at church, at your house. I got up in the middle of the night 'cause I couldn't sleep and I talked with Brother Neil and he prayed with me."

"Well, congratulations, I guess," Mark said then turned to me and asked, "What are you supposed to tell somebody when they get saved anyway? Congratulations, Bon Voyage, the more the merrier?"

"How about baa baa black sheep," I said.

"What does that mean?" Cain asked.

"Just means you're now another sheep in the flock," I said.

The sarcasm was mostly lost on Cain. He seemed like a very literal kid.

Mark said, "I got saved when I was five and a half."

"Jeesh," I said, "what the hell do you know when you're five?"

"And a half," Mark said. "What was I supposed to do? The preacher's son has got to be saved."

"Is that all anybody in this town ever talks about? Getting saved?" I asked.

"What's she doing?" Cain interrupted and pointed over at Grandma.

Across the cemetery, Grandma was pacing back and forth in front of Grandpa's grave with one hand holding her purse in the crook of her arm and the other shaking a finger at the headstone.

"I think she's yelling at him," I said. Though when I took a closer look, I couldn't really tell if she was yelling or crying. "Mom says they fought a lot."

That seemed to settle it and we started walking again and then Cain asked Mark, "Did you feel different after you got saved?"

"Heck if I remember," Mark said.

"I don't feel that different," Cain said. "I hope it took."

"Do you still hate Bobby Lee Brewster?" Mark asked.

"So far," Cain said. "But I'm working on it."

A bundle of fresh daisies in a cement urn sitting in front of one of the graves caught my eye. I recognized the name.

"Hey, look at this," I said. "It says McAllister."

The tombstone read, "Joseph Allen "Dip" McAllister, born June 15, 1948, died January, 1968," and Cain stopped dead in his tracks when he saw it.

"Did you know this was here?" Mark asked Cain, who just stood there and shook his head.

"I thought they never found a body," I said. "I mean—"

I shouldn't have said that. Just from the stories I'd heard, they all said that Cain's dad was MIA.

"Do you think maybe they found him and didn't tell you?" Mark asked.

"I don't care," Cain said. Then he walked off, not running, but fast. About eight rows over I saw him stop and sit down on one of the headstones with his arms crossed.

"Do you think we oughta go talk to him?" I asked.

"Nah, he hates it when people talk to him if he's mad," Mark said.

"I don't think he's mad," I said. "I think he's upset. Why do you think they didn't tell him it was here?"

"Don't know," Mark said.

"Let's get going, kids," Grandma hollered at us. "I got beans in the pot at home. Where's Cain?" She was walking toward us with her tiny steps that looked like little hops.

"Over there," I said.

"Come on Cain, time to go!" she yelled.

Mark and I took one more look at the headstone, then each other. By then Grandma had already hopped three rows over and said, "Come on now. You can all come back with me next week."

"Oh great," I said. Then Mark reached out and took my hand. I pulled away and asked, "What do you think you're doing?"

His face got all red and he said, "I was just going to see if you wanted to race back. Bet I'll beat you." Then he took off running toward the gate.

Jeesh.

I took the jonquil from behind my ear and lay it on the headstone and knelt down to touch the part that said "Dip" etched in the cold stone. Just then Cain walked up. He looked at me, then to the flower on the stone. We both walked back together toward the car without saying a word.

Chapter Twelve

An Army of Angels

Mrs. Odell Brinkley

Cain and I were at my desk at the courthouse working on another letter to Southern Lifestyles and I noticed he didn't seem quite himself. He had written faithfully since last year, with no response. Each month, with surprisingly precise grammar for a boy his age, he politely made a case for Lost Cain to the obviously uninterested editors of the magazine.

"Is everything okay, Cain?" I asked. "You've been awfully quiet today."

"I went to the graveyard with Macy's grandma on Sunday," he said.

"That was sweet of you," I said.

Mrs. Hollister bragged incessantly about how often she visited her husband's grave. She and Eupha Lovelady apparently had a rivalry going to see which widow was more devoted to their dead husbands. Each made the trip several times a week, depositing flowers, polishing the headstones and glaring at each other from across the rows, should they both happen to be there at the same time.

"Did you know there's a tombstone with Daddy's name on it out there?" Cain asked.

The memory of the day we had the graveside service for Dip rushed back. The family had waited several months after hearing word of his death, hoping something would be sent home. Finally giving up hope, young Lola, with Cain on her hip, stood by while each loved one dropped a flower of their choosing into the empty grave. Momma Jewel put in a rose, Trudy a tulip, Leon a chrysanthemum and other family members their own. Finally Lola dropped in a handful of daisies—the flowers she said Dip had always brought her. The thought could still bring me to tears, all these years later, but I didn't want Cain to see that.

"Yes, Cain, I did know. Did you?"

Cain just shook his head, tears forming in his eyes.

"It's okay, Sugar," I said, pulling him into my breast. He held me tight. "Your daddy would be so proud of you, Cain Joseph McAllister," I said.

We are all so proud of this boy.

It was nearly a week later when I finally received a response to all Cain's letters from the past year. The return address was printed with raised, embossed lettering that said, Southern Lifestyles Magazine above an Atlanta street address. It was so clean and stiff—very thin—but surprisingly heavy. It must be the quality of the paper.

I didn't dare open it without Cain, but hated to leave the courthouse in the hands of the Mayor. I could hear the steady rumble of snoring coming from his office. Randall Polk, our current Mayor, came in every morning at eight forty-five, drank a cup of coffee, burped, and then went to sleep on the couch in his office until lunch. Randall was the local veterinarian and widely known to be a notorious drunkard.

No one in Lost Cain paid any attention whatsoever to whom they voted for mayor because they knew I'd take care of anything that came up. For years now, I'd done every bit of work associated with the office. More often than not, it was me that made every major decision and signed all the papers in the perfectly forged signature of whoever happened to be mayor at the time.

It had been the Baptist's turn for mayor when Randall put his hat in the ring last spring. None of the farmers had time and it was either Randall, who, drunk or not, showed up to church every Sunday, or Leon, who, though a member, hadn't darkened the doors of Lost Cain Baptist in years. Most wanted Leon, but since he was already the acting fire chief, it was decided that Randall Polk would have to do.

Personally, I was relieved by the decision. I didn't want to share close quarters with Leon McAllister. I didn't know why I was still so uncomfortable around him. What we'd had was so long ago—years before he met Trudy. And though it was the closest I'd ever come to romance in my life, I'm sure Leon never gave it a second thought.

"I've half a mind to run myself," I said to Odell one night over the dinner table. Odell laughed so hard it started a coughing fit.

"Lost Cain ain't ready for a woman mayor, not by a long shot," he said.

"Well, they've had one for nine years, whether they were ready for one or not," I said right back.

Odell just laughed and dabbed some butter on his

roll, then asked me to pass the mashed potatoes. He was right, of course, which made it all the worse that he would come right out and say it. The man was honest to a fault.

As I gathered my things and put the letter from Southern Lifestyles in my purse to run show Cain, I couldn't help but think to myself, during all our twenty three years of marriage, Odell Brinkley has never once told me a comforting lie.

Trudy McAllister

Lola's latest thing was making plaster decoupage pictures. Mostly flowers, children kissing, and angels. Lord, the angels. She'd spend days on end doing nothing else but laying out mold after mold in the kitchen and put dozens at a time in the oven if she got too impatient for 'em to harden on their own. I'd gone over as early as six in the morning to find her in the kitchen working. They're pretty and all, but the number of angels that girl had in her house at any given moment was downright apocalyptic.

Not that it's bad to have a hobby. She'd give the pictures to shut-ins, mostly little old ladies from the church with broken hips or misshapen joints. That or she sold them for a dollar apiece at school auctions and cakewalks. What had me worried me was that she'd quit all the committees at church and took to staying at home all day, every day. Claimed she didn't have any time left anymore, she was so busy making pictures. It was getting to be like pulling teeth to even get her out for church on Sundays.

As much as I hated to admit Ida Pico might be right

about anything, I agreed that Lola needed to find herself a man. It's not the end all, be all, but it takes your mind off things.

I'd decided that we were going to have this out, so I took myself over there one morning and knocked on her kitchen door. I let myself in when there wasn't any answer and found the counters and table all covered with small plastic containers filled with white plaster. I figured Lola was sleeping so I started straightening up and noticed a piece of notebook paper on the fridge held in place by a little angel figurine. Across the top it read "Words Cain McAllister is not allowed to say, ever!" Underneath it: P*ss, f*rt, b*tthole, cr*p and p*ckerwood.

Good Lord, by the time the boy's in junior high, he'll be a mute.

I heard Lola holler from somewhere in the house, "Cain, get up."

"I'm already up," Cain yelled from the den.

"That's not up. Now go get a bath and get dressed. Just 'cause it's summer don't mean you can lie around all day like third base," she hollered and backed into the kitchen with a tray in her hands. When she turned around, she saw me and said, "Oh, Trudy, I didn't hear you come in."

I'm not one to be at a loss for words, but let me tell you, she looked a mess. Both her arms were covered in long plastic bags with patches of dried plaster all over them. Her hair was speckled with little white clumps that looked like dangling beads of cake icing when she turned her head.

Just then the front door bell rang and Lola set the tray down on the kitchen table and shrieked, "Good Golly,

I can't let anybody see me looking like this." She ran down the hall to her bedroom and called back, "Go get the door and tell them I'm on the toilet or something."

I finally collected myself enough to yell after her down the hallway, "I don't see how sitting on the toilet is a better excuse than making little plaster pictures."

Lord help us, I'm going to have to call Ida.

"It's Miss B," Cain yelled from the front door.

"The coast is clear," I hollered to Lola. "It's just Miss B come to see Cain."

Lola peeked back into the kitchen from the hallway.

"Now come in here and sit down," I said. At least let me make you a proper breakfast. You're looking downright pekid." She sat down at the table. It was the first time I'd seen her still in weeks. "You and me's about to have ourselves a talk," I said.

Just then Cain came running into the kitchen, tickled to death, and jumped into Lola's lap. He gave her a big hug and said, "They're sending a photographer to Lost Cain!" Lola held on to him tight and smiled that pretty smile I remembered so well but hadn't seen in so long.

"I knew you could do it, baby boy," she said.

"I'm not a baby," Cain said, standing up.

"I know. I know," Lola said, still holding onto his hand.

"They got all my letters and said they'd send someone next month! Did you hear, Aunt Trudy?" he asked.

"I'd have to be deaf not to hear that," I said. "Ain't that something."

"Can I go tell Mark?" Cain asked, pulling at her arm.

Lola stood up and hugged him again. "Of course, you

can," she said.

"Well, let go of me," Cain said.

That smile of hers just faded away and it about broke my heart.

"Momma loves you," she whispered and kissed his forehead.

"Can I go now?" he asked again.

"Go put on some clothes and don't be too long," Lola said and finally let go of his hand. Before she could even finish the sentence, Cain had bolted down the hall. She stood and listened as he ran to his room, then out of the house. When the screened door slammed shut, it was like somebody had hit her with a bullet. She sank back down at the table and said, "I'm not the person my little boy lives to tell everything to anymore."

I set down the skillet and went over and took my baby sister in my arms.

"It's going to be okay, Sweetie," I said. "Cain's growing up to be a fine young man. You did a good job."

I held her there for a good while and then she stood up, said, "I'm not hungry," and walked away. Before she got to the hallway, she turned back around.

"Trudy, Why does life give you something so precious and then bit by bit take it away?" Then she turned away toward her bedroom and left me there in the kitchen, surrounded by an army of angels.

Cain McAllister

I couldn't wait to tell Mark the news about the photographer. I ran by his house but Mrs. McElroy said she didn't know where he was. I figured he was at the church and ran over there as fast as I could.

Mark would have been at my house when Miss B came, but his mom said no when we asked if he could stay over. Mrs. McElroy had been saying no a lot more lately. Last week she made me sleep on the sofa in the living room when I stayed at their house. She said it was so we wouldn't stay up all night talking and keeping her awake, but Mark always fell asleep so early and so fast that it didn't make sense to me.

By the time I made it there, I was out of breath so I stopped just inside the side door. I heard laughter coming from the sanctuary and then a big splash, so I climbed the steps and ran through the choir loft to the hole in the back wall that looked onto the baptismal pool. Mark was underwater with all his clothes on, his eyes open and face pressed against the small section of Plexiglas that looked out to the sanctuary. With people getting saved left and right, Brother Neil had starting filling the pool almost every week. Mark smiled at me and waved while little air bubbles floated up over his face. I reached my hand over the rail and pulled him up by the hair.

"Hey, watch it," Mark yelled.

"Brother Neil's gonna kill you if he catches you," I said.

"I don't care," Mark said and pushed my arm away.

The only time Mark said anything against his daddy was when Macy Hollister was around. I looked over, and sure enough, there was Macy sitting on the edge of the steps, her bare feet in the water, with her hand over her mouth, holding in a laugh.

"Oh. Hey Macy," I said.

"Hey yourself, Cain McAllister," Macy said.

Macy always called me by both names and I didn't really like it.

"Jump over the rail, Cain," Mark said.

"No way," I said.

"Why the hell not?" Mark asked. Cussing was another thing Mark did a lot around Macy. Before Macy, Mark would only cuss when it was just the two of us. It was our joke and every time he did it, he would wink at me and laugh. Now he just looked at Macy after every single cuss word.

"Don't you want to come swimming?" Macy asked, but she didn't say it like a question. "Please, Cain," she said.

Macy Hollister

I knew the little shit wouldn't do something against the rules.

I could peg just about anybody, boys especially, but I didn't know what to make of Cain McAllister. He hated it when I called him both names like that, so I made sure I always did. Instead of jumping in, he just walked around the choir loft to the end of the baptismal pool opposite me.

"Go on," I said to Cain.

"I can't," he said, looking so scared it made me feel a little bad for being so mean.

"Suit yourself," Mark said, then turned to me. "I

dare you to get in, Macy."

When someone dared you to do something, nothing gets to them like acting as if it wasn't even worth a dare to begin with, so I jumped in like I didn't even have to think about it.

Mark laughed and started to splash me while Cain gave me that look he always did. The one that says, "I think I may hate you." I had learned to ignore it. I started splashing Mark back, then all of a sudden he stopped and I saw his eyes get wide.

Oh, shit! I forgot I didn't have on a bra. My nips were out to there. I ducked into the water as fast as I could and screamed, "Stop looking!"

"Looking at what?" Mark asked, smiling.

Cain just rolled his eyes. *You don't fool me, Cain McAllister. You look at my tits just as much as everyone else, but not like Mark.* Mark couldn't do anything but look at them. As soon as I walked into a room he couldn't seem to help himself. I thought it was funny. But Cain only stole glances when he thought I wasn't looking. I'd seen him in the mirror at my grandma's house or in the reflection off the glass in the meat counter at his uncle's store. He always looked thrilled and repulsed at the same time. As if he was above looking at a girl's tits or something. I may not have had him pegged yet, but that I could tell.

"Oh, shut up," I said back. *Jeesh.*

For ten solid minutes Cain went on about some photographer who was going to come to town to take some pictures for a magazine. He was real excited about it. Said Mark and I could help him make sure everything was ready. Just chattering away. I made sure that my tits were below the water but I started seeing if I could make Mark look by moving my hand away to touch my hair while Cain talked. Mark's eyes would try to sneak over every time. I guess I should have felt bad teasing him like that, but I didn't. What else was there to do in that place?

A reflection of light from the back sanctuary door swung across above us, and Mark said, "Damn, somebody's here."

"Can you see who it is?" I said to Cain.

"Shhh," he said and lifted his head up to look over the railing, then popped back down. "It's Brother Neil," he whispered.

There was no way we'd be able to get out without him hearing so Mark and I both stayed put. I tried not to move so the water would stop sloshing against the sides. In the quiet church even that little sound was a lot.

The colder it got, the more my nipples felt like they were going to poke right through my arms. I could hear Brother Neil whistling as he walked to the front of the church. The water lapped against the sides of the baptismal pool as we all sat where we were and didn't make a move. After a couple minutes, I saw the light from the door come back across above us and heard the click of heels in the foyer.

"Oh, Brother Neil, I'm so glad I found you," a soft, breathless voice said.

"Good morning, Mrs. Jasper, what can I do for you?"

"I wonder if I could steal you away from your work for a few minutes," Mrs. Jasper asked.

"Of course."

"It's Jimmy, we've just come back from the doctor," she said.

Jimmy Jasper? You've got to be kidding me. What is it with these people and names?

"They said he's going to have to have an operation," Mrs. Jasper said.

"What is it?" Brother Neil asked.

"Well, I can't really—it's just that..." Mrs. Jasper stuttered and stammered a few minutes before she went on to describe in detail that little Jimmy's pecker was too big for the hole at the end of it. The doctors would have to go in and stretch the thing out, then cut a little slit—anyway, I can't even go on, it was so disgusting.

Of course Cain and Mark were almost peeing in their pants, they thought it was so funny. Cain even smiled at me at one point, which I don't think he'd ever done before.

Brother Neil

I was called to preach, not pastor. Preaching was when I felt most alive. I had delivered my first sermon by accident when I was only thirteen at a youth service in a neighboring town. I was asked to give my testimony and said a prayer before I began. I then lost myself in the Holy Spirit for the next hour. Afterward, people of all ages that I had never met came up to me and told me how encouraged and challenged they had been by my words, most of which I couldn't even remember. By seventeen, I was leading revivals as a guest speaker in churches across Mississippi and Alabama.

Once I started a family, I had to become a pastor. There were bills to pay and it offered a stability that was too tempting to resist. I told myself that I would still be able to preach, but found that unlike the joy I felt in the pulpit, pastoring often seemed a distraction from my true calling. I handled this dissatisfaction by moving every few years to a new church, each bigger than the one before. My church in Meridian boasted over seven thousand members, though on any given Sunday, only around seven hundred actually bothered to come. It wasn't what I considered a respectable percentage, even taking into account that the rolls included anyone who had ever been baptized at the church. I tried once to get the rolls cleaned up but found that even a death certificate was a barely justifiable reason for the ancient secretary who worked there to take someone off the roll. I'd venture that many a soul in Meridian who met their final judgment years ago still got the annual Annie Armstrong missionary drive envelope at their last known address.

The decision to come to Lost Cain with a membership of only three hundred and forty seven was something that puzzled my church leadership in Meridian. As one of the deacons there put it, "God rarely called a pastor down the scale, but always up."

My wife, Patty agreed. She'd been a humble and obedient woman in our fifteen years of marriage, but wondered if a small town would satisfy my ambitions. My wife considered me ambitious, but I only knew myself to be called. I was constantly asking God to make that calling more clear to me. It was the subject of many a prayer.

That morning, I had left my office hoping to take some time to pray, but Mary Jasper had tracked me down and cornered me in the sanctuary. Pastoring seemed to always involve comforting overly dramatic women and I'd never been good at that. It was one of the reasons I married Patty—she was the least dramatic woman I'd ever met. A deacon or other male member of the church would, now and then, come to see me, but most always it was simply holding the hands of the women in church while they told me their troubles. I did my best to listen, but my mind was always somewhere else.

Like this morning with Mrs. Jasper, I sat there for as long as I could—I won't even go into what the discussion entailed—before I finally told her all was well, God was near, and politely led her out the door to her car.

She wouldn't leave until I prayed with her. She'd wanted to go to my office, but I was always careful about appearances, so there in the parking lot next to the church, she put her hands in mine and we bowed our heads to pray. *Lonely women have been the downfall of many a godly man.* I couldn't say I wasn't drawn to any of the ladies in my congregation, but Mrs. Jasper was not among those ranks. After a few words, she was finally consoled enough to go on her way.

Macy Hollister

For a half hour Mrs. Jasper wailed about little Jimmy Jasper's miniature urethra and whether or not he'd survive the surgery. I could tell Brother Neil was trying to get rid of her, but the woman just wouldn't leave. Every time she said the word penis, it was like she did it low and throaty. It sounded to me like she was hitting on the preacher. I could tell. By then I was so cold that my teeth started chattering. I didn't think they could hear me down in the sanctuary, but Cain shot me a dirty look anyway.

Finally, Brother Neil offered to take Mrs. Jasper back to her car. As soon as I heard the door close, I jumped out of the water with Mark right behind me.

"Quick, we probably only got a few minutes before he comes back in," Mark said.

"Here, take this," Cain said to me. He handed me one of the choir robes and I put it on over my clothes.

Mark bolted down the stairs and out through the back of the church, but Cain stayed behind and held out his hand to help me down the steps. Shivering, I took it and still almost slipped. Cain reached around my waist to support me and smiled at me again.

Twice in one day. That's got to be a record.

Brother Neil

When I walked back inside the sanctuary I noticed a glimmer from the baptismal pool as the water rocked gently against the glass. *A tremor perhaps*? Earthquakes were a sign of the the Second Coming. There would be wars, and rumors of war. Natural disasters. Suffering and persecution. All the things I saw in those troubled times. *Jesus could come back at any moment. I'll not be caught unprepared.*

When the sanctuary was quite like this, I enjoyed it, though it's strange how, in an empty church, you almost always heard something—never true silence. On the wall above the piano, hung a small black attendance board with white letters and hanging numbers like a tiny scoreboard keeping track of which side was winning. The Training Union numbers were shameful, but I saw that Sunday mornings were heading up. Last week we had

203. The week before only 178 and the week before that 165. The growing attendance humbled me. I was honored that God would choose me to do His work here.

I felt the Lord's presence during my sermons lately. I sensed a change. Each Sunday since I had started the book of Revelations, as I sat looking out just before the service, I could hear the congregation murmur and spark in their pews like hot embers working up through old wood. After the service last week, there had been nine saved and three rededications.

For the coming week, I had the secretary put in large bold letters on the back of the bulletin: "The End Times Are Coming..." and nothing else. That would get people's attention, I believed. All my sermons were to focus on Revelations leading up to the arrival in August of Professor Preston Stanley from the Southeastern Baptist Theological Seminary. He had written several books on the Rapture, Tribulation and Armageddon. The review on the back of his latest book called him, "A modern day John the Baptist, proclaiming the imminent coming of our Lord." He was one of the main architects in cleansing the seminaries of the false doctrines of Biblical criticism.

The Word is the only certainty we have in this uncertain world God's inerrant, infallible, voice. Our only shelter from wickedness. The only hope for redemption. There is none righteous, not one. I reminded myself of these things daily in prayer and knew that God wouldn't be satisfied with me until every believer in my flock was truly on fire for the Lord.

Chapter Thirteen

Shock and Moral Outrage

Mrs. Odell Brinkley

There was trouble brewing, I could tell. It had all started innocently enough when the Methodists began holding youth meetings on Saturday nights in their basement. I imagine the Reverend felt a little outdone by the enthusiasm over Brother Neil's sermons over at the Baptist Church. They played charades, and games where all the kids lined up, girl, then boy, then girl and passed an orange to each other using only their necks, no arms. Apparently as the night wore on, someone stuck a Bee Gees tape in the sound system for some background music during the games and one by one, the kids started swaying to the music. Next thing you know, they were all dancing.

Unlike the Baptists, we Methodists had nothing in particular against dancing. The youth minister decided it was harmless fun, so he cranked up the music and joined in as they all bopped around in the basement to the music of *Staying Alive*.

The next morning at First Methodist, the Reverend heard so many good things that he encouraged more to come, and let the congregation know that next week he intended to "cut a rug" himself, and asked for chaperones. Since Odell's idea of an exciting Saturday night was staying awake through an entire episode of *Barnaby Jones*, I volunteered.

The next week, nearly two dozen kids showed up and before long the dancing started. They were having a grand old time. There was Elton John, Donna Summer, and something called E.L.O. In spite of the fact that I couldn't understand most every song they played, I was thoroughly enjoying watching them from behind the kitchen counter when the Reverend and Youth Director came over and asked me to join the Conga line.

It wasn't like me to get rowdy, but I was having so much fun, I threw caution to the wind and hopped on in. As we made the second go-round, the teenagers all lined up behind us. I noticed Dulan Meacham, a city councilman and chairman of the deacons at Lost Cain Baptist, watching from the stairway, perched on the last step that led down to the basement with a horrified look on his face as if he was standing above a flow of molten lava.

Once the song ended, everyone laughed and the Reverend called us all in a circle for the closing prayer. Dulan just stood there in righteous indignation, but once he figured out we were no longer dancing, but praying, he bowed his head reluctantly. I imagine it was too great a struggle for a pious man like Dulan to resist any spoken prayer, no matter the circumstances. After the Amen, Dulan made his way, teeth clenched, through the crowd of teens over to the Reverend and myself. Dulan was a little stout man whose feet always pointed out from each other when he walked as if they weren't on speaking terms.

"Do you mind telling me what's going on here, Reverend?" he asked, a small, crooked vein throbbing at his temple. "I was just out for a walk, and heard all this commotion. Sounded like the world was coming to an end!"

The Reverend turned and took Dulan's hand in that effortless way of preachers and politicians and said, "Mr. Meacham, I'm glad you could make it to our little social, here."

"It looks more like a bar to me," Dulan said, then immediately turned, and stomped back up the basement stairs and out the door.

This isn't the end of this.

It turned out that Dulan was not "just out for a walk," but had been tipped off by a concerned mother. Her son had come home the previous Saturday night bragging about how much fun he'd had at church and she'd called Dulan, saying it sounded suspicious to her.

According to the noise complaint he filed with the County Sheriff the next morning, the sight of us all, "pelvically thrusting to a Satanic beat" –Dulan's words, not mine—had filled him with "shock and moral outrage."

Peggy Leggett

Before church started, Dulan Meacham pulled Belle Milow and myself aside and told us of all the goings-on in the Methodist Church basement the night before. He described, in great detail how all the teenagers, and even Mrs. Odell Brinkley and the Methodist preacher, were all lined up, their hands on each other's hips, jumping, thrusting and gyrating to some African sounding music right there in the house of the Lord. If a Methodist church could even be called that.

You could have literally knocked me over with a feather. Belle just stood there next to me with her mouth wide open—something she always did whenever she got to concentrating too hard, even though I'd told her a hundred times it was quite unattractive. I reached over and yanked my husband Bud's arm and he spilled his coffee on Belle's husband, Hickory.

"Did you hear all that, Bud?" I asked.

Belle said, "I've always suspected they use real wine in their communion. There was a distinct aftertaste that time I visited there last summer."

"That would explain why they do it every week instead of each quarter like any good Christian should," I said. The Baptist Faith and Message given out by the Southern Baptist Convention recommended the practice of quarterly communion, and I took that as gospel.

"We should send somebody to investigate," Belle said.

"I couldn't agree more," I said.

"Why don't we send Mayor Polk over to First Methodist to see if it's alcohol or not. He oughta be able to tell easy enough," Hickory chimed in.

Bud snorted what was left of his coffee and Hickory had a good laugh. As if having a raving alcoholic for Mayor was something to brag about.

"Wait 'til you hear this," Hickory said to Bud. I started to interrupt, but Bud pinched me on my arm. Bud and Hickory were both on the city council and Bud was forever reminding me that Hickory was one of the biggest farmers around and I oughta be more respectful.

Hickory went on, “Tuesday morning, I called Mayor Polk over to take a look at one of my cows that’s been ailing. He looked like twelve miles of bad road, I tell ya—the mayor, not the cow. Well, the mayor walks up to the cow lying there on the ground, and hitches up his pants and squats down next to it. He thinks on it a minute and says to me, he says, “Now, Hick, you go get me a pint of buttermilk mixed with six raw eggs and seven shakes of Tabasco sauce,” then looks back down at the cow. I thought to myself that’s the darnedest thing I ever heard—giving milk to a sick cow. So I go in and tell Belle here to put it all together and I take it out to him in a big bowl. The mayor just looked at me a little funny. Then he took the bowl from me, turned it sideways and drank the whole thing down in four or five gulps. He shook his head back and forth, and smacked his lips, and then he says to me, “Now that I got my wits about me, let’s see about this cow.”

Hickory and Bud busted out laughing and I just looked at Belle, who was giggling a little herself, failing to grasp the seriousness of the situation, as usual. If Belle Milow wasn’t my best friend in the world, I don’t think I’d have a thing to do with her, to tell you the Gods-honest truth.

“Now fellas, this is serious,” Dulan said. “Joke all you want, but drinking leads to dancing and dancing leads to premarital sex and the next thing you know, we’ll have a whole generation of bastard children running the streets of Lost Cain.”

Just about that time—I figured it must have been divine providence at the mention of the word bastard—

Lola walked by, looking all skinny and pretty. Bud and Hickory both nodded and smiled. I smiled too, but I could feel the muscles in my jaw just aching and waited for her to pass. Lola hadn't been to church for weeks. I forgot how nice it was to look out from the choir loft and not see her sitting out there looking like a dainty, delicate little flower.

Dulan said, "It'd be one thing if they were having dances for the adults, that would be bad enough, but I wouldn't say nothing about it. But for children? Something has got to be done!"

"I couldn't agree more," I said and pinched Bud hard.

"All right Dulan," Bud said, "don't get worked up. You just do whatever you want and we'll be behind you."

During services, as I sat up in the choir loft that morning, I looked out on all the young faces in the congregation and thought about the corrupting influence those Methodist dances could have on each of them. There on the third pew sat little Jodie Abernathy, nine-years-old with blonde pigtails. In my mind, God gave me a picture of that sweet little thing, just a few years hence, eight months pregnant and snorting cocaine off the hymnal. I teared up just thinking about it and wondered if Brother Neil knew what was going on right there in Lost Cain.

Ever since he had started his series on the Tribulation, Brother Neil had us all enthralled. As he made his way up to the pulpit, I wondered, *who knew talking about the end of the world could make a man so much more handsome and appealing?*

Before choir practice last week, Belle had confessed

to me that she listened to every word of Brother Neil's sermons with an enthusiasm that bordered on arousal. I admitted I'd found myself using the program as a fan more than I was entirely comfortable with. At every Baptist Young Women's meeting, we couldn't help but note Brother Neil's sensitivity and sincere devotion to God. It had inspired each of us to take up the cause of Christ with more fervor than ever before. LeAnn Hester had started a new Lottie Moon soup can drive. Tammie Johnston was going door to door witnessing to migrant farm workers down by the river. Even Rhonda Mason had volunteered the use of her van to pick up retarded children and bring them to church every Sunday. And everyone knew how ticky Rhonda was about her upholstery, what with the drooling and all.

While I sang the last stanza of *Thy Kingdom of Glory*, I could see all the other ladies in church, each looking admiringly at Brother Neil, who sat, with his eyes closed in prayer, in the big throne-like chair by the pulpit. I asked myself if I was doing enough for the Lord? Did Brother Neil think of me as a faithful servant? The music director signaled the finale and I made sure my soprano lilted just a little above all the others. Brother Neil smiled at me and this drove my voice to even greater heights. As the song ended, I breathlessly took my seat and watched the back of Brother Neil's head as he opened the sermon with a prayer. It was during that prayer that I found a new calling.

Trudy McAllister

It did my heart good to see Lola in church that morning. I had told her on the phone, “I’ll come over there and drag you out of that house if I have to,” and hung up before she could tell me any different.

Now if I could just get Leon here, I could die a happy woman. Fat chance of that. Leon swore the walls would come tumbling down if a sinner of his magnitude were to show up. *That man.*

Lola looked good too. Some folks, when they’re going through a tough spell, just go all to pieces. But not Lola. She was put together perfect.

After closing prayer, Peggy Leggett hopped down from the choir loft with a yellow notepad in her hand and started yapping with the gaggle of ladies that always pooled around Brother Neil after his sermons like some teenagers waiting for the Beatles to come off a plane.

After a few minutes, Peggy made her way over to us. She barely gave Lola a look before she shoved that yellow notepad at me with one hand and held her pen out to me with the other.

“How about you sign our petition, Trudy?” she asked.

“Depends on what we’re petitioning for,” I said.

Peggy huffed and shifted to one hip, letting me know she was offended to even have to explain. I noticed about a dozen or so signatures already on the paper.

“The Methodists are throwing wild dance parties in their basement and letting in all ages,” Peggy said, her face all contorted.

“You mean their Saturday Socials?” I asked. Working

at the store, this was all old news. Sounded pretty harmless, if you ask me.

"Socials, hmph," Peggy said. "For all we know they're big drug orgies."

I laughed so hard at that one I snorted.

"It's not funny," she said, shoving that pad and pen at me again. "You going to sign or not?"

"I don't think my mind's made up, one way or the other, Peggy," I said, proud of myself for sounding halfway polite when the Lord knew I was thinking otherwise.

Peggy just clicked her pen at me, and said, "I see." Then she stomped off, ignoring Lola completely, like Peggy always seemed to make a special point to do. I took Lola's arm in mine.

"You going to come by for lunch?" I asked.

I could tell she'd rather think up some excuse to get back home, but she didn't. We all had a nice afternoon together. I'd like to think it did her some good too.

The next week, Peggy and her bunch at the church went door-to-door, collecting signatures for their petition. Leon was always talking to me about word of mouth marketing and now I finally understood what he meant. By Saturday, thanks to the hard work of the good Baptist ladies, every teenager in the county was lined up outside the Methodist Church for the next dance.

Lola McAllister

I wouldn't let Cain go to the dance, but it wasn't because of that silly petition of Peggy Leggett's. I had grounded him on Wednesday after the cleaning lady at church told Brother Neil she walked in on the boys simulating what she called, "lewd and lascivious behavior" between the Apostle Paul and Mary Magdalene puppets during practice for Children's Church. Cain was so mad at me he'd barely said three words since.

"Cain, don't be upset," I said through the door. "You can go to the dance the next weekend."

"Leave me alone, I wanna die," he said.

I went back to the kitchen and lit a cigarette. Then I called up Ida on the phone just to punish myself for smoking and being a bad mother. I wedged the phone against my shoulders and rubbed my temples while she went on.

"You are doing exactly the right thing, Lola," Ida said. "A week means a week, end of story."

The next morning at church Brother Neil went over all the reasons good Baptists should easily see the dangers of young people dancing together in a basement. He didn't exactly badmouth the Methodists, but it was pretty clear where he stood on the issue. After the sermon, there was a special closing announcement and Peggy Leggett came down to the pulpit with her little notebook.

"I'm proud to say that I recognized this menace early on and thanks to the good work of most of the ladies in our congregation—"

It was pretty clear the way she said "most" what that implied about us good ladies who hadn't helped.

"We have gathered one hundred and thirty three signatures!" Peggy said, holding the notebook up in the air like a banner, making sure Brother Neil noticed. As a matter of fact, she wouldn't quit waving the thing until he finally gave her a little nod. Then she said, "And thanks to all this hard work, and your prayers, my husband, Bud, who most of y'all know is a city council member, and Hickory and Dulan, have all agreed to hold a special meeting of the city council this Friday night to take up this dire issue."

Then she walked over and practically yanked Brother Neil's arm out of the socket, raising both their hands up like they were Jimmy and Roslyn Carter at a campaign stop.

Cain McAllister

The Saturday before, I had snuck out while Momma was on the phone with Mammy Pico and looked at the crowd waiting outside the Methodist Church. It reminded me of the movie magazines I read at the store with pictures of people lined down the street waiting to get into Studio 54. After that I started practicing my dance moves every single day.

I had picked out what to wear on Monday night, even though the social wasn't until the next weekend. There was going to be a dancing contest and everything. I'd watched Denny Tario on *Dance Fever* every Saturday for two years. I almost always picked the couple that won. I'd never actually danced in front of anyone—Baptists weren't supposed to—but I figured I'd love it.

As much as I didn't want to, I asked Macy if she'd

come over and practice with me. I didn't really ask her if she'd be in the contest, just if she'd practice. She was the only girl I really knew who might know anything about dancing. *I bet they do it a lot up in St. Louis.*

Since Mark followed Macy everywhere, he invited himself along as well. He said that as much as I made him watch *Dance Fever* on Saturday mornings before we went to the creek, that he was practically an expert himself. I didn't mind that he came, but after the first day he got so bored watching us that he left early and didn't come back all week.

Macy was good. We worked up a routine from stuff we'd seen on TV and a few things we just thought of at the time. We'd lock hands, then put them over our shoulders and spread apart. I pulled her into me and then swung her out and back in to dip her down. I tried to put one leg out, bend down and flip her over but she was so much bigger than me and kept falling. By the time Friday came around we had it down. It lasted about four minutes. That afternoon we did the routine for Momma Jewel, Aunt Trudy and Momma. They all said it was real good.

Please, God, I prayed in bed each night that week before the city council meeting, *don't let them shut it down before I get a chance to show everybody.*

Mrs. Odell Brinkley

So many people had shown up for the special council meeting that we were all forced to walk from the courthouse over to the gymnasium at the school. As the mayor's secretary, it was my job to keep minutes at all the meetings, so I sat at the table up front with all the council members while a sizeable crowd of about fifty, mostly women, took their seats in the bleachers behind where Brother Neil sat next to Reverend Jenkins from the Methodist church. After I read the minutes from the previous week, Hickory Milow called the meeting to order. To open the discussion, he called on Dulan Meacham.

Dulan, like a crazed carnival barker, spouted out statistics and examples of rampant youth crime and debauchery in the world. While he was doing that, Peggy Leggett passed out fliers showing a young pregnant white girl standing with a black boy at a tattoo parlor. Across the bottom it asked, “Are you ready to be a grandparent?”

She gave me a copy and said, “I think this should be included in the official record.” I took it, smiled and dropped it in the waste basket beside me as soon as she turned away.

Reverend Jenkins was then given a chance to respond. He approached the podium and explained that their intentions had been only to give the children something to do on Saturday nights. The dancing had occurred spontaneously and, contrary to the earlier comments of Mrs. Leggett, was not engineered by secular humanists.

As if Peggy Leggett has a clue in her empty head as to what a secular humanist is.

The three Methodist council members asked sympathetic questions and tried unsuccessfully to point out that in America a church should be allowed to decide for itself what’s permitted within its walls. To this, Dulan Meacham quoted a verse about the sin of one rubbing off on all, and called for a vote to stop the dances immediately. Belle Milow, on the second row, asked for Brother Neil's thoughts.

When Brother Neil took the podium he tried to be respectful of Reverend Jenkins' theological interpretations, and insisted that his concern was not with the dancing, but the music. He pointed out that though the Bible was full of examples of people dancing in praise of the Lord, that the music being played was secular, with subversive and sometimes sexual lyrics.

Predictably, when the time came to vote, it was split, three Methodists for the dances and three Baptists against. I suspected Hickory would have liked to have joined the Methodists, but the look on his wife's face as she nodded her head up and down when Brother Neil spoke probably made him toe the line.

One of the Methodists suggested we table the issue until next month so that both sides could talk more about their stance. Dulan insisted that someone go find Mayor Polk to break the tie and they started discussing where he could be. I looked at my watch, which said six thirty. *I can tell you exactly where he is. Passed out drunk and dead to the world, in the den he made out of his carport last spring.*

The Methodists knew the Mayor, being a Baptist, would vote against them anyway, so one of the councilmen suggested that the socials could continue if Brother Neil's concern about the music was addressed.

In the end, a compromise was reached that, like most, pleased no one. The dances could go on but the Baptists would supply the music. The kicker being, that the music would take the form of Mrs. Mary Brown Conaway, the seventy-eight-year-old retired Baptist church organist.

Cain McAllister

Macy and me showed up thirty minutes early and sat on the steps at the church along with about twenty other kids. I had on a pair of tan corduroy pants, a bright green long sleeved shirt, a thick white belt and my Sunday shoes. I figured it was the closest thing to Studio 54 I might ever get, so I'd better make the most of it. I thought I looked pretty good, except after five minutes on the steps, I felt awful hot. I wished Mark could have come, but even with the music changed, Brother Neil wouldn't let him.

Finally the Methodist youth director opened up the door and led us all down to the basement. It wasn't as big as our fellowship hall, but it was nice. They had it all decorated with purple and gold streamers, and little old ladies stood behind the counter in the kitchen handing out Dixie cups filled with punch.

In the corner, Mary Brown Conaway was already stooped over, sitting at the organ, and as soon as we stepped down, she pounded out the first notes to *Onward Christian Soldiers*. The Methodist kids jumped right in and started dancing together, while most of the Baptists held back and watched. Mary Brown banged the keys and picked up the tempo on the next verse.

I was dying to dance, but didn't want to be the first Baptist. About eight of us were standing around just looking at each other, me tapping my foot and doing all I could to stand still. Just then Macy grabbed my hand and led me out to the dance floor. At first I just kind of stood there snapping my fingers and moving my arms a little bit.

Macy lifted her hands over her head, while she twirled her hips to the beat of the organ.

On the chorus, Onward Christian soldiers, marching off to war—she took my hand and said, "Come on, Cain, just cut loose."

And so I did. For I don't know how long, I just danced and danced. It was the most fun thing I think I'd ever done.

By the time I came back to myself, *Holy, Holy, Holy* was just ending and I was drenching wet with sweat as the youth director stood up to announce that it was time for the dance contest. Macy smiled and took my hands and we started our routine.

Just as we did our big finish, I saw Bobby Lee Brewster walk down the steps into the basement. He looked straight at me and grinned. I stopped in my tracks and Macy asked, "What's wrong?" I wanted to run away, but couldn't seem to move.

Macy Hollister

I know what it feels like to dread someone that much. Cain's face went white and all the joy ran right out of it at the sight of Bobby Lee.

As soon as we finished our routine, Bobby Lee came over to us.

"Congratulations PeePants," he said. I heard a few snickers from several of the kids who had been cheering us on just a few minutes before.

"You going to get lucky tonight?" he continued,

giving me a wink.

Then the youth minister came up and announced that Cain and I were winners of the couple's dance contest. He handed us each a little trophy that read "First Place, Praise the Lord," and a miniature copy of the New Testament.

Bobby Lee backed off while we accepted them and the old lady playing the organ started another hymn.

When everyone went back to dancing, I looked for Cain, but didn't find him at first. Then I spotted him across the room and saw Bobby Lee walk over and yank the trophy out of Cain's hand. Bobby Lee took a look around to make sure no adults were watching, then spit in the little trophy cup and handed it back to Cain. I decided right then and there that I hated Bobby Lee Brewster too.

Mark had told me about how they were always planning revenge on Bobby Lee for picking on Cain. They even had a book full of stuff they'd been copying down for the past year.

Bobby Lee doesn't know who he's dealing with. But I didn't want him to know that. I walked over and said to him, "That wasn't very nice of you." But I didn't say it in a mean way.

"It's just PeePants. He likes it, don't you," Bobby Lee said.

"I'm Macy," I said and smiled at Bobby Lee. "I'm visiting my grandmother this summer."

"Hey," Bobby Lee said, finally ignoring Cain, who was giving me a hard look.

"You wanna dance?" I asked.

"Sure," Bobby Lee said, looking me up and down.

"Could you hold this for me, Cain?" He just yanked

the trophy out of my hand and ran toward the steps.

While we danced, Bobby Lee kept trying to put his hands on my waist. I just smiled and pushed them away that flirty way you swat at boys' hands that makes them think you're still deciding. I wanted Bobby Lee to think I was a little curious. The song playing was *Up From the Grave He Arose* and from the look of the little tent in Bobby Lee's pants, it fit the moment.

I danced and talked with him long enough to make him think I was good at acting good. By the end of the song, it was enough to confuse him as to whether I was a good girl acting bad or a bad one acting good.

"Well, I gotta get home," I said.

Bobby Lee took a step toward me and said, "I'll walk you."

"Then when my grandma hears some boy walked me home, I'll never get out of the house for the rest of the summer," I said. I reached out my hand and touched his arm just above the elbow.

"Maybe I'll see you soon," I said, then walked away, making sure to turn my feet with each step so that my dress would sway.

When I got outside, I looked for Cain but couldn't find him. On the ground were two trophies lying in the dirt, broken and stomped.

Cain McAllister

I couldn't stop running. I went past the store. Past my house. Past the church, and the edge of town where the bulldozers and heavy equipment to pave the road were parked in front of the levee. I just kept on. I climbed over the top of the levee and went all the way to the bank of the river, down past the grass ledge, into the dried mud that was still soft from where the river had flooded a few weeks ago.

I couldn't catch my breath and fell down on my knees in the dirt. I put one hand in one of the big dried up cracks in the ground and threw up. I felt too hot and tired to get up, so I just laid down instead. The ground felt cool and damp against my face. I'd never been this close to the river at night. The water was dark and unmoving and the sky was almost black with no moon in sight. The river always scared me, that was true, but not as much as other things.

Like if the rest of my life was always going to be like it was right now.

PART III

Chapter Fourteen

Imagine the Indignity

Mrs. Odell Brinkley

Every inch of my body ached as I polished the antique light post outside the courthouse. I ran inside to turn on the switch and then back out to see how it looked. *Not too bad. Not too bad at all.*

Looking down Main Street I couldn't help but feel a little proud. We had finally managed to get the road paved, and it was all going to be done well before the photographer's visit to town. There wasn't money to get any of the side roads done, but that was next on my list. The vote to pave Main Street had been the closest in the history of Lost Cain. The measure passed 101 to 98. Suffice it to say that roughly half of Lost Cain wanted nothing to do with paved roads.

I'd been working diligently for ten years to see this, and took great pride in cutting the ribbon that September day when the work started. Myself, Brother Neil from First Baptist, the mayor, and Reverend Jenkins from the Methodist church, smiled brightly for the picture taken by the reporter sent over by The Courier News over in Blytheville to cover the event.

The Pastor and the Reverend hadn't truly patched things up since the dustup over the socials, but they acted cordial enough in public. It got better after the dances had petered out on their own. Turned out that the attention span of teenagers didn't go much beyond a week or two. I wish I could say the same about the adults involved. Peggy Leggett never forgave me for throwing that flier of hers in the trash.

The day after the ribbon cutting, the state sent a prison crew from the county jail down in Luxora to begin work on the road. The rumblings from the rest of the town started almost immediately. Though most of the people under fifty worked with whites and blacks daily on their farms or over in Blytheville, the older people in town weren't accustomed to being in close quarters here in Lost Cain. Some of the places an hour or so west toward Crowley's Ridge were "sundown" towns—meaning anyone not white was expected to be out of town by sunset. Lost Cain had never been that kind of place, but the prison crew of roughly ten men had one black deputy and two black prisoners among them and their presence put some people on edge.

As much as I loved Lost Cain, the attitude toward anything or anyone different was downright shameful. As individuals, the people were as generous, loving and kind as any you'd find in this world. However, we were in a southern state and had all the baggage that came with our geography.

Thank God for Momma Jewel. The first day the prison crew started work on the road, she sent out Cain and Mark with big pitchers of lemonade and iced tea. You could see the eyebrows arch on the people who looked out from their front windows and porches as the two boys passed around the little Dixie cups to all the men. Every single afternoon the boys would make their rounds passing out the cups and Momma Jewel would follow, thanking each and every man for the work he was doing.

Mark and Cain found the whole thing fairly exciting and would come over to the courthouse to talk to me afterward.

"I lived with black folks all the time down in Mississippi," Mark said. "But they were never prisoners or deputies either!"

"This is the first time I've ever seen one close up," Cain said. "I see lots of them when Aunt Trudy takes me to Blytheville, but I never talked to any before now."

"Boys!" I said, "they are just people like you and me, so stop talking like that."

"Like what?" Cain asked.

"Like calling them 'one of them'," I said.

"I didn't mean anything bad by it," Cain said, his eyes starting to tear. Cain could cry at the drop of a hat when you hurt his feelings.

"I think it would be cool to be in jail," Mark added, "at least for a little while."

"It certainly would not be cool, young man," I said. "Now you two boys take these pitchers back to Momma Jewel's and let those men do their work."

In less than a week we had a paved, freshly painted road that led all the way through town. I made sure that rather than a patch of rough asphalt, a proper street was made, with sidewalks, drainage pipes—that led to nowhere really—and even three lampposts. There was one on each end of town and another here at the courthouse.

We could only afford three, so the others would have to be added to each block, first one end then the other, until they met someday at the courthouse in the middle.

Trudy McAllister

I had told Leon that I was going to meet Glenda and do some shopping, which wasn't exactly a lie itself. I *was* going to meet Glenda and we'd go shopping after the tests. I hadn't felt well for months. Couldn't seem to get warm. I hated going to the doctor's. Every time I did, my blood pressure would go up and I'd get sweaty all over. I didn't consider myself stupid, but I felt so uneducated there. The fact was, I never graduated high school. I left my sophomore year just to spite Momma and got married to Leon. I went back to get my GED a few years after that, but I never felt it was the same as a real diploma.

My regular doctor wanted me to see a specialist and I called Glenda to go with me. I told myself it was probably nothing and that Leon worried too much about me as it was. Glenda was the only one in the family that I told about the tests. She had always been so practical and distant, I didn't have to worry about her overreacting or flying off the handle about anything.

On the drive to Memphis I thought a lot about Ida for some reason. I wondered sometimes if she was softer in the days before us kids were under foot. I'd seen pictures of her and Daddy in old Model Ts, caught in mid-laughter, holding empty liquor bottles for a joke. Daddy never liked to drink, but I suspected maybe Ida used to. Nothing to excess, mind you, but I liked to imagine that Ida Pico wasn't always the stickler for appearances that

I'd known her to be.

Before I knew it, I had made the hour long trip to Memphis. Glenda must've been waiting at the window 'cause as soon as my car pulled in the drive, she popped out the front door and turned to lock it behind her. She didn't even invite me inside to use the bathroom before we went. That bathroom of hers was bigger than half my trailer. It had a big tub and even a separate shower. I liked to look at people's bathrooms, I don't know why. To me, that part of the house told you more about a person than just about anywhere else.

For example, Brucie Lunsford had wallpaper with little leprechauns in hers and stacks of true detective magazines hid under the sink. Ida's had everything covered in little knitted doilies or macramé cozies—the suggestion being that anything that went on in there should be hidden and covered up. That was just like Ida. Lola's always looked like she lived in it, everything strewn about and half leaking on the counter. Mine was sparse, just the essentials—soap and tissue. There wasn't room for much else.

After the tests were done, Glenda and I spent an hour on the fifth floor of the Sears Tower in the lady's section. She bought a real pretty jumper with a matching jacket. I was happy just to look around, save my money and think about what Buckingham Palace would look like in person.

Cain McAllister

I wouldn't talk to Macy for a whole week after the dance. She came by my house a few times but I told Momma to tell her I had a rare tropical disease and that I was quarantined until further notice. Momma shook her head when I said it, but I heard her telling Macy just that in a dramatic tone when she answered the door.

Mark had told me what Macy was doing the night of the dance, but it didn't make me any less mad. When I got mad like that I just couldn't seem to get un-mad without a lot of work. Finally Macy caught me when I was helping Aunt Trudy at the store. I was carrying a load of bottles in the wooden slates we kept out by the table on the front porch.

"You ever going to talk to me again, Cain?" she asked.

The bottles clanked together when I stopped and Aunt Trudy, behind the meat counter, looked up from behind a big slab of country ham and smiled at me through the glass.

"All right," I said to Macy and led her to the back of the store, where I motioned for her to open the back door.

There was a separate room off to the left of the screened porch where I sorted the bottles and we went inside. I slapped the case down on some other full ones and then turned over an empty and put it on top. Macy sat and I pulled up one of the others and turned it long ways, set it on its side and sat down myself.

"Mark told me what you were doing," I said.

"Then why the hell haven't you been talking to me?" she asked.

"I don't know."

"When Bobby Lee took that trophy from you and spit in it, I got so mad," Macy said. "I decided right then and there we were going to do something. People like that never get what they really deserve."

As much as I wanted to get back at Bobby Lee, part of me worried that it would just send him off after me even more than he already was. On top of that I kept listening to Brother Neil talking at church and wondered if I was supposed to go ahead and forgive Bobby Lee.

Next week Brother Neil was going to talk about secular humanists, Jimmy Carter, and the Equal Rights Amendment and how it meant men and women would all have to use the same bathroom if it passed. That's not what the whole sermon was going to be about, but it was the part Mrs. Thompson told us about in Sunday school with an appalled look on her face.

"Just imagine the indignity," she had said to the class. I looked over and tried to picture Gayla Mason taking a pee and agreed it wouldn't be a walk in the park.

Macy and I sat on the porch for a while not saying anything while I sorted bottles. All of a sudden she leaned over and kissed me. Not on the cheek, but on the mouth.

"What'd you kiss me for?" I asked.

"I don't know," she said. "Do you gotta have a reason for everything you do?"

"I guess not," I said. "But that don't mean you have to ever do it again."

"You're the first boy, Cain McAllister, to ask me not to kiss him anymore." Then she laughed. And I did too.

Macy Hollister

I can't believe I kissed Cain I walked home to Grandma's from the store. *Jeesh. Maybe I just felt bad about being nice to Bobby Lee no matter what my reasons were.*

I was so distracted thinking about it that I ran right into Miss B standing on the sidewalk across from the courthouse.

"Sorry," I said.

She was just standing there in a dark blue pantsuit with little white cuffs on the wrists, studying the front door across the street. It was the first time I'd ever seen her without a dress on.

"Oh, Macy. I'm so glad you came along," she said as she took me by the arm and turned me toward the building. "Do you see anything different about the courthouse, Darlin'? Are the bushes on the left a lot bigger than the ones on the right?"

On either side of the door was a row of big bushes that went about halfway up the building. I didn't really see any difference that I could peg, but I kinda saw what she meant. Something about the two sides was definitely different, but I couldn't say how exactly.

"Yeah, I guess," I said.

"Hang on a second," she said. She let go of me and put her hands on her hips, then grunted a little before she went back across the street. For a second she disappeared inside, then came back out with a tape measure in her hands.

She called me over to hold it while she measured each row up and down. I held one end of the tape and moved wherever she said, but was only half listening while she went on about getting ready for the *Southern Lifestyles* photographer that was coming to town. I was still thinking about why I had kissed Cain and why I did a lot of the things I did. When I did something stupid back home, it was usually to piss off my parents.

Cain was different than any other boy I'd met. He didn't seem to want anything from me the way most boys did. And just the fact that he didn't, made me like him. I'd never had any close friends back home. Daddy wouldn't let anyone spend the night or for me to stay with anyone else. Mom didn't think it was healthy for a girl not to have close girlfriends, but Daddy told her that there were all sorts of people in the big cities and you just couldn't let a young girl go staying at people's houses like you did when they were growing up. Mom agreed about that.

"You can let go now," Miss B said.

I did and the tape zinged back into the square silver holder. Miss B kept going on about all the places she was going to take the photographer once he got in town. "We'll put him up at the Holiday Inn over in Blytheville," she said. "And Cain and I will run get him first thing in the morning. On the way to town we'll take him by Chickasawba Mound. I bet that will sell him on the idea before he even makes it into town, don't you think?"

I didn't give an answer, but just looked at her.

"You do know the history of Chickasawba Mound, don't you Macy Hollister?" she asked.

I vaguely recalled something about Hernando DeSoto and a bunch of Indians that my grandma had told me, but I could tell when Miss B was about to go into a history lesson, so I nodded and said, "My grandmother told me all about it."

"That's good," she said. "It's important to know where your people are from. Can you imagine what it must have been like to be there, all those hundreds of years ago, and see the Indians performing rituals and pagan prayers right here in Lost Cain? I get chills down my spine every time I think about it."

That's when an idea hit me. Not a full-blown idea, but at least the start of one.

Bobby Lee Brewster better look out.

Mrs. Odell Brinkley

When I came into work the next morning it was even more pronounced. The left row of bushes outside the front door was markedly different than the right. The proportions were still the same as when I measured yesterday, but the density didn't match. It looked a little like Mayor Polk's hair—it was all still there, but you could almost see right through to the scalp.

I was studying it again when Momma Jewel walked out onto her front porch across the street. I'd been meaning to check on Trudy, so I walked over.

"Morning, Sadie Lynn," she said. Momma Jewel was the only one left in town who called me the name I had in childhood. It always made me feel good when she did. Even Odell just called me Sadie.

"Morning Momma Jewel," I said. I'd called her that ever since I dated Leon back in high school—practically everyone in town did by those days, related or not.

"How's Trudy?" I asked. Momma Jewel dipped her chin down and shook her head. When she brought her eyes back up to me they were filled with tears.

"I'm afraid"—she started but couldn't finish.

I hurried up the steps and reached out for her. She folded me in her arms and squeezed hard.

"It's cancer," she said.

My stomach fell and I squeezed her back as we stood there in a long embrace. Momma Jewel could never stand still too long on her bad leg, so she leaned on me and we walked over to the rocker where she sat down. I kept hold of her hand and sat on the swing next to her.

"How's Leon?" I asked.

"Oh, Sadie Lynn, I'm afraid this is just going to be too much for him. My boy's never been as strong as he makes out. You know that better than anyone."

It was hard to say what made me first fall in love with Leon back in high school. He was the only boy who really listened to what I had to say. When people asked how it was that Leon always had such good luck with ladies, given his condition, I always told them that he listened better than any man you'd ever find.

Momma Jewel held onto my hand and rocked back and forth in the chair.

"My family's got more than its share of troubles in this world, I think sometimes," she said.

"What can we do to help?" I asked. "These days they have more ways to treat things than they used to."

She just shook her head and I took that to mean they'd checked into it and the news must not be good. We sat together on the porch for the rest of the morning and talked about times gone by. I imagine Momma Jewel wondered sometimes if I had any hard feelings. I think she knew I never stopped loving Leon. She must have. I didn't know if Trudy had any idea or not. I could still remember the day when I turned eighteen and I told Leon that if he wasn't going to marry me right then that I'd find somebody who would. I was in such a hurry to grow up. Leon told me how much he loved me but that he was too young to get married. He asked if I couldn't just wait a year or two while he did some traveling.

I was so mad and hurt that I slapped him as hard as I could and determined I'd marry anyone as long as it wasn't him and as long as it was soon. Two months later, Odell proposed and I accepted. By then Leon was down in Memphis working for the highway department and playing poker at nights. *For all I knew, I never crossed his mind. For all I know, I still don't.*

As hurt as I was, I never begrudged him what he had found with Trudy. It was clear from the start how much they loved each other. Even if I had hard feelings, they melted the first time I met the young redhead from Frenchman's Bayou, as everyone used to call Trudy when they first came to town. All the men teased Leon about robbing the cradle, bringing home such a young girl with him almost forty. Leon would just laugh and say they wouldn't say that if they'd met her. And when they did, the teasing stopped. At sixteen and a half, Trudy had a sense of herself anyone twice her age would envy. I always hoped we'd become closer someday, but life has a way of steaming by and before you know it, twenty years was gone.

Chapter Fifteen

He Demands Blood

Macy Hollister

It's finally cooling down a little. I stood underneath a tree by the bottom of Chickasawba mound and looked down the road. My dress felt sticky against my skin. It was still hot, but the sun was about to set, and it was starting to feel almost bearable.

"Can you see him?" Cain asked from behind a tree further up toward the top of the hill.

"Not yet, and shut up or he'll know something's wrong," I said back.

The mound was a little hill covered with trees in the middle of a field about forty yards off the dirt road that went toward Blytheville. Nothing special to it, if you ask me. Grandma's Nova was parked on the side away from the road. I had lied and told her I was taking Cain and Mark out to look at how work was coming on the new bridge over the Mississippi. "Stay off that interstate, and I don't mind," she told me as I left. I didn't have my license, but Grandma let me drive almost anywhere as long as I stayed on the gravel roads. She said she started driving at eleven and thought sixteen was too old to learn anything new.

I heard Cain and Mark moving up above. "Shhh," I said, "I see him coming." Bobby Lee was walking down the road about a quarter mile away. I could tell his swagger even though I couldn't see his face. I leaned up against the tree and put one foot up against it like I'd seen in some movie with Natalie Wood. Bobby Lee waved and started to jog toward me. I kept the pose and when he came across the field, he hollered, "Hey Macy."

Waiting until he was closer, I finally said, "Hey."

He took a look at me then at the mound of trees. "I ain't never been up close to this thing before, if you can believe that," he said.

I don't believe anything from you, then said, "They say it's haunted. What do you think?"

"I guess anything's possible," he said, looking around.

The mound was steeper than it looked. As we walked up, I said, "Mrs. Brinkley says the Indians used to come up here for all sorts of rituals." The trees were pretty thick, but there was still plenty of room to walk. "Some folks even say they had human sacrifices at the very top." That wasn't anything I'd heard anyone claim, but I thought it sounded good.

"Probably sacrificed 'em some virgins," Bobby Lee said following me up.

"Then I guess it's a good thing I'm not one of those. Are you?"

Bobby Lee got a look on his face and I'd bet you a thousand dollars he was. Boys like him always talked big until it came down to it, then they acted as scared as a mouse. I sped up and said, "Let's see what it's like at the top."

When I was almost to the top, I turned around and leaned against a tree again while Bobby Lee made his way up to me. Just beyond where I stopped was a large open space that made up the top of the mound. I could hear Bobby Lee panting a little as he covered the last few steps. I was facing toward him and watched his face when he saw the lit candles arranged on the ground behind me.

"What the hell?" he said.

Earlier Cain and Mark had laid out all the sticks they could find and put them in the shape of a big pentagram with a lit candle at each end of the five points on the star. The pentagram was a nice touch. Cain thought of it. My original plan was just to scare the shit out of Bobby Lee by spooking him with some Indian stories, but once Cain warmed up to the idea he spent a lot of time thinking about it. He said that people in movies on TV were always running up on some coven of Satan worshipers in little towns like Lost Cain.

"I just wanted to get things ready for us," I said to Bobby Lee with an intense look on my face.

"Ready for what?" Bobby Lee asked.

I just winked and walked over to the middle of the circle and sat down cross-legged. I motioned for him to come sit in front of me on the other side in the middle of the symbol. He hesitated.

"There's nothing to be scared of," I said.

"I'm not," he said, and then came over, carefully stepping over each line of sticks. He started to sit, but I stopped him.

"Wait," I said. "For this to work right you have to be naked."

For a second, he looked at me like he didn't quite hear right, then smiled before he said, "You first."

I was real proud that I didn't even flinch. I hadn't planned it, but I knew it might come to that. I pushed one, then the other strap from my shoulders and let my dress fall down to my waist, exposing my breasts.

Cain McAllister

When Macy's dress fell, Mark grabbed my hand and squeezed it so hard it hurt. He looked at me with his mouth gaping, his eyes wide open. Bobby Lee had a similar reaction and quickly peeled off every stitch of clothing he had on and flung them over by a tree just outside the circle of sticks. Macy just sat there, her hands in her lap, and her boobs squeezed against the inside of her arms.

That hadn't been part of our plan. Macy was supposed to meet Bobby Lee and start talking about all the spooky things the Indians did on the mound years ago. Once they got to the top, she was going to freak out when they found the pentagram and try to get Bobby Lee worked up enough to get so scared he'd run away when Mark and me started making noises. Mark looked at me as if to say "what do we do now?" I just shook my head and shrugged my shoulders.

I guess Macy was running the show now.

Once Bobby Lee was stripped he stood there like he'd done something important. His skin was so white it reflected the light off the candles almost like a cat's eyes. There wasn't a hair on his chest or stomach, just a small patch of blonde where his pecker stood out from his body, long and skinny, pointing toward the sky. Macy nodded her head and motioned for him to sit. Bobby Lee never took his eyes off Macy's chest as he crossed his legs and sat, the tip of his pecker bobbing up from his lap like a cobra in a wicker basket.

The sun was gone now, and in the candlelight I saw Macy roll her eyes back and start to swing her head in small circles. When she did, her boobs swung back and forth, her nipples pointing out from large brown circles that covered most of the front of them. She started to mumble under her breath and swing harder and harder around. Bobby Lee reached a hand across toward her when suddenly she threw her arms in the air and screamed so loud that Mark and me both grabbed hold of each other. Bobby Lee yanked his hand back, then I saw his eyes look up at Macy's arm.

In her hand, she held a big knife, dripping with ketchup that we had left under the sticks for Bobby Lee to find when they came up on the pentagram. Our idea was that the whole thing would scare Bobby Lee so much he'd run back home and tell everyone around about it. Then we'd clear everything away before anyone came to look and Macy would swear she didn't know what he was talking about. Though I didn't know where this new plan of Macy's was going, I couldn't say that I didn't like it so far.

Looking up at the bloody knife in her right hand, Bobby Lee screamed. Then Macy threw the other arm up, and grabbed the knife with both hands above her head. She opened her eyes and looked straight at Bobby Lee and said, "Anything for you, Oh, Satan!" She pulled the knife back like she was getting ready to come down and Bobby

Lee jumped to his feet.

Just after he left the spot, Macy brought the big knife down and into the ground. "He demands blood!" she screamed.

Bobby Lee, still naked as a jaybird, ran down the side of the mound hollering his head off. Macy's boobs just hung there while she leaned over the hunting knife buried in the ground and smiled. I started laughing so hard I thought I was going to choke. Then Mark punched me in the side with his elbow to try and make me stop. Macy winked at us before straightening herself up and pulling the top of her dress back over her chest.

"Listen to that, Cain. Stop laughing for a second," Mark said.

There was a bunch of loud cracks like when a deer takes off in the woods, then more screams coming from down the hill, but these were different. Mark and me looked at each other and knew something was wrong. We came out from behind the tree.

"Did you hear that?" Mark said to Macy. She looked a little worried.

"Yeah, what do you think happened?" she said.

"Maybe we better go look," Mark said.

We all just stood there looking at each other. Mark grabbed Bobby Lee's clothes up off the ground, underwear and all, and said, "Cain, you stay here with Macy and y'all clean up all this stuff." Then he said to Macy, "Take it all and put it back in the trunk of your grandma's car. I'll go see what's wrong."

As soon as he went off down the hill, Macy and me started scrambling to pick everything up. Mark hollered back to us, "And make sure you scatter all those sticks around so nobody can tell anything!"

We could still hear Bobby Lee hollering in the distance. Macy and me looked at each other, then dropped the sticks on the ground and ran down the hill to follow Mark. About three quarters of the way down, we started to see the blood. There was a big patch on the ground, then little spots on the leaves leading down to the field.

When we got to the bottom, I was running so hard that I fell where the edge of the field started. Mark was there and reached down to help me up.

Macy pointed out into the field and said, "There he is!"

About twenty yards away, we saw Bobby Lee hobbling along, holding one hand over his face and the other trying to cover his crotch.

"Bobby Lee! Wait, I got your clothes," Mark yelled. When Bobby Lee turned around all I could see was the blood pouring down the side of his face before he fell to the ground between the empty rows.

Lola McAllister

I had just gotten home from Trudy's and sat down on the porch when Macy pulled her grandmother's car into the driveway and then straight across the front yard. I ran up to see what was wrong and saw all the blood on the rear door. My heart jumped to my throat and I searched for Cain, who hollered back at me from the passenger seat.

I threw open the door and was surprised to see Bobby Lee Brewster, his face bloody and swollen, lying there in the backseat with his head on Mark's lap. There was so much blood that I didn't want to chance moving him, so I just pushed Macy over, jumped in the car and went straight to the hospital in Blytheville.

"Thank God I was home," I said. "Now what happened?" Bobby Lee was moaning and the other three just looked at each other and wouldn't say a thing.

"Cain Joseph McAllister, you tell me what happened, you hear me?" I said, but Cain was crying so hard I knew it was no use. In about fifteen minutes we got to the hospital, and I noticed that Bobby Lee's shirt was on inside out when the paramedics pulled him out of the car and loaded him onto a gurney. Cain, Macy, and Mark still hadn't said a word. I assumed they were waiting for me to go inside the emergency room to get their story straight.

On the way home, I tried again to get Cain to tell me what really happened. He just sat there in the passenger seat, his eyes red and puffy. In the rear-view mirror I could see Macy and Mark just staring out the back windows, afraid to look me in the eye.

"Well, we'll just see what Bobby Lee has to say," I said loudly. "If he lives," I added. Cain bolted up and started crying again.

"Is he gonna die, Momma?" he wailed.

"No, he's not Cain," I said, "but the doctor says there's a good chance he'll lose that eye."

I never got a story I believed out of any of them, but I was just too tired to push it. I dropped the boys off at Brother Neil's, and then took Macy back to her grandmother's.

"I'll say goodbye here and just walk on home, Macy," I said on the Hollister front porch.

"I'm sorry to have bothered you, Mrs. McAllister," Macy said with a sincerity that wasn't her usual tone.

"Are you going to be okay?" I asked. For a moment, it looked as though she might cry. I reached out to put my hand on her shoulder, but she pulled away.

"I'm always okay," she said, her guard back up.

As I walked home in the dark, I decided to go check in on Trudy. I'd been staying with her most nights. Every day she was a little weaker than the one before. There wasn't a cloud in the sky and the stars shined from every direction on the horizon as I walked through town. When I got to the trailer, I stopped myself before I knocked. Leon would call if he needed help with anything and I wanted them to have some time alone, so instead of going inside I sat down on the steps and looked up to the sky.

My entire life, I'd never felt like I was the person most people needed me to be. Not the wife or the mother, or especially the daughter.

Please help Trudy, I asked God. *My big sister is the one person in this world that I've never let down.*

Chapter Sixteen

Any Hand I'm Dealt

Peggy Leggett

I made sure to come to church early every Sunday and watch the people come in. From where I sat in the choir loft, I could see the whole congregation. Trudy McAllister was there for the first time in weeks.

"I'm not afraid to tell the truth," I said to Belle, sitting next to me. "She looks like death warmed over."

"It's so sad," Belle said.

"At least she gets to keep her hair," I said. "Thank God for small favors, I guess."

Trudy had always been so proud of her red hair—I don't know what it is about those Pico girls and their hair. Lola was the same way about hers, though you'd never convince me she didn't dye it blonde. I had poked around a little with the girl over at Thelma's Cut and Curl to see if maybe Lola came in after hours. But either she didn't or she only saw Thelma herself. Lord knows, Thelma was locked up tighter than Fort Knox. Which is silly for a hairdresser, if you ask me.

Anyway, Trudy looked so unlike herself sitting there between Lola and Momma Jewel that I couldn't help but almost feel sorry for them. There were a few moments when Lola looked so tender and loving, holding the hymnal for Trudy and helping her stand for the opening prayer, that it almost made me a little jealous too.

I bet I would have made a wonderful sister.

During the opening hymn I leaned over to Belle and whispered, “I notice that Leon McAllister is nowhere to be seen.” Belle nodded her head, smiling out to the congregation as she sang. “I suppose it’ll take more than a dying wife to get him back on the straight and narrow,” I said. I couldn’t help but wonder if the McAllister family wasn’t exactly what it seemed, given all the punishment they’d been doled out over the years. I was about to say something to that effect to Belle, when the congregation broke out into applause when Brother Neil stood up for the announcements.

The church was certainly packed full. As the ushers collected all the plates for the offertory, Brother Neil got up to share prayer requests. He went through a list of names. Ruth East had broken another hip. *She just broke the other one a year ago.*

“She’s eighty-seven-years-old, for crying out loud—at a certain age shouldn’t you just take to the bed and be done with it?” I whispered to Belle.

Brother Neil continued. Betsy Oxford’s grandson was in the hospital. *Drugs.* One of the Brewster kids had gone and poked his eye out. *Aren’t the Brewsters supposed to be Pentecost? Seems like he’d be on their prayer list, not ours.* And Bertha Hornbuckle had an “unspoken need.” *I shudder to think what that might be.*

I never did well with doing two things at once, so I usually just picked one of the requests and concentrated my prayers. So when everyone bowed their heads and took a silent moment to pray. I ran through them in my head.

Definitely not Bertha's unspoken. Not Betsy's druggie grandson. Ruth East practically had one foot on the other side already. *I guess I'll pray for the Brewster boy. Was it a boy? I think so. Anyway, Dear Lord, please bless that little Brewster—um, child, and help him to not feel like a freak with that one eye gone. If they don't know you Lord, I ask that you bear down on them with your loving rebuke and make them see—at least the boy with the one eye he's got left—that your way is*—Brother Neil said Amen before I got the chance to finish. *Oh well.*

After the special music—Amanda Gilbow sung a lovely rendition of *We Shall Behold Him*—Brother Neil stood up to start his sermon. Before I knew it he was twenty minutes in and I was all flushed with the love of the Lord. Brother Neil looked so handsome standing there in the shadow of that big wooden cross with the light from the stained glass windows streaming over his rugged face. I'd never heard as energetic a preacher as Brother Neil. He'd prance from one side of the stage to the other; his well-worn brown Bible in his left hand and his right raised up in a fist.

Today's sermon was on the first four angels sounding the trumpet to begin Tribulation. Brother Neil reached to the sky as he told of the first trumpet and the hailstorm of fire mingled with blood that would scorch a third of the trees and all the green grass on the earth. Then tears came to his eyes as he followed with the second angel's trumpet and a great mountain of fire falling to the sea, turning a third of it to blood, killing a third of the creatures and sinking a third of the ships. He held out his arms and called out in a voice of the stricken, "Help us, oh Lord!"

It was all I could do not to stand right up and shout Amen. No sooner did that thought leave my head, than someone behind me did indeed shout, "Amen." To which Brother Neil replied back, "Yes, Brother!" in his booming voice. I was both shocked and thrilled. Spoken Amens, always hushed, had all but disappeared in February when Dewey Ledbetter got gout and died. I wasn't quite sure what to think.

Leon McAllister

I'd been coming in during the special music the past few weeks and sitting in my wheelchair in the foyer listening while the preacher talked. I always left during the invitation and so far I'd got away with it. Only time anybody noticed was the Sunday before when Wilbur Sellers come through sneaking out for a smoke and invited me along. We went over to the side by one of the thick stained glass windows, and Wilbur didn't flinch when I pulled out my Old Charter.

"I wouldn't mind church so much," I told him between swigs. "If I didn't have to talk to all those damn Christians before and after it." Wilbur wasn't one to talk but he smiled at me like he understood. He didn't let on to nobody that I been coming.

I shoulda gone inside, I suppose, and sat next to Trudy. I know she'd have liked that. If I did though, the whole place would make a big to do about it, and I'd never been one for show. Half those people couldn't stand each other during the week but just put on the dog every

Sunday.

The last time I'd come, about five or so years ago, Harlan Sparks came up to shake my hand during the sing and greet and said how proud he was to see me. I told the sumbitch to take that outstretched hand of his and shove it up his ass. The whole congregation stopped singing *In the Garden*, mid-stanza, and Brother Ben, the preacher at the time, suggested to Trudy that I might oughta consider becoming a Methodist.

No less than three days before, Harlan had took a swing at me 'cause I finally cut off his credit. Man hadn't paid for six months. Kept drinking his paycheck, is what it was. When Trudy got onto me for using that kind of language in church, I told her, "I'll be damned if I treat somebody any different in church than I would on the street." Trudy'd always been after me to come to church, but after that, she let up.

I could hear through the doors that Brother Neil was on a tear. Once that man got worked up there was just no stopping him. He was going on about the evils of soap operas and I could just picture the ladies all looking at each other then back up at him.

He's opening a can of worms there. Talking about the fiery end of the world was one thing, but you best tread lightly when you get between a woman and *The Guiding Light.* It reminded me of something Daddy used to always say when we was kids. He'd carry me in his arms as we walked home from church and look over at Momma and say, "Jewel, that sermon today has done gone from preaching to meddling, don't you think?" Momma'd just say, "pshaw" and swat at him with her hand.

When Brother Neil come to the end of the sermon, I told myself I oughta head out, so I could make my way back home before anyone saw me. Something seemed to be holding me in place, though. It was like my wheels was bolted to the ground. Must be something in the spokes, I thought. But when I looked down, I realized that I didn't even have my arms on the wheels. The next thing I knew, I was crying.

During the opening of invitational hymn, I said to myself again that it was time to head home. Even as I was thinking it, my chest was heaving and I couldn't hardly catch my breath. I took my cane from beside me and pulled open the door to the sanctuary. Soon as I got it open, I pushed through into the aisle that went down the middle of the congregation. I could see a blur of people out of the corner of my eye, but it was only Trudy that was in focus when I saw her turn and look back at me. Seeing her like that tore at me and I pushed myself ahead with big thrusts, passing two or three rows.

When I got to where Trudy was sitting, I stopped. Lola stepped out from the pew and guided her over to me. Trudy took my hand, then got behind me and leaned on my chair, pushing me toward the front of the church. Brother Neil was standing with his arms out a little from his sides, his palms facing us. Everything next come in flashes. Brother Neil took my hand in his. Trudy was kneeling in front of me and I pulled her close. Brother Neil's arms was wrapped around us both.

For I don't know how long, we just sat there, all together while the music played and the folks sang. Brother Neil prayed and I cried. Trudy stroked my back, and I thought to myself, *You gotta pull it together, Leon.*

But I didn't. I just kept crying and told God that if he'd just let me keep her, I'd be a better man.

I'll play any hand I'm dealt, Lord, but not this. Please don't let it be this.

Mrs. Odell Brinkley

Cain hadn't seemed himself lately. I image this business with Trudy was upsetting him more than he ever said. He spent most all of this time at Momma Jewel's house now that Lola had been staying with Trudy and Leon full time.

Leon couldn't do nearly all that had to be done to care for someone in Trudy's health, and Billy Ray was still just sixteen. Plenty strong enough to lift Trudy, but a boy shouldn't have to do those things. Lola had moved in to the spare bedroom and spent most all her time with her sister.

The doctors didn't really say how much time there was. It was maddening for me to even think about it, so I could only imagine it was so much harder for the family. I'd been coming by and working in the store most afternoons. Leon wouldn't ask, but he accepted my help. Given the circumstances, I hated to admit that I enjoyed being around him again. He was the only man in my whole life that I ever felt knew me, and even though that connection was long since gone, I found something comfortable about being in his presence. Nostalgia, perhaps.

Is it wrong for me to hope that my being here to help somehow comforts him as well?

"Can you hand me the Windex?" I said to Cain from

inside the icebox case, where I was on my knees and leaning in while I cleaned out the display window. Cain took his time finding it. "Now hurry up, Sweetie," I said. "We can't let the meat set out too long or it's liable to spoil." I'd wrapped each of the meats tightly with cellophane and put them on the back table while I gave the icebox a good cleaning. I never realized how much work Trudy did around the store to keep things moving smoothly.

As I wiped down the glass, I could see Leon sitting on his stool at the cash register adding up tabs on the electric adding machine. His face looked blank as he clicked in the numbers. The whir of the printer sounded like a distant birdcall from inside the icebox.

I wasn't there but I had heard about Leon getting saved at Lost Cain Baptist the Sunday before. Every person I'd talked to said there wasn't a dry eye in the church by the time the invitation was over. Since then I didn't know if I'd say there'd been an improvement in his outlook as much as a shift to something different. That first week afterward, he acted a little like his old self, teasing and laughing. He seemed to have it in his mind that Trudy was going to beat this. Each day that she hadn't improved, his mood had gotten steadily worse. Now he'd gone past a bad mood into almost no mood at all. Just a robotic movement through the particular business of the day. He tried to be sly about it, but I could smell the whiskey on his breath by the time I arrived every afternoon.

Lola McAllister

Ida came every Monday night so I could stay at home with Cain and to give me a break from taking care of Trudy. *As if Ida Pico coming to town would give anybody a break from anything.* I scrubbed the linoleum kitchen floor at Trudy's. Every Monday, I had to spend all day scouring every last inch of the place so Ida wouldn't pull me aside and ask how I could let my big sister die in a filthy trailer.

"It's bad enough she's living like this," Ida would say. "The least we can do is make sure it's decent when the folks have to come pay their respects."

Ida hated that trailer.

I imagine it reminded her of everything Trudy didn't do with her life that Ida had hoped for. Sometimes I thought Cain reminded Ida of everything I didn't do. I don't know why I thought that—Ida had always been good to Cain. For Ida, she was about as loving as it was possible for her to be, I suppose. But sometimes I saw her look at Cain and I caught that same disappointment in her eye that Ida always had when she looked at me. It had started the day I told her I loved Dip McAllister and had been that way ever since. *Always would, I guess.*

Glenda was the only one of us three that'd come close to being what Ida needed us to be: respectful, obedient, well-off, and socially connected. And where had Glenda been in all this? She certainly hadn't come up to lend a hand. She called and talked to Trudy every few days on the telephone. She barely said six words to me.
Probably because she was scared I'd ask her to come help out. Glenda had always been as cold as ice. She was

already fourteen when I was born, so I never spent as much time with her as I did Trudy.

My earliest memories of Glenda were the pictures of her on the walls more than her as a person. Tall, with chestnut brown hair, striking some pose in a fancy lace dress with a boy on her arm about to go to some dance. The same dresses that I'd wear to my own dances fourteen years later, smelling of mothballs and cedar clippings. Momma had pictures of Glenda all over the house. Glenda always did exactly what Ida said. To Ida, this was all that was expected of a child, to obey your parents and then your life would surely fall into place perfectly, as Glenda's seemed to have done.

I heard Trudy call from her bedroom, "Lola, can you come in here a second?"

As sick as she was, her voice was still strong and clear. I stopped dusting, stuck the rag in my pocket and wiped my hands on my pants. When I walked in to the room, Trudy called me over to sit by the bed.

"What is it Tru?" I said once I sat down.

"I want to have a little talk with you before Momma gets here."

If it's much of a talk, I won't have time to finish dusting before Ida arrives.

"Stop that," Trudy said when she noticed me looking at my watch. "I don't give a good damn what Ida thinks about my dirty house." I looked a little surprised that she knew about my cleaning frenzy.

"I'm sick, not deaf," she said. "The walls in this thing are like tissue paper and I hear every word said in the place. I can hear Leon sneaking a bottle out of the cupboard in the kitchen. I can hear Billy Ray jacking off in his bedroom every night, God bless his little horny heart."

"Trudy! I'm in the room right next to his and I've never heard any such thing. That's disgusting!" I said. Unfortunately, I *had* heard but you're not supposed to talk about those things.

"Lighten up Lola. It's just what boys do."

I was appalled at this thought and seemed to detect an implication that my little boy did such things, and said, "Well, not Cain."

"He will soon enough," Trudy said. "I see him sneaking looks at the magazines under the board over to the store."

"Trudy, is this the conversation you called me in here for?" I asked. "Because if it is I can tell you I have no need or desire to hear another word." I stood up and pulled the dust rag from my pocket.

"No, it isn't what I called you in here to talk about, but it's not that far off either," she said. "Now sit back down, please."

I did, but kept the rag in my lap, wringing it with both hands.

"Lola, I've been noticing things that I should maybe have said something about a long time ago. Or maybe I shouldn't say anything now, to tell you the truth, I just don't know," she said. Trudy wasn't normally one to question herself about anything.

She went on, "I'm worried about you."

"About me?" I said. "I'm right as rain." I cringed a little when I said it because it's a phrase Ida often used.

"That's exactly it," Trudy said. "Right as rain. I swear Lola, some days it's like you're turning into Ida Pico, Junior right before my very eyes."

"Trudy Mae McAllister, you take that back!" I said and threw the dust rag at her.

"I will not. You need to hear it before it's too late. I don't have much time left, and I'll be damned if I'll sit here and see my favorite person in the world turn into someone that I know she's not. Baby sister, you've got to get over whatever this is that's going on with you. You need to think about getting a man back in your life. Hell, even if you don't get one in your life, you need one in your bed now and then."

"Would you stop using that language?" I yelled. As soon as I said it, I caught myself and my hands went up to my face and I started to cry. Ida couldn't tolerate "language" as she called it. For a second I thought about telling Trudy the truth. That I couldn't have another man. That sleeping with me is deadly to men.

Instead I just yelled, "Shut up! You shut the–heck up!" and ran out of the room.

I went straight for the front door and slammed it hard as I left. I stomped down the steps and over to the store. When I walked in, Cain was sitting on the floor looking at a movie magazine. I walked over and jerked it out of his hands.

"Have you finished your homework, young man?" I asked.

He looked up at me like I was crazy and said, "It's summer Momma. There's no school."

"Well, all right then," I said and handed the magazine back to him. I turned on my heels and said to Leon, "You need to go over and look after your wife 'til Ida gets here. I'm going home." Before he could say anything, I went out the door and walked down the street toward my house. As I was walking, I got a little worried about myself, thinking maybe I was starting to see things. I could have sworn that back in the store, when I was yelling at Cain, there was a head in the meat box that looked just like Sadie Brinkley.

"Shitfire!" I forced myself to say right out loud, and then got embarrassed even though there wasn't a soul around. *Oh, God. Maybe Trudy's right. I might be just like Ida.*

Ida Pico

When I got to Trudy's place, Lola was nowhere to be found. I walked over to the store and asked Cain, "Where has your momma gotten off to?"

"She ran home, Mammy Pico," Cain said without even getting up to give me a kiss.

"What for?" I asked.

He just shrugged his shoulders. I never could stand a child not answering polite like God intended and was about to tell him so when Mrs. Odell Brinkley popped up from around the meat box. Her hair was pulled back in a sloppy ponytail and she had a bottle of Windex in her hand.

A woman over forty shouldn't wear a ponytail, ever. However, of all the people in Lost Cain, Mrs. Brinkley was about the most tolerable that I'd met. The only tolerable one, to tell God's truth about it, including my own two daughters half the time, sad to say.

"Hello, Mrs. Pico. It's so good to see you," she said.

"It's nice to see you too, Mrs. Brinkley. It's so nice of you to help out around here. I know it must be a lot of trouble," I said.

"I'm happy to do it. And please, you can just call me Sadie."

I feigned a smile and asked myself, *are we all fourteen around here?* What's the use in having a married name if you never get to use it?

"All the same, it's greatly appreciated," I said.

"Leon's with Trudy right now. Can I get you a coke?"

"No thank you. I only drink tea," I said, then I reached down and grabbed the movie magazine from Cain who was sitting on the floor, cross-legged like a perfect heathen. "Get on home and spend some time with your mother," I said to him. "And another thing, it's not good for a boy your age to be reading movie magazines. They'll put ideas in your head." He just looked at me like I had slapped him across the face.

"What's wrong with ideas?" he asked.

"Don't talk back. Go see your momma. She's had a lot on her plate and this is her only night to get to spend with you."

Lola thought I didn't know what she was going through, but I did. I had buried two sisters and my momma before I was even twenty-five. I wished there was more I could've done for Lola. I'd have come more than once a week if I thought it would help ease her load. But I knew that me being around only added to it.

"Don't I even get some bye-sugar, since I got none at hello?" I called out to Cain who was headed for the door. He came over and gave me a peck on the cheek. "Thank you, young man," I said and reached out to put my hands on either side of his face. "You're going to be as handsome as your Daddy was. Now go on."

Dip was handsome. And I didn't dislike him near as much as Lola always said I did. My girl was just seventeen. I'd have felt the same no matter who she married at that age. She was too young. I thought I could talk sense into her back then. She had always been such a sensible girl up to that point. Made good grades, came home right after school most every day and helped out around the house. Why, when she was a baby, the girl would stand at the screen door hollering her head off while I hung laundry until I came back inside. And now when I walked into a room she tensed up like I'd just sucked every bit of oxygen out of it.

"Would you like to sit down, Mrs. Pico?" Mrs. Brinkley said to me, reaching out and touching my arm.

Good Lord, I've done almost gone and let myself tear up right here in front of some rank stranger.

"No thank you," I said. "I'll just go on over and see about Trudy."

When I walked over to the trailer I kept thinking, I just want to curl up and die rather than lose Trudy. She thought I favored her big sister, and I'll admit that Glenda pleased me more often. But Trudy had always been the fire in my life. It was everything I could do not to let my emotions run away with me. When I got to the door of the trailer, I could hear Leon crying inside.

I took a deep breath and said to myself, *somebody's got to be strong for Trudy.*

Cain McAllister

The next day I was helping Uncle Leon at the store when Miss B poked her head in the door and asked me to keep an eye on the bushes in front of the courthouse that night.

"I'm there all day, so it must be someone coming under the cover of night," she said.

"I'll ask Mark if he can spend the night with me at Momma Jewel's house tonight," I told her. I'd been staying there every night except Mondays since Aunt Trudy got sick.

"That's wonderful," Miss B said and closed the door. I watched her walk down the little path that led to Aunt Trudy's trailer. Whenever I'd ask Momma about Aunt Trudy, she just said that it was nothing for me to worry about and then made up a reason to leave the room.

Macy's grandma, Mrs. Hollister, stopped by to pick up a case of Diet Rites and a can of snuff like she did every week. She never asked for the snuff, I just knew Uncle Leon kept it under the counter and that when Mrs. Hollister came by I was supposed to put it in a sack and add it to her bill, but not say nothing to her about it.

"How's Trudy?" She asked, but didn't wait for an answer. "Everybody seems to be dying from cancer these days." Then under her breath so Uncle Leon wouldn't hear, she asked, "Are y'all making arrangements?"

I just shrugged my shoulders and wished she'd hurry up. Later on when Miss B came back in to help us get ready to close, I waited until Uncle Leon went out back to check something in the stock room and asked her, "Is Aunt Trudy going to die?"

"What does your mother say?" she asked.

"She don't say anything, really," I said.

"She doesn't say anything," Miss B corrected.

"Doesn't," I said. Sometimes I'd say things the wrong way just because I knew Miss B liked correcting me.

"Cain, you know I always try to be truthful with people, no matter what," she said.

I nodded my head and figured I knew the answer to my question even if she didn't say another word.

"Your Aunt Trudy's very sick. She's got cancer and yes, it's possible that she could die," she said.

"Possible?" I asked.

I could tell when Miss B wasn't really lying, but she wasn't really telling the truth either.

"The important thing is that you spend some time with her, and that we all help out as much as we can," she said.

When Mark and me ate supper at Momma Jewel's that night, I kept thinking about Aunt Trudy being dead. Usually Momma Jewel would poke at me and do her best to get me talking because she always said she didn't like the idea of a quiet child. But tonight she just talked to Mark most of the time and reached over and smoothed down my hair now and then.

Miss B had probably told her about our talk. They didn't think I knew, but I could tell they gave each other updates on my moods now and then. Like if Miss B knew I was thinking about my daddy, then Momma Jewel would tell me a story about him later that day. Or if Miss B gave me a new book, Momma made sure to ask me about it.

After supper Mark and me got a can of OFF out of the pantry and went to the front porch and sprayed each other down. When the sun would set in Lost Cain, you had about an hour before the mosquitoes came up from the river where they'd been hiding from the heat during the day. After that they were everywhere. We sat on the front porch swing for awhile, holding out our arms and watching them try to land, then jump back.

"Gotcha," Mark said was he swatted one between his hands. When he opened them, blood was splattered in the middle of both his palms.

"Cool," I said. "I wonder if it's mine or yours?"

"Could be either or both," he said, and tried to wipe his hand on my jeans before I pushed him away. Then he pushed me back and we lost our footing so that the swing jerked back and forth, rattling the chains.

From inside the house, Momma Jewel's voice called out, "No scuffling on my swing!"

"Yes, ma'am," we both said then got real quiet and smiled at each other.

After we went to bed that night Mark and I snuck out of the house once Momma Jewel was asleep. We put on a fresh coat of OFF and instead of watching from the porch swing, decided it would seem more like real surveillance if we lay down by the fence in the front yard and used our binoculars.

At daybreak I woke up all wet from the dew on the grass. I shook Mark awake and dragged him back inside so we could get in bed before Momma Jewel woke up to make breakfast.

Chapter Seventeen

Room in the Human Heart

Mrs. Odell Brinkley

With the cherry cobbler in my hands, the door was a little tricky, but I finally managed to get it open and let myself in at Momma Jewel's house. Once in the entryway, I saw several of the McAllisters I hadn't seen since Easter milling around the living room. Lola sat on the sofa in a dark gray skirt with a matching jacket, her face swollen and red. She had her arm wrapped around Cain's shoulders as one of Leon's other cousins stood by the couch talking to her. Lola nodded her head up and down, but from the look on her face I could tell she didn't hear a thing. Ida Pico darted in and out of the room, with dishes and drinks in her hands.

Across the room, in a corner, Leon sat in a rocking chair, looking out the side window. Underneath the chatter of the room I could hear the air-conditioner humming in a sustained strain. He looked like a little boy with his feet tucked under himself watching out the window, waiting for his mom to come home.

It was Momma Jewel who had called to let me know that Trudy had passed. Odell and I had just finished supper when the phone rang. She said it had happened around an hour ago. Trudy had gone in the hospital a few days earlier. Her breathing was so uneven and the pain so much that there was really no other choice. Once they had her there and on pain medicine she came back to herself after a day. Momma Jewel said that the last day and a half were very pleasant. Trudy got to spend some time with everyone. Then she slipped into a deep sleep around noon and couldn't be roused. Lola, Leon, and Ida Pico sat with her the whole afternoon while Momma Jewel went home and made sandwiches to take back for everyone. She said when she got back she tried to get Leon to eat, but he wouldn't. He hadn't left Trudy's side for over twenty-four hours. Just before seven he left the room to smoke a cigarette.

"It was as if Trudy wouldn't leave with Leon in the room," Momma Jewel had said on the phone. "Leon hadn't been gone two minutes when we heard her take about four deep breaths, then stop. Poor Lola was holding Trudy's hand to her face and just wouldn't let go. Ida Pico didn't show it, but I know'd she was hurting. I run down the hall to get Leon. When he got back—"

Her voice broke off. She couldn't continue and I didn't think I wanted to hear, so I said, "I'm so sorry. Is there anything I can do?"

"I just wanted to let you know. Trudy thought so much of you, and how much help you've been."

"Thank you," I said and then we said our goodbyes.

That night lying in bed next to Odell, I thought about Trudy and the last conversation we'd had. It was on Tuesday and I had come over to ask her how she did the candy orders. I didn't want to bother her and had spent several hours trying to figure out the order forms. It seemed like there was some kind of system to it, but try as I might, I couldn't make heads or tails of it. Finally, I went next door and when I poked my head in her bedroom I thought she was asleep. Just as I was pulling back, she said, "Come on in, Sadie."

"I don't want to bother you, Hon, I can ask later," I said.

"I've got something to give you," she said.

From the nightstand drawer she pulled a stack of notebook paper. I walked in and sat next to the bed.

"I've written out all the things I can think anyone would need to know about the store and how things work," she said. I guess she could see something on my face because she went on, "It's okay. It's something that had to be done. Lord knows Leon's a good man, but between you and me, you're looking at the brains of the operation," she said and smiled, handing me the papers. Trudy's fluid, neat handwriting covered page after page.

"Leon is a good man," she said again. I nodded my head. "I've always thought that if he and I hadn't fell so hard all those years ago that you two would have somehow gotten back together," she said.

"I don't know what Odell would have had to say about that," I said, trying to smile. "That was a lifetime ago."

"Yes it was," she said and I cringed when I thought about how that could sound.

To her it was a lifetime ago.

"I worry about Leon after I'm gone," she said. "How he'll manage."

I still didn't feel right talking about it as if her death

were a certainty. But I sensed that she needed to say something.

"We'll make sure he's okay, Trudy. You don't have to worry about that. Every single person in this town will do what they can."

"I don't doubt that. But Leon don't care about everybody in this town like he does you," she said.

The breath went right out of me. "Now Trudy, surely you don't think..." I started.

"Oh, no," she said. "I'm just saying that even though Leon and I have had a wonderful marriage, a beautiful marriage..." She reached out and took my hand. "There is plenty of room in the human heart for more than one love in a lifetime."

I squeezed her hand and said, "Trudy, I wish I could tell you what you want to hear. I can assure you that I will do what I can for Leon. We'll make sure that the store is taken care of. We'll make sure that he doesn't go to the bottle too much." At this she squeezed back. "But I'm a married woman."

"I know, I know," she said. "I wouldn't ever—it's just that should there ever come a time when nothing stands between you, I hope you'll know that it would make me very happy to see Leon with someone who loves him so much."

Instinctively, I pulled my hand back with a jerk. Was I that transparent? *That pathetic?* Tears formed in the corner of my eyes.

"I didn't mean to upset you," Trudy said.

"It's okay. There's nothing about this whole situation that isn't upsetting," I said and reached for a tissue from the cozy on the stand by the bed. I dabbed my eyes with a corner, then folded it in my hands. We sat there for a few minutes before Trudy insisted I read through her instructions to make sure they were clear enough.

As I stood there in a room filled with her grieving family, I suddenly felt like an intruder. I'd seen Trudy McAllister almost every day for the past twenty years, yet we had never been close. Never shared coffee or gone on shopping trips together. Still, she knew me well enough to see how I had felt about Leon all that time.

I felt arms around my waist and took my eyes away from Leon over by the window. I looked down and saw the top of Cain's head resting on my chest. I put my chin against him and caught sight of Lola looking in our direction. She smiled at me, her eyes warm and wet.

Macy Hollister

She was a nice lady. Cain walked up from the front row and stood next to the hole in the ground. He grabbed a fist full of dirt and dropped it in. The rest of the family did the same, one at a time.

After the service, we went to his grandmother's house and the three of us sat on the porch while all the adults were inside. Cain sat in the big rocker while Mark and I were on the swing. There was a constant buzz of voices inside and now and then a burst of loud laughter.

"I don't guess I've ever known anyone that really died," I said. "Except Grandpa Hollister, and he was dead way before I was born, so I guess that doesn't really count."

Mark said, "I've been to a lot of funerals with Daddy preaching."

"Do y'all think what we did to Bobby Lee was wrong? I mean really wrong?" Cain asked.

The three of us hadn't talked much about what all went on with Bobby Lee since it had happened. After Cain's mother took him to the hospital, she dropped off Cain and Mark at the preacher's house and took me to my Grandma's. When she asked me on the porch that night if I was okay, I almost said something to her. Told her a secret I hadn't told a soul. It was the first time anyone had asked me if I was okay in as long as I could remember. For a second, I thought maybe I could. But then I ran inside.

Later that night my grandma got a call on the prayer chain to pray for Bobby Lee, saying they had to take out his eye and put in a glass one. I called Cain and we agreed that we oughta all three take an oath never to speak of what went on that day. Bobby Lee came home in a couple days but as far as we could tell, he must have been too embarrassed to tell anyone what made him run into that branch out on Chickasawba Mound.

Some people inside the house laughed so hard that the picture window vibrated.

"Well, Bobby Lee had done some pretty nasty things in his life. I guess you could say he had something coming to him," I said.

"Daddy says nothing happens outside the will of God. So I guess that means God meant for Bobby Lee to lose that eye like he did," Mark said.

"Since when did you start believing everything your daddy says?" I asked and stopped the swing.

"Didn't say I believed, just said I guess," he said.

"Do you think God meant for Aunt Trudy to die?"

Cain asked.

"Daddy says there's a purpose for everything under the sun. That if it happened, then God means it for something," Mark said.

"You sure got an answer for everything today don't you?" I said as I hopped up off the swing.

"What you getting mad at me for?" Mark asked. "I'm just saying that when bad things happen there might be a reason for it that we don't understand."

"Some bad things happen for no reason at all, you hear me? No reason at all. God ain't got nothing to do with it. And if He does, then He's a mean son of a bitch!" Before Mark could say anything back, I grabbed my purse from the swing, stomped down the steps and out the front gate.

Lola McAllister

After the services, I went home and kept going over in my mind what Trudy said to me about getting to be just like Ida. I had planned on not saying a word to her all that week. I went over the next morning just as Ida was making breakfast. We all ate together; the three of us, sitting in Trudy's bedroom while Leon went to open up the store.

Before Trudy had died, Ida had set up a little workstation around the bed so Trudy could write cards or letters if she wanted. On one end she put up pictures of our family that she brought from her house. There was one of our father in his uniform. One of Trudy, Glenda and me, all in matching dresses that Ida had made for us the summer I was seven. And one of Ida combing Trudy's hair, trying to get out the curls. Trudy was about fifteen, rolling her eyes while Ida pulled her hair straight with one hand and held a brush to her head with the other with an intent look on her face.

"The years I spent trying to tame that hair of yours," Ida had said to Trudy as we looked through old photo albums together.

I said, "Oh, Lord, do you remember all those trips we took with Daddy and every single time, Trudy would get so carsick."

"Johnny Pico drove like a demon," Ida said. "Never would stop for nothing."

"Ida would have us all dolled up for Easter," Trudy said. "Down at cousin Bigger's old house in Tupelo, and like clockwork, I'd get sick just on the other side of Memphis and tell Daddy I was gonna throw up."

"Stick your head out the window, Sister," Ida said, trying to imitate Daddy's gravelly voice. "We're making good time."

The sight of Ida imitating Daddy, had set Trudy to laughing so hard she could barely get out the words, "I'd climb over Lola—why on earth did I always sit in the middle? Then I'd stick my entire head out the window and vomit all the way down Highway 71 at ninety-five miles an hour."

"Just looky here," Ida had pointed to one of the photos and said, "in every blasted Easter picture I've got, Trudy's hair is practically standing straight up on her head like a wild woman—" She pointed to another picture and I laughed so hard, I bent over in my chair.

"While Lola and Glenda look like little carved dolls," Trudy said, reaching out to put her hand on my head. I looked up at her and she patted my face. "Beautiful little carved dolls." Ida reached out and took each of our hands and turned her face away.

It was the first time in so long that I could recall the three of us in the same room without bickering. For the rest of the morning, we had just enjoyed each other's company.

Trudy sitting up in bed, nibbling on a biscuit, Ida drinking coffee with honey and melted peppermint candies, and me holding Trudy's hand like she always did mine whenever I was scared. For that morning at least, the room wasn't filled with sickness. Just laughter and talk of other days. *That's exactly how Trudy would want me to remember it,* I tried to tell myself.

Ida Pico

On my way home to Frenchman's Bayou, I stopped by the cemetery and stood next to the grave for a mighty long time.

The epitaph read:

Trudy Mae Pico McAllister
Born August 4, 1944—Died July 19, 1979
Daughter, Sister, Wife, Mother, Friend
May God Keep Watch Over Her and Those Who Will
Always Love Her.

We buried my girl today. It was clear outside. Not too hot. *Pleasant. Real pleasant.*

Chapter Eighteen

Like a Lamb, Lying on the Alter

Brother Neil

The scriptures say that we are to avoid even the appearance of sin, so I did all my counseling sessions in the main sanctuary. I believed anytime a man—preacher or not—met with a woman who wasn't his wife, it should be in as public a place as possible. I'd known too many pastors who let sin creep into their thoughts and lives by not taking precautionary steps. So when I walked in the sanctuary that morning, I took my usual spot on the front pew and waited.

Things at the church couldn't have been any better. Each Sunday's attendance was higher than the one before. Every week when I stood before the congregation for the invitation, I saw people getting ready to come forward even before the music began. Often there were so many they had to sit on the front pew, forming a little line to pray with me. As soon as I'd finish with one, I'd hand them off to one of the deacons and move on to the next. People were getting saved, they were rededicating their lives, asking for special healing. I could truly feel the Lord at work. A real revival.

Just a week before I had preached about the rapture of God's people before the Tribulation. I pointed out that all the signs signaled the return of Jesus sooner rather than later. There were false prophets. Rampant idolatry. Paganism and witchcraft were on the rampage. The humanists, feminists, homosexuals, and liberals were aggressively seeking to end the American way of life as we knew it. All this was happening, yet many women—servants of God in this very congregation—were spending hours each day sitting in front of their television sets watching the sinful goings on of fictional characters in soap operas that had no God but mammon.

"You might as well bow down on your knees and lay yourself prostrate in front of the television set every day from eleven to three o'clock. There is your God!" I said in my last sermon. I hadn't even prepared for that in my outline. It just came to me from the Holy Spirit. Several ladies came forward after the sermon, rededicating themselves to God. Peggy Leggett had started a women's Bible study that met every weekday from eleven to noon in the fellowship hall. I heard through the grapevine that I offended more than one, but so be it. God's message was rarely pleasant, and His conviction usually resisted. Now was the time to fight even harder. Satan is angered to action when God's people are on fire for the Lord, I reminded myself.

I heard the doors open behind me and stood as Lola McAllister walked down the aisle toward me.

"Good morning, Lola," I said.

"Good morning, Brother Neil," she said. When she reached the front, I steered her to the end of the second pew with my outstretched arm. I sat on the first pew, put my elbow over the back and turned toward her. I imagined the pew between us as God's protection against sin. A man had to be diligent with women like Lola McAllister. She was twice widowed, alone, just lost her sister and in a vulnerable state. And one of the most attractive women I'd ever met. *Satan is ever ready to tempt the faithful.*

"I appreciate you taking the time to talk with me," she said. I nodded and waited to see what she had to say. "I don't think I'm handling things very well." She seemed on the verge of tears.

"What things?" I asked, reaching my hand over to pat her shoulder.

"Everything I guess," she said. "I feel like I'm a bad Christian. That I wasn't a good enough sister."

At that the tears came. I reached across the pew and put my arm around her shoulders. Her tears turned into sobs.

"From everything I've ever heard, you were a wonderful sister to Trudy," I said.

That was true. The two women always seemed to be genuinely fond of and devoted to one another. "What do you think that Trudy would say to you right now if she could?" I squeezed her shoulders from both sides in a comforting gesture and she seemed to give the question genuine thought.

Before I realized what was happening, she kissed me. I was so taken by surprise that I kissed her back.

Peggy Leggett

I woke that morning with an inspired thought. God wanted me to give myself to Brother Neil. To volunteer my time in whatever way he thought would be most useful for the church. Now that I wasn't watching soap operas anymore, (except for *The Edge of Night*, which really wasn't a soap opera, but a crime show and only lasted thirty minutes) I had all this extra time on my hands without a thing to do. I started a women's Bible study every weekday. I named it The Devout and the Faithful—weekdays at eleven. That's how it appeared in the bulletin. It's a play off of *The Young and the Restless*, which, back when I was backslidden, was my favorite show. But even with the Bible study, I found that from twelve to three I was just lost as a goose.

Anyway, I had come to church that morning to let Brother Neil know that he could use me whatever way the Lord led. And what did I see when I walked into the side door of the sanctuary, but Brother Neil, bent halfway over a pew kissing Lola McAllister!

There they were in a passionate embrace, arms flailing and clutching, him on the front pew and her in the one behind it. I looked up at the cross over the baptismal to make sure it hadn't fallen from the blasphemousness of it all. Or if it was hanging upside down for that matter—for all I knew I'd stumbled into some satanic sexual ritual held every other Saturday morning on the second pew.

In the doorway, I stood there waiting to see what was going to happen next. They kissed for what seemed like an eternity. He had one hand behind her neck, gripping her entire head in its grasp. It wasn't just any kiss, but a soap opera kiss. I reached up and touched the back of my own head and wondered what that would feel like. *I've never been kissed like that once.* Bud kissed like a woodpecker, darting his tongue in and out, poking at my teeth.

After a second, Lola pulled away. She backed out into the aisle, saying, "Oh. Oh no. I'm sorry," leaving Brother Neil sitting there on the pew with a stunned look on his face. Then she turned and ran down the aisle toward the front of the church and in two seconds flat she was out the door. Brother Neil put his face down in his hands and for a full minute he sat just there.

That's when I thought about going to him. Offering myself. Like a lamb lying on the altar, ready to be sacrificed. Before I had the chance, he stood and walked out the back door toward his office, leaving that kiss hanging in the air of the empty sanctuary like a clean, crisp apple waiting to be picked.

That afternoon, I drove over to Jonesboro and spent nine hundred and eighty three dollars on one of those video tape recorders they had just come out with so I could record my soap operas. Every weekday from then on as I headed out the door to go to Bible study, I punched the record button and from eleven on it ran 'til all the tape was used up. I kept myself busy during the afternoons but most every night I'd sit in front of the television and watch the kind of life I'd never have.

Macy Hollister

This is torture. Grandma had made me go to the Ladies Bible Study every morning that week. She said she didn't like the mouth I was getting on me. She, on the other hand, had not come. She said she was making care packages for the Homemaker's Club to take to the jail in Luxora. That may have been true, but I'd bet anything she had on *All My Children* while she worked. She had tried to make me wear slacks, but I won that one. I left the house wearing a button down oxford shirt and jeans. As soon as I got out of sight, I took the shirt off and tied it around my waist. I had on a halter top underneath.

When I walked in, there were twelve or so ladies standing in small groups around the room. One of them crossed both her arms, clutching a Bible in front of her like it was her boobs on display and not mine. I went in without talking to anyone and sat in one of the empty chairs arranged in a circle. They all kept chatting, but threw looks my way and smiled every now and then. Mark's mother walked over and turned up the air conditioner and looked at me like maybe I should cover up, but I didn't pay her any attention.

When Brother Neil walked into the fellowship hall, the ladies all scattered to their chairs, giggling with excitement. Once a week, Brother Neil gave a talk about some issue of the day. He stood at the front of the circle and told us we were going to learn about the "homosexual agenda," then opened the meeting in prayer.

While he prayed I kept my eyes wide open. I didn't even bow my head. Several of the women snuck looks up at Brother Neil, then as soon as they saw me staring at them, they ducked back down real quick. Once he finished praying, Brother Neil took a long pause, like an actor before a big soliloquy.

"Ladies, right now across this country, there are forces at work," he said. "They would have you believe that there really is no such thing as right or wrong. They say that everything is relative and that God should be taken out of the schools and the government. If they have their way, many of your own children would turn into homosexuals." A couple of the ladies sucked in deep breaths at that.

I'd seen queers in St. Louis. The past year at the school I went to, two of the boys in my grade were caught jerking each other off in the locker room after gym. Everyone teased them so bad their parents took them out of school and put them no telling where. I heard somebody say that one of them had run away to California. My father called California "the land of fruits and nuts—where the nuts are fruity and the fruits are nutty." Brother Neil went on for what seemed to me like a day and a half. The ladies all gasped and shook their heads now and then.

They took turns raising their hands and sharing some story they'd heard, each trying to top the others. Brother Neil listened and nodded his head while they talked.

"When I was at my brother's house once, I found a dirty magazine in his son's sock drawer," a lady in a blue dress said.

What's she doing in her nephew's sock drawer to begin with?

"I had never seen such a thing. It was filled with

naked women. In the back of it there were advertisements for homosexual pornography." *Whatever it was, I guess she took the time to look it over all the way through*. The lady took a pause like the preacher had earlier, then said, "It even had a black and white picture of two men doing horrible things. Together."

At this several of the ladies squirmed in their seats and one made a disgusted face and started to fan herself with her pocketbook.

"They sell those magazines right here in town at Leon's store," another lady said.

"I've told Jim that if I ever find one in my house that I'll skin him alive."

After this they started clucking one after the other.

"I'm surprised Trudy ever let Leon sell those things anyway."

"Trudy wouldn't sell them to anyone, I know that for a fact."

"Do you think now that he's saved, Leon'll get rid of them?"

"Maybe we can ask him to give 'em to us and we can have a service and burn them?"

"We could call Channel Eight and they could come film it."

"What about rock records too?"

"Magazines, records, whichever, but something ought to be burned," said the lady in blue who had started it all.

Then Peggy Leggett finally joined in. "What do you think ought to be done about it, Brother Neil?" All the ladies looked over to Brother Neil the way I looked at Shaun Cassidy's picture. Except for Peggy Leggett. She just kept the same straight look on her face while she waited for him to answer.

"It's funny y'all should mention that. I had planned on having a talk with Leon about those magazines this very week. If we want a true revival, then I think we should do our best to keep sin out of our midst."

"Amen," one of the ladies said, then blushed.

"However," Brother Neil said. "I don't think we need to make a spectacle of it by burning them." Then he quoted some verse about not showing off righteousness and one of the ladies quoted one about not keeping your light under a bushel. The whole discussion went on forever. *I got to stop mouthing off to Grandma.*

Cain McAllister

It was the second night Mark and me had slept at the courthouse. Miss B thought I didn't know what she was doing. She kept me busy all day long so I didn't have time to be sad about Aunt Trudy. As soon as we finished up at the store, she had me running errands to get ready for the photographer's visit. Then at night she got Mark and me to stake out the courthouse so she could figure out who was trimming the bushes so ugly.

Miss B was obsessed with those bushes. Every day they looked a little more thin and uneven. The ones on the right side of the courthouse looked like a big green dog with patches of mange all over where the sun shined through. There was just enough gone to make you think you were seeing crooked, but not enough for it to stand right out unless you knew where to look.

Something hit the front window of the courthouse

and I got so scared I jumped over and got under Mark's sleeping bag, lickety split. Mark jumped too, but not as much. Then he just laughed and pointed at the window. I peeked from under the covers and saw Macy standing there, with a big smile on her face.

"Let me in," Macy said from the other side of the window.

Mark jumped up and unlocked the door. Macy came in wearing her pajamas and a pair of tennis shoes. "I come for the slumber party," she said.

"It's not a slumber party if it's for boys. It's a bunkin' party," I said.

"Fine," she said. "Mark don't mind if I call it a slumber party, do you?"

"What do I care what it's called," Mark said.

Macy flirted with Mark all the time, but it was me that she kissed. When she got mad after Aunt Trudy's funeral, I went over to see if I had said something wrong. Her grandma was still at Momma Jewel's house cleaning up for the family.

Macy let me in and we sat on the couch. I could tell that she'd been crying. When I told her I was sorry, she told me that it wasn't my fault but that there's some things you couldn't talk about with anybody. I said I wasn't just anybody and that she could tell me whatever she wanted. She smiled and told me I was the nicest boy she'd ever met. Then she kissed me again.

This time I kissed her back. When she leaned in and put her lips to mine, I moved toward her and put my arms around her shoulders. I had never kissed a real girl before. Not a girl with breasts. She parted her mouth and I felt her tongue brush against my lips. I was a little surprised and at first didn't know what to do. Then I opened my mouth and did the same thing she was doing. I liked it, but at the same time I didn't think I was doing it right. After that time, we kissed now and then. It was the only secret I'd ever kept from Mark since he came to town and started being my best friend.

"I don't want to stay at your old bunkin' party anyway," Macy said to me. "I just snuck out of Grandma's to bring you some Little Debbie Swiss Cake Rolls and see if you found out anything about the bushes?"

"Hell, no," Mark said.

I was still a little mad at getting scared like that so I didn't say anything.

"Well, I just thought I'd check," Macy said. "Want to walk me home?" She kinda said it to no one in particular so I wasn't sure if she meant me or both of us.

In the second that I was trying to figure it out, Mark jumped up and said, "Sure, I will. You stay here and watch the bushes, Cain. I'll be back before too long," and dragged her to the door.

Macy looked back at me and smiled. "G'night Cain," she said.

I wondered if Macy kissed Mark and he was just not telling me about it either?

Mrs. Odell Brinkley

What Trudy said to me that last time we talked kept going over in my mind. Leon had been a mess since she died. I found myself thinking about him all the time. Hoping that he was okay. It broke my heart, knowing he was all alone in that trailer with no one to console him.

I felt so devastated I could barely function. Of course Odell didn't notice anything. Most days, I could've lit myself on fire and he'd have just thrown on another log. I tried to keep myself busy getting ready for the Southern Lifestyles photographer who was coming the next week. But, I'm ashamed to say, my thoughts were never far from Leon McAllister.

Leon McAllister

The preacher come in late one afternoon before I was about to close and waited around as my last customer left before he asked me if he could have a word. I was in no mood, but figured I was lucky he'd left me alone this long since Trudy had passed. I can't blame him for giving it a shot.

"We've missed you at church, Leon," he said.

"Can I get you a Coke?" I asked.

"That'd be nice," he said and I grabbed one out of the cooler, then flipped the sign from open to closed in the window by the register. I didn't bother to go lock the door. *This ain't gonna take too long.*

"Before you get going Brother Neil," I said. "I appreciate you coming by, but I got no interest in heading back to church."

"Why is that?" he asked.

"I wasn't myself that day I went down. Don't get me wrong, I don't regret being there with Trudy and making her happy, but as far as religion goes, I figured I'd give it one more shot if it meant I could keep her," I said.

"God doesn't work like that. We work on his terms, not ours," he said, reminding me of the reason preachers piss me off so much. *People'd be a lot better off if more folks talked to God instead of for Him.* Out of respect for Trudy, I held my tongue.

The preacher walked over in front of my magazine counter, took a look, then turned back to me. "Grief can be overwhelming, I'm sure. It must be comforting to know Trudy was right with the Lord," he said.

"No sir, it's not," I said, which surprised him a little. Most folks don't tell preachers the truth, I reckon.

"I appreciate your honesty," he said. "Can I be just as honest?"

"Have at it," I said.

"I'd like you to stop selling these magazines," he said, pointing to the girlie books under the wooden plank on the top shelf. It was something every preacher and upstanding citizen in town had probably been dying to say, so I'll give it to him for gumption.

"Well, Brother Neil," I said, "some people's got God, and other's got Penthouse," thinking maybe it'd lighten the mood. I was wrong about that.

"We must choose who we serve in this life, Mr. McAllister, God or money," he said.

I don't like a sermon that much when I'm in church, but I put up with it. *I don't have to in my own place.*

"All due respect, Brother Neil, but I think it'd be best

if I run my business and you run yours," I said.

"My business is the spiritual welfare of my community," he said.

His community. Man's been here all of two years and he thinks this is his community more than mine. Hell, half the deacons in his church come in when they see my light on after hours just to pick up a little something from behind that plank.

All those church folks act like sex is the worst sin there is. But you go down to some strip joint in Memphis or a Holy Ghost revival in Jonesboro and tell me one ain't just another way of saying the other. People's got needs that's going to be met.

If I figured keeping my mouth shut would end this conversation, I was wrong again. The preacher went on, "Make no mistake, God can't abide sin, brother."

Here I'd gone from Leon, to Mr. McAllister and now to brother. Preachers is just like salesmen, always working out which angle gets at you best.

"This perversion has no place in a decent community," he said. "I'm saying this for your own good as well. Sin has consequences."

"Consequences? What do you think God's going to do to me, Brother Neil?" I asked real loud. "I got no legs, can't walk, a stump for a hand and my wife's dead. You're barking up the wrong tree with me, talking about God punishing sin, preacher. God punished me before we ever met. Now get the hell out of my store."

Trudy'd be mad at me for hollering at a preacher like that. *But then she ain't here to tell me no different, now is she?*

Chapter Nineteen

The Key to the City

Cain McAllister

Miss B had sent Mark and me to every house along Main Street to pick up trash the whole week before the photographer's visit. The entire town was pretty much spotless. At seven o'clock in the morning, I was waiting outside the courthouse for her inspection. It was already a little warm, so I moved over next to the building under the shade.

The sun poked through all the holes in the bushes so there was no relief there. When I got closer to the door, I heard a loud clank inside, then saw the doors shake back and forth. I put both my hands up against the glass and peered in. Mr. Polk was staring back at me, his eyes blinking as they adjusted to the light. He had a big red spot on his head that matched a greasy patch on the door where I figured he'd just walked into it.

"Let me outta here, son!" he yelled through the thick glass and pulled on the door again.

"Turn the lock, Mr. Polk," I said, pointing my fingers down toward the latch just above the handle.

"Well, hell," I heard him say when he saw what I was talking about. He turned the latch, and pulled the door open wide.

"Good god, if it'd been a snake it woulda bit me," he said, laughing. He smelled funny when he walked past. "I was up late working and must have fell asleep," he said. "I don't know what I could have done with my keys."

He patted his dark brown polyester jacket and the pockets on a pair of pants that looked too big and rode up high on his waist, then started looking around on the ground. Over next to the bushes, he saw his keychain and went to pick them up.

Miss B had made a little bedroom out of the conference room for the reporter to stay in that night. She was going to have him stay over at the Holiday Inn in Blytheville, but they got flooded a week before and when she went by to check, she said the rooms smelled like a swamp. So, instead, she moved a bed, nightstand, and couch into the conference room and made Mr. Polk swear he wouldn't sleep things off in his office while the reporter was here.

"You'll never guess what I've discovered, Cain," Mr. Polk said as he put his arm around me and led me over to where his keys had been laying. He got down on one knee and motioned for me to look, pointing underneath the wooden steps that led into the building. "Looky right in there," he said. His breath was so bad it made me jerk my head back before I looked. "Just there, behind that block."

I could see something dark moving up and down slowly. "What is it?" I asked.

"Beavers!" he said loudly. "That's what's been chewing up these goddamned bushes, my friend! Won't Sadie be happy? I came up on 'em in the night—uh, sometime—I'm not exactly sure when, but it's them, sure enough."

"What are we gonna do about them?" I asked.

"Don't you worry a bit. I'll just set out some traps before midnight. Maybe give them a few tranquilizers before I take them out to the river. Beavers get nasty when they've been caged. But they'll be fine, don't you worry," he said.

Just then Miss B walked up in a hurry.

"Cain, I'm so glad you're on time. We've got two hours until he gets here," she started, then noticed Mr. Polk. She looked him up and down. "Randall, tell me you didn't sleep in our guest quarters in the conference room?"

"I simply fell asleep at my desk, working on the..." Mr. Polk fished for a second, then said, "the budget plans."

Miss B rolled her eyes in my direction and said, "That's fine, but tonight I don't want you within a mile of your office or your bottom drawer, do you understand what I'm saying?"

Ignoring this, he said, "You'll be glad to know that I've made a discovery about your bushes—"

Before he could go on, Miss B interrupted, "I've decided that we're going to tell Mr. Daubs that the bushes are part of the church's coming revival with that Armageddon theme," she said. "Kind of a scorched earth, Apocalypse scene," she added. "Now, Randall, go home and come back here at four o'clock sharp so you can give him the key to the city at the ceremony."

She put her hands on the mayor's shoulders and turned him in the direction of his house and pushed. Then she took me by the hand and led me into the courthouse.

Mrs. Odell Brinkley

This day couldn't have gone any less like I planned. I stood next to the reporter, who snapped photos of a barge as it slowly passed us on the river. The barge was filled with heaping piles of garbage, the smells of which were downright overpowering. The heat had ruined my hair already and to top it off, the barge seemed to have gotten stuck on a sandbar.

"Maybe we can come back a little later so you can get a good shot of the river," I said. "It's really quite beautiful at dusk." I made a mental note to make sure I picked up a few cans of OFF at the store. I'd hate for the mosquitoes to carry him away. He was just a little bit of a fellow, bald on top and thin as a pixie stick.

"Actually pretty interesting," he said, then mopped his face with a handkerchief and fanned it front of his nose before continuing to snap photos.

I couldn't imagine what might be interesting about a big slab of rotting garbage, but just smiled as pleasantly as I could. He certainly didn't seem interested when I gave him a tour of the mounds earlier. I had prepared my lecture on the lifestyles of the indigenous cultures for weeks. I planned all the dramatic moments to coincide with the revealing of particular scenes. All of which he greeted with a "hmm," and snapped an obligatory photo. Now there he was taking a whole roll of pictures of an old barge.

Cain had suggested I take him to Barfield point, where the Indian village sat at the fork of the river and Big Slough. It was a significant location, but quite frankly, I got ill at the site of bones, human ones in particular. I've yet to go out there when I didn't run across some, and I had hoped to keep this visit as tasteful as possible.

"We better head back to town. We don't want to be late for the ceremony," I said, moving just slightly into the frame of his camera to try and get his attention.

"Sure. Sure," he said. "Right into the river, huh?"

"Pardon?" I asked. He pointed down to the road, which led straight down from the levee and disappeared into the water.

"The road," he said. I had yet to hear the man speak in a full sentence. One with a subject and a predicate.

"Yes, it does," I said. "Of course the river's high this month, we've had a lot of rain. The road ends just about twenty feet from there. Most of the time it's not covered with water."

He snapped another picture. "Something," he said, swatting at a mosquito.

I drove back into town with the air on as high as it would go, and we stopped at the school where Cain and Mark had set up the chairs for the ceremony in the playground. It was a good turnout for a hot afternoon.

Once the ceremony started, it became painfully obvious to me and everyone else that Mayor Polk, while not entirely inebriated, was a good two sheets to the wind. Liquor made the mayor think he was funny, which I assure you, he was not. Before presenting Mr. Daubs with the key to the city, Mayor Polk goosed him with it, causing the little man to nearly jump off the stage.

With two word sentences, he accepted the key, then took me to the side and asked if it'd be okay if he went to sit in the courthouse under the air-conditioner. I said of course and deposited him there while everyone milled around waiting for me to give them the go ahead to go home, which I quickly did.

I had planned on hosting a dinner at my home with several of the ladies in town, but the young man told me that he was "wiped out" from the drive and the heat, and hoped it was okay if he just "fell out" in bed. I thought about the twenty-four salmon patties in my oven, but told him it was no trouble at all and to go get some rest. Then I called Emmie Phelps to ask her to put out the word that the dinner was off.

"Of course, darling," she said. "It's no trouble at all. That fella's a little squirt of a thing, ain't he?"

"I really appreciate it," I said.

"I'll just use the prayer chain, that way it'll make the whole rounds," she said.

Does the prayer chain ever get used for actual prayers.

The entire day seemed lost to me. Everything I thought would make a good picture, he barely noticed, and everything that seemed old, out of place or unpleasant, he just snapped away. He must have gotten thirty of V.R.'s, which is by no means an attractive building, and none of First Methodist, which is quite quaint.

To be perfectly honest, I was just ready for it all to be over.

Peggy Leggett

Mrs. Brinkley had asked me to bring breakfast over to the courthouse that morning. Everyone in town bragged on my homemade biscuits and chocolate gravy. I guess she wanted to send that reporter off in style. Personally, I didn't see what all the fuss was about. I couldn't give two hoots if we get pictured in that magazine at all. Frankly, I was relieved when Emmie Phelps called me on the prayer chain the night before to tell me that the dinner was cancelled.

I told her, "I don't want to do anything these days that involves me having to put on a pair of panty hose." Then Emmie told me about Ella Odem's daughter getting arrested over in Blytheville at The Dew Drop Lounge.

"I hear it's an awful place," I said into the phone.

I wasn't about to tell Emmie how I knew—I'd had to pick Bud up there more than I cared to admit. Besides, Emmie was a horrible gossip. I wasn't one to care much for gossip, but I enjoyed being next in line behind her on the prayer chain, all the same. Seems Ella's daughter, Tish, pulled a knife on another girl in some altercation over a man. Poor Ella certainly did need some prayer. That daughter of hers had been nothing but heartache since she first drew breath.

Anyway, I was carrying a whole tray full of biscuits and gravy when I approached the courthouse around eight that morning. Mrs. Brinkley was standing next to that little reporter, from wherever, while he was taking a picture of the courthouse. Little Cain McAllister, who, by all rights should have been my child, was standing next to her. I looked over and Mayor Polk was standing on the steps, with four beaver carcasses lying in front of him!

As I walked over, I heard Mrs. Brinkley say, "I really don't think this is appropriate."

"Let the man get my picture, Sadie," Mayor Polk hollered from the steps. He flashed a proud smile and said, "Hurry up, I think one of 'ems waking up."

I looked down at the four beavers lined up in a row and sure enough, one of them was twitching. That reporter was just smiling and snapping pictures.

"Hush up, Randall," Mrs. Brinkley said. Cain reached over and took her by the hand. She just shook her head back and forth while Mayor Polk struck a pose next to the beavers like one of those pictures of Teddy Roosevelt in my history books back in school.

"I've got breakfast," I said, not at all sure what was going to happen next. Mayor Polk got up and said, "Yippee, I'd love some chocolate gravy. Just let me get these fellas back in the cages."

He picked up one of the beavers by its tail.

Seeing the look on my face, he said, "Oh, now don't worry. It's just knocked out, is all. Little tranquilizer. After all, I'm a humanitarian!" Then he took the beaver and placed it gently in a cage setting to the side of the steps.

"Come on in, Peggy," Mrs. Brinkley said, all defeated like. "I'll help you get things set up for breakfast." She walked inside, and I followed, gingerly stepping over one of the beavers, careful not to spill my gravy.

Mrs. Odell Brinkley

It was the first time I'd seen Leon laugh in all the weeks since Trudy got sick.

"Now, stop that Leon, it's not funny at all," I said.

He just kept right on as I told him one thing after the other about the photographer's visit. When I got to the part where Mayor Polk had the four tranquilized beavers laid out on the steps of the courthouse for a photo, Leon spit out his Dr. Pepper all over the floor and pounded his fist on the counter.

"Well, laugh all you want, but it was one of the most embarrassing moments in my life," I said.

"Oh now, Sadie Lynn, don't be so sensitive," he said.

"I am not sensitive!" I screamed. Leon didn't say anything, but I could hear him snickering under his breath. "Let's just pray to God that Southern Lifestyles has the good sense not to print that picture," I said.

"Hell, Randall Polk would frame it and stick it up on the wall at City Hall, don't you know it," Leon said.

I just rolled my eyes, knowing that it was the gospel truth.

"Sadie Lynn, your problem is that you expect too much. This is just a little piss-ant delta town that nobody's ever gonna pay much attention to, and that's all there is to it," he said.

"But I want people to appreciate it here," I said.

"People that live here appreciate that it's a nice place to be. A nice place to grow up. What's it matter what anyone from outside thinks about it?"

"It matters," I said, then stopped for a moment to collect myself. "Because it's a beautiful place."

Leon smiled.

"What?" I asked.

"Just thinking about something Trudy always said about you," he said.

I wanted to hear, but at the same time the thought of it made me nervous. I busied myself with cleaning out the empty candy boxes behind the counter.

"What did she say?" I finally asked.

"She said that you were the kind of person who always left things better than when you found them. People included."

"When did she say that?" I asked.

"Years ago. Always stuck with me," he said. "Cause it's true."

"That was sweet of her," I said.

Leon didn't say anything for several moments. "Sadie Lynn, I know it's a lot to ask, but I was wondering if you would help me do something with some of Trudy's things?"

"What things?" I asked.

"Her clothes mainly," he said.

"Have you asked Lola or her mother? I'm sure they might want to take care of that."

"Lola says she can't do it. I asked her last week what she thought I ought to do with them. She said she tried to start once the week after Trudy died and that everything she looked at in the closet reminded her of some shopping trip. That'd she'd like to help, but she just couldn't do it. And you know I don't like to ask Ida Pico for anything. Besides, if there was anything particular Ida wanted, I'd bet anything she's already snuck in and got it."

I could imagine that being true. "What do you think

Trudy would want to do with her things?" I asked.

"Give them to someone who needs them, I imagine. The church mission over in Gosnell is always asking for donations," he said.

"That's a good idea," I said. I knew it was hard for Leon to ask for the help, so I figured we best do it soon. "I'll go get some boxes out back and meet you over there." He nodded. "I'll close up," he said.

I walked to the back room and started to collect a few medium-sized boxes. Instead of going back through the store, I went out back and into the trailer from the doorway closest to the master bedroom. I sat the boxes on the bed and opened the closet door, not sure if Leon wanted me to start without him or wait. I decided to take the clothes and start dividing them into piles.

As I pulled out some of the dresses, I saw one that I recognized immediately. It was a green summer dress that Trudy wore often. It set off her emerald eyes and I had complimented her on it many times. I held it up to me and looked in the mirror. When I turned to put it on the bed, I noticed that Leon was in the doorway, tears in his eyes. He moved forward, his hands balancing his weight and climbed up to sit on the bed. I turned back to the rest of the clothes in the closet.

"Sadie Lynn, do you think Trudy was happy, being married to a cripple?" he asked.

In all the years I'd known Leon, I'd never once heard him call himself that. Something about the word—cripple—stabbed me. I turned back and knelt down in front of him.

"I think Trudy loved you. That made her happy," I said.

Chapter Twenty

Butt Ugly, Arkansas

Mrs. Odell Brinkley

The lady on the phone gently let me know that *Southern Lifestyles* had decided not to do an article on Lost Cain for their "Landscape of the Delta" pictorial. Quite frankly, after the debacle of the reporter's visit, I was more relieved than disappointed.

"We just appreciate you taking the time to have someone come take a look at us," I said.

"About that," she said. I waited for her to continue. "The reporter who visited you last month is a freelance writer and not technically an employee of *Southern Lifestyles*."

"Oh, he was quite polite," I said, thinking she might be under the mistaken impression that he was to blame. "I'm not sure how much he told you, but there were several complications during the day."

"Yes," she said. I could just tell from the way she said that one word that he told her all about it. "What I'm trying to say, Mrs. Brinkley, is that Mr. Daubs is a freelance writer and photographer and therefore he works for other magazines in addition to accepting assignments from us."

"Okay," I said. I had no idea at all where this was going.

She took a breath then continued. "And it seems that he's decided to write an article about Lost Cain for another publication."

My heart jumped a little with excitement. "How nice," I said.

"Well," she said. If I thought I could tell a lot from the yes she said earlier, I could tell even more from this. "On behalf of *Southern Lifestyles*, I hope you will accept our deepest apologies if you or anyone in—"

There was a pause while she had to shuffle some papers and find our name, I'm sure. "If you or anyone in Lost Cain may be offended by the article," she said.

"Offended?" I asked.

"Mr. Daubs sent us a copy of the article he's submitted for publication elsewhere. I'm sorry to tell you that it isn't particularly flattering," she said.

I took in a breath and asked, "How unflattering is it?"

She took a lengthy pause. "Quite," she said. "I just thought that you would want to know."

"I appreciate that, Mrs. White. If I may ask, who is publishing Mr. Daubs' article?" *The Democrat* and *The Gazette* were the two state papers and I prepared myself for the worst. Or so I thought. Even over the six hundred miles of phone line between there and Atlanta, I could feel the tension as she said, "*The New York Times*."

"Oh dear," I said. "Do you think you could send me a copy of the article?"

"I'd be happy to drop it in the mail, Mrs. Brinkley, but I don't think it would do you much good. *The Times* is printing it in tomorrow's weekend section."

"I see. Well, I do appreciate you letting me know, Mrs. White," I said. By this time I just wanted to get off that phone and forget all about the entire conversation.

"We hope you don't let this experience keep you from continuing to be a *Southern Lifestyles* subscriber—"

I felt guilty before the receiver even hit the phone, but I hung up on Mrs. Sharon White, assistant to the editor of *Southern Lifestyles* magazine. I'd never hung up on anyone in my life. *Who around here even reads The New York Times?* I wouldn't have known where to go about getting one if my life depended on it. Maybe it would come out and just blow right over without anyone in Arkansas ever getting a look at the thing. Oh sure, a few hoity-toity Little Rock folks might see it, but we were four hours from Little Rock. They didn't pay any more attention to us up here in the northeastern part of the state than the man in the moon. And Memphis was too big a city to care anything about a little town across the river. *Everything will be fine.*

In any case, I decided I'd like to see what it was I was dealing with, regardless. I'd just drive down to Memphis in the morning and find me a copy to see what the damage was. I knew I'd have to tell Cain. He'd be disappointed, but I'd always told him it was a long shot.

After making some calls to see where in Memphis I could buy a copy of *The New York Times*, it turned out the only place in town that got the paper was *The Commercial Appeal.* The lady on the phone said their staff usually got about ten copies. Heaven help me, but I made up a story about a niece from up north getting married with her picture in the paper.

"I'll be happy to set you aside a copy tomorrow morning. Her picture in *The New York Times*!" she said emphasizing every single word in *THE NEW YORK TIMES*. "Ain't that something else!"

"It certainly is," I said.

Cain McAllister

"Butt Ugly, Arkansas." That was the title that read across the headline of the Lifestyle section of *The New York Times* on Friday, July 28th, 1979. I read it out loud to Miss B, driving up Interstate 55 in her Lincoln on the way back home from Memphis. She sent me in to pick up the paper from the lady at *The Commercial Appeal* while she stayed in the car out front. When I asked at the desk, the dark-haired lady behind the counter asked me what my cousin's name was. I just looked at her kinda funny.

"Ain't it your cousin whose picture is in the paper?" she asked.

I shook my head and said, "No ma'am," not sure what she meant.

"Oh, okay," she said and gave me a copy of the paper. I held out the quarter Miss B gave me to give to her.

"Now, you keep that and buy yourself a candy bar," the lady said.

I said, "Thank you," and went back to the car.

Before I even found the right section in the paper, Miss B was driving us over the Mississippi on the downtown bridge. Mark and me and Macy went to the new bridge they were building up in Missouri a lot. Her grandma let Macy borrow the old Nova and sometimes we'd take a picnic and watch the builders as they worked out on the beams stretched out about halfway across the river.

"Butt Ugly, Arkansas!" Miss B said. I remembered her using that phrase when she was apologizing to the reporter about the bushes in front of the courthouse before we caught the beavers. She had said that someone trimmed them butt-ugly and the reporter got a real kick out of that. *I guess the phrase stuck with him.*

I hadn't even showed her the picture under the headline yet. It was of Mayor Polk with a huge grin, standing in front of the courthouse steps. At his feet were the beavers, laid out like they were dead. Underneath the picture it read, "Not to worry, no beavers were harmed for the making of this article. They have merely been rendered temporarily immobile by mayor, veterinarian, and humanitarian, Randall Polk." When I pulled the paper up to my face to get a better look at the picture I noticed that Mayor Polk had forgot to put in his lower dentures that morning.

When I showed the picture to Miss B, the car suddenly swerved onto the side of the interstate, kicking up gravel. After she got it back in the lane she said, "Read on."

I read it to her out loud. "If you ever find yourself in the unfortunate position of driving from Memphis to St. Louis, as I recently did on assignment, you may want to take a few moments to veer off the beaten path to Lost Cain, Arkansas, a tiny community on the banks of the mighty Mississippi. One might call it a 'wide spot' in the road, but that would be a stretch, as the little two lanes of pavement keep a straight path right through town before disappearing into the waters of the Mississippi."

"That's not entirely true," Miss B said. "Main Street is a good six feet wider in town. I know 'cause I drew up the plans when we got it paved."

I wasn't sure if she wanted me to keep going, so I just looked at her. "Go on," she said.

I did. "Literally, the road goes up the levee, down the other side and vanishes straight into the Mississippi river. Talk about on the way to nowhere. Lost Cain boasts two churches, one set of gas pumps, and no shortage of walking, talking stereotypes."

"What's a stereotype?" I asked Miss B.

She poked her finger at the picture of Mayor Polk and the beavers. "That!" she said. "Keep going."

The article went on to explain the reporter's entire day in Lost Cain. Starting with the "nearly histrionic history lesson" given to him by a Mrs. Odell Brinkley, "the city secretary, member of the Daughters of the Confederacy, president of the Lost Cain Homemaker's club, and Sergeant at Arms of the Eastern Star," who, according to the reporter, "seemed to cling to the belief that the area's non-existent cultural significance somehow made up for the utter lack of trees." He gave a brief rundown of a Christmas parade from years earlier, in which Miss B played the starring role.

"Now how the hell did he hear about that?" Miss B said. I looked up from the paper, wide-eyed. It was the first time I had ever heard Miss B cuss.

"I'm sorry about that, Cain. I'm just starting to get a little riled," she said. "I'm not even a member of the Eastern Star. So much for fact-checking these days."

The rest of the article talked about the condition of the town. He pointed out that it wasn't that the town was run down. In order for it to be that, it would have to have been something to begin with. Miss B sank in her seat a little when I read that part. He talked about a young boy who wrote a prominent Southern magazine asking them to consider the town for an upcoming issue. I was a little disappointed he didn't use my name.

After covering the whole day, beavers and all, he ended with a commentary he called the "illusion of the mythical South" that read, "I left Lost Cain, or as I refer to it, Butt Ugly, Arkansas, thinking I had just stepped away from the poorly designed set of a bad Tennessee Williams play or a morbid Faulkner short story—only without the style, grace, or even the garish depravity those authors infused. It seems that perhaps this is the underbelly of the real South. The South they don't want us to see. Not the Margaret Mitchell tourist tours or the spruced up plantation homes. Merely the plain, impoverished, unpropitious, dull reality of life in a Southern town."

We didn't say much the last thirty miles or so. Miss B stared ahead while she drove and I copied some words from the article that I wanted to look up when I got home, like unpropitious. As I got out of the car in front of my house, Miss B said, "I'm so sorry I let you down, Cain."

"You didn't let me down," I said to her. "We got in *The New York Times*! How many towns can say that? That bastard don't know nothing about this place. I bet he wouldn't know real beauty if it came up and bit him in the ass." It was the first time I'd ever cussed in front of anyone over fifteen.

"Now, Cain McAllister," Miss B said.

"I'm sorry," I said.

"*Doesn't* know anything," she said. "That bastard

doesn't know anything."

"Yes, ma'am," I said. We smiled at each other and Miss B pulled the car away and waved out the window as she left, "I'll see you tomorrow, Sugar Cain."

Peggy Leggett

"We were the laughing stock of the entire country, I'll tell you that," I said to the handsome man from Channel Eight over in Jonesboro who was interviewing several of us out in front of the church. "Them Yankees got no business coming down here and making fun of us."

They were doing a segment on Lost Cain after all the uproar about the article in that paper in New York City. "Who in blue blazes reads a paper from New York City anyway," I added. The reporter tried to move the microphone over to Belle, who was standing next to me in a loud floral print dress the color of ochre that'd been boiled too long. I reached out and yanked the microphone back. "I'll tell you another thing. If that reporter shows up around here again, he's liable to get his butt kicked."

The reporter smiled and turned back to face the camera. "You heard it here. *The New York Times* is not welcome in Lost Cain. This is Jim Austin reporting from," he winked at the camera, "Butt-Ugly, Arkansas." I looked over at Belle and she was giving me a dirty look. Well, what was I expected to do? Belle was so ignorant that if she got a microphone in front of her there's no telling what she would have said. I think we'd suffered enough embarrassment as it was.

I don't know what Sadie Brinkley was thinking, inviting that photographer to town anyway. I told her as much at the city council meeting when all this hit the fan. Seems that she knew all about the article when it first came out and didn't tell a soul. At least that's what she said. I bet she told Leon McAllister all right. She was working at the store just about every single day. If I didn't know Sadie better, I'd have thought there was something going on. I told her that after the council meeting as well. "It just doesn't look quite right, honey," I said.

Well, the look she gave me could have peeled paint. I don't know why it is that people get so worked up when you just try to let them in on what everybody's probably thinking anyway. She just said to me, "Leon's hurting a lot right now, Peggy. He needs all the friends he can find." *Friends like Jim Bean and Jack Daniels.*

"When am I going to be on the TV?" I asked Mr. Austin as the crew from the television station was packing up their things.

"We'll be editing everything this afternoon, so it should run on the six o'clock news tonight," he said.

"I'll have to make sure I record it," I said. He didn't say anything but I bet he was impressed that I had a video tape recorder.

I heard Belle laughing and turned around to see her talking to Brother Neil, who must have come outside from his office in the church. It was shameful how he flirted with every woman in the congregation but me. I had half a mind to tell the whole place about him and Lola McAllister kissing. I'd been watching them both like a hawk. For a week or so after, Lola didn't come to church at all. Brother Neil didn't seem much different, but I did notice that when people weren't looking, he'd get a sad look on his face.

Then, when Lola came back to church the next Sunday, I noticed that she didn't so much as look in the preacher's direction, nor he in hers. At the Fourth of July dinner on the grounds, they stayed on clear opposite ends of the fellowship hall. Back in the old days we had dinner on the grounds outside, but it just got so hot in the summer that nobody could hardly breathe. Brucie Lunsford said that air-conditioners had made us all soft and that she'd rather eat tacks than spend good money on an air-conditioner. I told her she was gonna die of a heat stroke in that house of hers one of these days, sure enough. She just waved her arm in the air at me and told me I had potato salad on my collar.

Anyway, whenever Brother Neil came into a room at church, Lola went out. When he looked up, she looked down. If I were of a suspicious nature, I'd think they might be sneaking around or something and just doing what people call overcompensating by not talking in public. But I'd spent several nights in a row sitting by my window 'til well on three o'clock in the morning watching Lola's house to see if there were any comings or goings and there hadn't been a bit. I'd have my soaps running on my recorder, but I just listened and kept my eyes on Lola's side door. She had the lights in her bedroom on well into the night, but from everything I could tell, there'd not been any visitors.

Chapter Twenty One

Nothing Would Ever Be the Same Again

Cain McAllister

So many people had been getting saved that Brother Neil had to drain the baptismal pool every week to keep the water clean. There were only a few inches of water in the bottom or else I'd never have been able to get this close. Even with just a little water, I still kept my feet on the second step leading down. I heard stories all the time about people getting knocked out, falling down face first and drowning in puddles. I got shooting pains up the sides of my legs if I just imagined my feet sliding down near the water.

Next thing I knew my eyes were covered by arms from behind and I jumped up. "Don't scare me like that," I said to Macy.

We met there sometimes when Mark was at baseball practice. He tried to get me to play baseball with him that summer, but I wouldn't. The summer before I had and they didn't even put us on the same team. As soon as I found out that I wasn't on Mark's team I told Momma I wanted to quit, but she said that if I didn't want to play that I shouldn't have signed up in the first place. "You can't go through life quitting ever little thing that don't go your way. You're almost a teenager," she said.

I said back, "I don't see what that's got to do with anything." She just told me not to talk back or she'd send me to stay the summer with Mammy Pico to learn some manners. I shut up after that.

Macy sat down on the steps beside me. She had on a tight tee shirt covered with little yellow daisies and a pair of jeans. The week before last she had let me touch one of her breasts while we were kissing. I hadn't really planned on it, but had just lost my balance while I was leaned over kissing her and that's where I grabbed. She let out a little puff of air into my mouth and then breathed in deep, her breast pushing out into my hand. I kept it there in the same place the whole time that we kissed, not moving it an inch, just gently squeezing in and out.

"Did you see Mrs. Leggett on Channel Eight?" she asked.

"Yeah. Momma says Peggy Leggett would crawl naked across five lanes of broken glass to get a little attention," I said.

"Your momma's funny," Macy said. "You're lucky."

"She don't seem too funny to me," I said.

"You should meet mine. Then you'd see what I mean," Macy said. She looked down at the puddles of water and I put my hand on hers. When she looked up there were tears in her eyes and then she kissed me.

Every time Macy kissed me she cried. The first time I asked what was wrong and she said it was nothing—that lots of women cried when they got kissed and I'd see someday. Then I asked her why she let me kiss her.

"Cause you're different than anybody else," she said.

"How?" I asked.

"You don't expect it," she said. "Some boys expect you'll let them do whatever they want. And if you don't, then they get mad and say mean things to you. You're not like them."

"How do you know that?" I asked.

She pulled away.

"If I told you we couldn't kiss anymore would you still be my friend?"

I didn't want to look at her for some reason, but thought about it and then nodded my head. She took my chin in her hand and turned me to face her. "Not every boy would say that," she said.

"Do you kiss Mark?" I asked. I had wanted to ask for the longest time but I didn't really want to know the answer. If Macy told me she did, then we couldn't kiss. I would still be her friend, but if she told me that she kissed Mark, then I couldn't kiss her anymore.

"No," she said. "I like Mark and all, and he's my friend. But if I let Mark kiss me, then I don't think we could be friends like you and me. Sometimes kissing changes things."

Then she leaned over and we kissed a little while. Her lips felt slippery against mine. She started to use her tongue, then so did I. When I put my hand on her breast, she put her hand over mine and pressed it up against her tighter. This time I moved. I ran my hand all over and got big scoops of her while she moved her hand down my arm to my elbow and pulled me toward her. My tennis shoes squeaked against the fiberglass steps and I dug my hand into her breast. I worried that maybe I'd hurt her, but she just moaned and pulled on me harder. She lay back and I moved myself on top of her. When I tried to get my balance, I lifted up my head and saw Mark standing in the doorway, holding his baseball glove.

Macy Hollister

It was like I wanted to pull Cain so far into me that we melted into each other and he'd be in there with me and I wouldn't be alone. I didn't love Cain that way. Not the way I'd had crushes on boys back in school. But I did love him in a way I didn't recognize. A way that made me not hurt so much.

The first time I kissed him I didn't know why I did it. The next time I just knew that it made me feel better. I felt like when I kissed Cain that he was a part of me.

"Don't stop," I said, but he pulled away again, this time harder. He tripped down the steps into the shallow water of the pool. He sprung back up real fast and grabbed my arm, like he was standing on a tall building afraid he might fall. I followed his eyes and saw Mark running toward us. Mark grabbed Cain away from me and pushed him straight back down the steps. Cain fell into the bottom of the pool and Mark climbed on top of him, his fists balled up in Cain's shirt.

The water came up to just over Cain's ears. I could hear the panic in his voice when he screamed, "Mark, please!"

"Leave him alone, Mark," I screamed. "You know he's scared!" I jumped down into the water and tried to pull at Mark but he seemed as solid as stone.

Cain's face, sat like an island as the water got closer

to his mouth. He started taking gasping breaths. I pulled at Mark, but he held Cain down. I started to hit Mark in the back, then got down on my knees, trying to get under Cain's head so that he wouldn't go under. Cain just wailed and thrashed his arms and legs.

All of a sudden Mark jumped off of him and hunched down on the bottom step into a little ball. Cain pulled himself up holding on to me, still clutching at the air with every breath he took.

"You said you were my friend," Mark said, his voice cracking.

"I'm sorry," Cain said, getting to his feet and going over to stand by Mark.

"Get away from me," Mark said. Now it was Mark who was breathing in deep gulps. "I hate you," he said to Cain.

"Please don't say that, Mark," Cain pleaded as he pulled on Mark's arm and buried his face in his sleeve. Mark just looked over at me, his eyes red and sad.

"Mark," I said. "Don't be mad at Cain. It was all my fault."

Mark said to me in between sobs, "How come you like him and not me?"

"I do like you, Mark," I said. I walked over and stood next to them. "I like you both, so much." I realized for the first time maybe how much. Both of them meant more to me than anybody I had ever known. I loved them more than anybody in my family. They were the only real friends I'd ever had.

I bent over and put my lips against Mark's forehead. He looked up, and I leaned down and kissed him on the lips. I pulled him and Cain both up until they stood next to me with the cool water around our ankles. I kissed Mark again, this time slower. I put an arm around them both. Then I reached over and kissed Cain lightly on the lips as well, tasting the salty tears streaming down his face.

With our arms around each other, the three of us stood there in a circle without saying a word. Cain kissed me gently back. I tightened my arms and pulled them both closer. Cain moved away from my lips, then slowly moved toward Mark. He put his lips to Mark's mouth, barely touching. Mark didn't react. Cain pulled back and ducked his head down, a new tear running down his cheek. Mark kissed me again, and looked at me with a faint smile. Then he reached across and lifted Cain's face up toward us both. Mark leaned over and kissed Cain tenderly on the mouth.

That's when I heard Brother Neil's voice from the other side of the baptismal.

Cain McAllister

"Stop that right now!" Brother Neil screamed. Before I knew what was happening, he jumped down into the baptismal, grabbed me by the arm with one hand and Mark with his other. He yanked us in opposite directions and turned around, walking toward the steps, dragging both of us as he went.

"Leave them alone," Macy called out, as Brother Neil pushed me up the steps and dragged Mark from behind. When we got to the top, he shoved Mark down on the floor and put both his hands on my shoulders.

"I want you to get out of here right now and go to

your house, do you hear me?"

At first I didn't know what to say and then Brother Neil shook me so hard it sent little drops of water from my hair flying. "Do you hear me?" He said in sharp shots with each word.

I still couldn't say anything, but nodded my head up and down. Brother Neil pushed me toward the door and I ran down the steps, but I didn't go home. Instead, I ran out the side door and around to the front of the church. I jiggled the locked doors that led into the foyer until they opened like Mark had shown me how to do. Then, as I crawled up the steps to the small balcony overlooking the sanctuary, I heard Brother Neil screaming at Mark. When I looked over the edge of the balcony, Macy was still standing on the other side of the baptismal, wet and shivering, her arms clutched around herself. I couldn't see Mark or Brother Neil, but I heard Brother Neil say in a low voice, "You get your ass home," before I heard a door slam.

Macy looked up at the balcony and our eyes met. Then Brother Neil came down the steps of the baptismal pool toward her, his face red and hard. In the hollowed out baptistery they were framed like a picture. Macy and Brother Neil with the wooden cross suspended above them gently swaying in front of the wall of stained glass.

Over by the piano, I saw Mark crawling on his hands and knees through the doorway. He crept up the steps leading to the stage and then behind the choir chairs, so that he was sitting just under the baptistery opening, not more than two feet from them both. With his back against the wall, Mark looked toward the balcony and I ducked down, not wanting him to see me. Against the back wall of the church, Macy and Brother Neil's shadows spilled across the darkened sanctuary from the light through the stained glass wall behind them.

"Don't think I don't know why you're here in the first place," Brother Neil's shadow said. "Your father told me all about what's been going on with you in St. Louis."

"No, he didn't!" Macy's shadow yelled back.

"He was so repulsed at what you did that he could barely stand to even look at you anymore."

"That's not true," Macy said, this time without any emotion in her voice.

"What you did will follow you the rest of your life. There's a consequence to that kind of sin. What you've done is an abomination in the sight of God."

"I know that," Macy said.

"Everything you do in your life will be tainted with that sin. I won't have you bring that filth to my son. I should have known better than to let him associate with the likes of you. If you had your way, you'd take him straight to hell along with you," Brother Neil said.

Now Brother Neil wasn't talking, he was preaching. Mark told me that every time he got upset Brother Neil fell into the rhythm of a sermon and sicced hell on a person.

"God can't change what you've done," Brother Neil's shadow said to Macy. "You will have to live with the knowledge that you killed your own child for the rest of your life. But if you repent, if you ask for redemption, God can offer forgiveness."

"I don't want God to forgive me because I don't forgive him," Macy said, her voice low and strong.

"Then nothing but heartache will follow you

wherever you go," Brother Neil said.

I heard the water slosh and the sound of wet footsteps making their way up the steps as Brother Neil's shadow walked away. Macy's shadow stood alone while the cross above her still gently swayed, then slowly moved and disappeared into the straight black line of the dark.

Too afraid to move, I hid behind the railing and waited, knowing that nothing would ever be the same again.

Brother Neil

All that afternoon I sat in the sanctuary and prayed. I pleaded with the Lord to erase from my mind what I had witnessed. I will not have a son who defies me. *I will not have a son who is perverse.*

When we had picked up the Hollister girl at the beginning of the summer, her father had told me what the girl and her mother had done. With tears in his eyes he told me how he discovered the bills for the procedure in his wife's purse. In Illinois the laws were much looser, and only one parent was needed to sign.

While I was repulsed by the situation, I asked God at the time to give me compassion for the girl, and He had. I had hoped that being in Lost Cain might bring her to repentance. That spending time with Mark and Cain would lead her closer to the Lord. They were both good boys. In retrospect, I suppose I was naïve. After all this time I should have known that Satan only needed a thin crack in our armor to work his way inside.

It confirmed to me all that I had read and been preaching about the insidious nature of our perverse society. None of our children were safe. If my own son, having been taught and sanctified his entire life in God's Holy Word, was vulnerable to this kind of sin, then how much more so this nation's vulnerable youth? God was using my own son to show me His repulsion at the sight of our sin. Mark must be brought into submission to the authority of God's Word. *I would rather he be dead than a homosexual.*

Chapter Twenty Two

Sooner Die

Lola McAllister

Cain was lying on the bed where he'd been for almost two days. I didn't know what was wrong with him and it was worrying me sick.

"Cain, why don't you get up and have some breakfast with me," I said.

"I don't want nothing," he said.

Even though I knew it was something else, I reached out and put my hand against his forehead to see if there was a temperature. I cupped my hand to his cheek and asked, "Did you and Mark have a fight?"

He shook his head.

"Then what's going on? You two haven't gone this long without seeing each other since you met."

"I just want to be by myself," he said, pulling his covers up over his face.

"Cain Joseph McAllister you're going to tell me what's going on this very minute, you hear me," I said and yanked the covers down.

Big tears welled up in his eyes and started to pour down his cheeks. It took a few more minutes of cajoling and prodding, but finally he told me what happened at the church. I had already halfway figured out that Cain and Mark had fought about Macy. They were both crazy about her and I knew how boys were at that age. I could tell though that there was more than what he let on.

I had to practically threaten his life, but eventually he told me everything. When he got to the part where he kissed Mark, he searched for a reaction from me. I was surprised, but then not. I couldn't say I hadn't worried about Cain that way. He'd always been a sensitive boy and I knew enough to know that many like that do turn out—well it just broke my heart to think about it.

I knew it didn't matter to me, I only worried about my boy. At the same time I knew that I had kissed my best friend Maggie Payne in the 6th grade because we both thought we needed to practice before trying it on a boy. Kids do things all the time. I held on to the thought that maybe nothing was set in stone, even though inside, I knew different. By the time he finished the story, Cain was so upset again that he was practically hysterical. When he told me about Brother Neil walking in and seeing the whole thing, well then everything made sense.

"Is that where those bruises came from? Brother Neil?" I asked.

The morning before at breakfast I had noticed purple bruises on both his arms, just below the sleeves of his shirt. When I asked, Cain said that he and Mark were wrestling at church between the pews. I scolded him for not being more careful, and remembered thinking that it wasn't like Cain to be roughhousing hard enough to leave bruises. He was always such a careful child.

"Cain, you listen to me. This will blow over in no

time. No time at all. I want you to get up out of this bed, get in the shower and do something. I don't care what it is you do, just do something that requires leaving this room or else."

"Yes, ma'am," he said.

I kissed him on the forehead. "I'm going to go check on Momma Jewel. I'll be back in a little while." I closed the door, walked down the hall and grabbed my purse before I headed to see Brother Neil. I hadn't said anything to him since that day in the sanctuary when we kissed. When I'd see him at church or around town, I said a polite hello and excused myself for some reason or the other. When I had trouble coming up with a quick excuse to leave, he'd jumped right in with one of his own. I'm quite sure that both of us would be happy if the subject never came up. I suspect it had very little to do with either one of us, but more what each of us was going through at the moment. *A kiss isn't the end of the world.* I planned on telling Brother Neil exactly that when I talked to him.

I'd not have him manhandling my son for any reason. And I wouldn't have him making Cain feel like something's wrong with him just because he did something without thinking about it. Cain kissing Mark meant no more than when I kissed Brother Neil that day. *Kids ought to be free to figure out who the hell they are in this world.*

Macy Hollister

I miss them. I hadn't seen Cain or Mark for four days. Mark tried to talk with me that day after I left the church. I was walking down Maple Street, toward my grandmother's house when I heard him call for me.

"Macy, wait up," he said. At first I didn't look back or stop walking. I just wanted to go to my room, get in bed and never move again. He caught up to me and grabbed me by the arm. I pulled away, never stopping.

"Macy, it doesn't matter what Daddy said. It doesn't matter what he thinks about anything you did," Mark said.

That got me to stop. "You heard what he said?" I asked.

"I was behind the choir loft. I wanted to make sure you were okay," he said.

Even though I wasn't mad at Mark, I was so upset with everything that I lit into him. "You didn't have any right to listen!" I said.

"There's nothing wrong with what you did. It ain't against the law," Mark said.

I was almost at Grandma's so I didn't say anything else, but just took off running toward the house, leaving him behind.

When my mom found out I was pregnant, she hit me so hard I thought something had broken. She called me every name she could think of and told me I had ruined my life and that now I'd find out how lucky I'd had it. Being married and having kids meant that any good times was over, she said. "Now you'll see what it's like."

I told her that I wasn't going to get married and that

if this was supposed to be my good times then I was glad they were done and finished. For three days she pestered me about telling her who the father was. She wondered if I even knew, calling me awful names. She always thought I was too old for my age and she hated to think of all the things I had done.

My mom grew up in Caruthersville, Missouri, just about thirty minutes across the state line, north of Lost Cain. She met Daddy when her family moved to Memphis and he went down there to go to college. Grandma always bragged about being able to send Daddy to college, even if he never did finish. "It was college that saved him from that war," she always said. Daddy never could make good grades, but he stayed in school five years anyway to avoid the draft. My mom lived next door to the house where he rented a room. They went to the same church.

I had been to that church a couple times when we'd go to visit my other grandparents. They cast out demons from people there. Usually demons in kids. The time I saw it, they had a little boy about eight-years-old sitting in a chair while eight men all stood in a circle around him, each with both hands laid somewhere on the boy. Some were on his head, his back, and his chest. There was even a man sitting in front with his hands on the boy's shins. I figured out later he was there to hold him down. The pastor led a prayer and all the men started mumbling words I couldn't understand.

They went on for several minutes until one of the men shouted, "I cast out the demon of rebellion!" The others kept mumbling and each shouted out words like, laziness, idolatry, and stubbornness. Then all the men would speak, each casting out different things while everybody in the congregation prayed and some wailed. The boy started to shake and convulse. After ten minutes or so he started screaming out and the people got excited and prayed harder. The pastor started saying how this showed that the demons were leaving and they were breaking the spirits that bound the boy. By the time they were finished, the boy was sobbing. He had red marks where some of the men's hands had dug in. They carried him out and the pastor turned to the congregation and said, "And all God's people said." Everyone but me said, "Amen."

Mom had suggested a few times that maybe they should take me there. At first she used to joke about it when I was being bad. Then later, when things got worse, she said it like she was serious. I heard her and Daddy talking one night about it. Daddy said that he knew I was rebellious, but that he didn't think I was beset by demons. That's why he came and prayed with me each night, he told her.

I used to wonder sometimes if my mother knew. I hated her if she did. When Daddy left my room each night I would pray. I would ask God to please not let it ever happen again. After a while I stopped believing in God at all. After that though, sometimes, during it, I'd still pray. Trying to keep my mind off what was happening. But I knew by then that God wasn't listening.

When I finally told Mom the truth, I could tell by the look on her face that she didn't know. She went all white and nearly fell to the ground, so that I had to hold her up. For a few minutes she didn't say anything. She just sent me to my room. The next day she took me in the car over the river to East St. Louis, Illinois. Afterwards, she gave me some pills to take and told me to never tell a soul about any of it. I ran away the next week. I was gone for about four days before they found me. I stayed with a nice woman who ran a motel downtown. She saw me at the bus station without any money and gave me a room.

By the time they found me, Daddy knew everything that happened in East St. Louis. He never hit me but I could tell that he wanted to. They sent me down to Lost Cain the next week.

I won't ever go back there again. I'd sooner die.

Brother Neil

I had increased my prayer time to three hours every day. With everything that was happening, I could see the clear hand of Satan at work. Instead of being discouraged by this, it spurred me on and fueled my resolve and desire for the Lord. The past Sunday was our highest attendance yet. We had fourteen souls won and nine rededications. There were so many people who came forward during the invitation to pray that there wasn't enough room in front. They began to kneel down at the end of the aisles along the church walls. Standing there at the pulpit on the stage, seeing God's people on their knees in holy reverence and devotion, my heart swelled.

In spite of all that had happened, Mark remained obstinate. I'd always felt the boy never heard a word I said. He'd always been obedient, at least initially, though I saw the little ways he defied me after I turned my head. I'd let this slide because he'd never caused me any real trouble. In fact it was exactly the opposite—wherever we'd gone he had drawn people in with his affable way and good nature. But I could see that the chickens of my lax discipline had come home to roost. For his own sake, I knew that had to change.

I forbade him to see either of those children. He tried to argue, but I let him know that I wouldn't even have him utter their names in my house. I knew he had no intention of following my orders, so the only way I could control him was to keep him in sight. He'd been grounded all week. The only times he could leave the house were to come to church with me. I'd unplugged all the phones except the extension in my office, and that room remained locked. Patty complained that even she didn't have a key, but I told her if there was an emergency she could get help quicker by running out the front door than getting on the telephone.

I'd not told her the extent of what I saw that day in the church. I hoped it wouldn't come to that. I prayed that perversion hadn't taken root in my son, and I would do all I could to see that it had not. As for the other boy, his mother came by a day or two after the incident to see me in my office. Seeing her there made me think of my earlier transgression. It was the first time she and I had been alone since it happened. She was upset about bruises on her sons arms and rightly so. I apologized for my rough handling of the boy, but at the same time suggested that perhaps a little more rough handling wouldn't be entirely harmful in his case.

She went on to justify the three, saying that they were merely exploring as all adolescents will do. I let her know that I never did any such thing when I was an adolescent. That there were some territories a decent person left untouched.

"However," she said, "there certainly are times when we all venture into places we wished we hadn't."

I understood the implication immediately. I took the opportunity to apologize for my part in the kiss that we had shared. It was true that she had kissed me first, but I could not justify or explain my eager, yes lustful, response. For the first time since we began the talk, her anger subsided.

"It was a mistake all around," she said. "I hope you'll remember that when you deal with Mark. Don't punish the boys too much for what was a simple mistake and probably doesn't mean a thing."

Until I sensed true repentance in Mark, he would be at home with me. And he'd never associate with her son again, repentance or not. I ended the meeting politely, but had no intention of treating this matter as anything other than what it was. Sin. And sin must be confessed, repented and given to God.

As for the girl, I'd called her father in St. Louis and explained to him the situation—naturally leaving out any mention of what went on between the boys. He asked for my spiritual guidance and counsel, as he and the mother had very nearly divorced over all the trouble the girl had caused. I explained to him that shipping this girl off to a lenient grandmother was no way to correct a path so far from God's plan. That I understood the impulse to remove her from the situation, particularly if the marriage was truly in trouble.

However, now that some time had passed—time for he and his wife to fortify their relationship and present a solid Godly front—it was time they reined this child in. I suggested he come to Lost Cain immediately to take his daughter back home.

Chapter Twenty Three

The Way it Is

Cain McAllister

I saw Macy once on a Thursday in her grandmother's car as they drove by the store. She was looking out from the car with her face in the bright sun. Just as they passed, her head tilted and it seemed for a second that maybe she could see me. But before I could wave, the taillights of the car disappeared over the old railroad tracks and she was gone.

Later that day a man came in the store who knew Uncle Leon. He wore mirrored sunglasses that he never took off the whole time he was there.

"Hey Leon, sorry to hear about Trudy," he said. "Could I get a pack of Lucky's?"

"Appreciate it, Trent," Uncle Leon said as he reached under the counter and pulled out the pack without even having to look. "How's everything up in St. Louis?"

"Fair to middlin' I guess," the man said.

"We've gotten to know Macy while she's been down. She seems like a real nice girl," Uncle Leon said as he took the man's money.

The man hit the cigarettes on the counter a few

times, then tore the top off and tapped one of the cigarettes from the pack. He leaned his head down and pulled one from the pack with his mouth. “Well, I better get back to Ma’s. Good to see you,” he said as he lit up the cigarette that moved up and down as he spoke. He walked out the door, letting it slam hard behind him.

“Was that Macy’s dad?” I asked Uncle Leon.

“Sure was. Ain’t seen the SOB in almost fifteen years and he’s just as talkative as ever,” Uncle Leon said.

I sat next to Momma Jewel in church the next Sunday and tried to get a glimpse of Mark or Macy across the sanctuary. I saw Macy walk in a few steps behind her father with Mrs. Hollister. I tried to catch her eye but she was looking down while she walked. Her dad stood next to one of the pews closest to the back then Macy and her grandmother slid in before he sat down on the end next to the aisle. He wasn’t wearing the sunglasses anymore, but had them hanging from his shirt pocket with the front turned out. In the two mirrors, I could see the reflection of the overhead lights. He put his arm on the back of the pew around Mrs. Hollister, who smiled at him, but Macy never looked up.

Desperate to at least see Mark, I scanned the rest of the church, but couldn’t find him anywhere. I’d been too scared to go by his house to ask to see him. Even when I knew Brother Neil was at the church, I still wouldn’t go check. I was afraid that Mrs. McElroy wouldn’t let me in, but mostly I was afraid that Mark wouldn’t want to see me even if she did. I didn’t know if he was mad at me for what I did or not.

Momma Jewel handed me a piece of Juicy Fruit, which I unwrapped immediately. As I was about to put the wrapper into the little holder for the visitor's cards, I saw something written on one of them and pulled it out. Across the back it read, "Come see Barnabas."

Barnabas was one of the hand puppets we used during the skits that Mark and me did for children's church. I wanted to jump up, but realized the service was already starting. For the next ten minutes it was everything I could do to sit still. At least I knew that I'd get to see Mark again, even if he hated me for what I did. Finally, Wilbur Sellers led the opening prayer and I snuck out. Momma Jewel would think that I'd gone to sit with my friends, which I sometimes did during the prayer. It was the one time after the service started where everybody had their eyes closed and was almost always long enough to make it across the room or even out the door.

Once I was in the foyer, I could still hear Wilbur praying as I opened the door and went outside. I ran around the front of the church to the back hallway entrance. Brother Neil had suspended children's church for the summer, so nobody was there.

I took the steps two at a time. When I got into the room, I didn't see a soul. Then Barnabas, with his ragged blonde hair and a nose that used to be a button but was now just a crookedly drawn black spot, appeared on the puppet stage, smiling wide with one hand waving in the air. I busted through the curtain and sat down cross-legged beside Mark.

"What did your daddy do to you? Did he get real mad? Are you ever going to get to go anywhere again?" I asked all in a row.

"Well, he's not thrilled, that's for damn sure," Mark

said.

I wasn't really worried about Brother Neil, but only afraid of what Mark was going to say about the kiss. I hoped he couldn't tell that.

"Have you talked to Macy?" he asked.

"No. I went by to see her a couple times, but Mrs. Hollister told me she wasn't feeling good and maybe I should come back next week. Have you?" I asked.

"No," Mark said.

"She's in church today with her dad," I said. For a little while we just sat there and didn't say anything. I felt like I was going cry, so I turned my face away from him. "I wish things could just be like they were," I said.

"Things are like they were," Mark said, but I couldn't look at him. He put his hands on my head and turned me to face him. "You're still my best friend, ain't you?" he asked.

He doesn't hate me. Relief poured over me and filled every empty spot, like one of Momma Jewel's big bear hugs. *Mark doesn't hate me*. I smiled and said, "Yeah," but couldn't stop crying for the longest time while he sat next to me and held my hand.

"Cain," he finally said. "When Macy kissed me, it was like something sent sparks all over me and I thought I might catch on fire. But it didn't bother me none what you did. I felt bad about holding you down in the water like that. I know it scares you. That's why I kissed you back. I like you just about more than I do anyone else I ever knew. I guess I love you, though sometimes I don't think I really know what that is. It don't matter that we're different that way. At least not to me. You're always going to be my best friend, like it or not."

He held the Barnabas puppet out in front of me and moved its mouth while he said, "And that's the way it is," trying to sound like Walter Cronkite. Then he put the puppet down.

"So no matter what else changes Cain, that one thing will always be the way it is," Mark said.

Peggy Leggett

You could have parked a station wagon in my mouth, my jaw dropped so low. Brother Neil had just stood up in front of everyone in the congregation and admitted to kissing a woman other than his wife. I looked around me and everyone else was doing the same thing. Looking around not sure what to do.

Brother Neil went on, "I know that it's a lot to ask, but I have to beg you all for your forgiveness. When God is at work, Satan doubles his efforts."

I heard a few uncomfortable Amens. I looked over at Patty McElroy and the woman looked no different than she did when her husband was making the announcements for prayer requests. *She must be a cold woman.* I tried to get a look at Lola McAllister from where I sat up in the choir, but I couldn't quite see her face because Pam Lovelady was so fat you could barely see around her. I figured Lola was sweating in those cute suede boots I noticed she had on that morning. She ought to be.

Dulan Meacham got up and put his arm on Brother Neil's shoulder. "Brother Neil has made a full confession to all the deacons," he started. I shot Bud a look that could kill. *That man never tells me a thing*. It's not natural to be so good at keeping things to yourself. Dulan kept going, "We all agree there is no need to go into the particulars of this incident," he said. *No need? I most certainly think there is a need!*

"We have heard the entire story and are satisfied that Brother Neil is sorry and truly repentant," he continued. "We're in a time of great revival in our church, like nothing we've seen before. We believe that indeed dark forces are hard at work to stop that revival. We don't intend to allow that to happen."

It was all I could do not to jump up and shout, "It was Lola McAllister! She's the one he kissed!" Lola was gonna get out of all this scot-free without a single consequence to her actions like she always did.

Brother Neil talked a little more about how troubles could bring us closer to God. It wasn't really a sermon he was giving, but it was awful close to one. I looked around and could tell that everyone had already forgiven him. They were wiping their eyes and nodding their heads. I had not forgiven him, though. *That should have been me he kissed and not Lola.* I tried not to cry. I hated to think something like that in church but it was the God's honest truth.

After Brother Neil finished, they gave the invitation and people started going down front to pray. I saw Trent Hollister leading his daughter down the aisle. I used to have a crush on Trent back when I was in ninth grade and he was a senior. Well, let me tell you—he hadn't held up well, that's for sure. There was a big bald spot on the back of his head and what used to be a football player's build was now just chubby. He pulled that daughter of his—the one that always dressed so trashy—tears in her eyes, up to the stage and knelt down with her to pray.

All across the church people were praying. The front was full, the side aisles were full. People were kneeling down right where they sat. The only two people without their heads bowed in the whole entire place were me and Lola McAllister. I could see her fine then. Pam Lovelady had kneeled her fat self down on one knee—Lord knows how she'd ever get up—and there was Lola, looking oh so pretty and proper, eyes straight ahead. I locked my eyes and didn't budge 'til she saw me looking right at her. I wanted her to know that she wasn't fooling me. No siree. Not me.

Cain McAllister

Mark and me made a plan to meet when Brother Neil locked himself in his study each morning to pray. "He's always in there for at least a couple hours," Mark said. "I heard mom telling him that she thought it was too harsh, him not letting you and me see each other. So I think she'd let me come over to the church while he's in there, and you can meet me here. She's still mad that he took out all the phones in the house except the one in his office, so she'll do it just cause of that I reckon."

I knew that if Mrs. McElroy knew the real reason that Brother Neil hated me so much, she probably wouldn't let me see Mark either.

"When you get to the church," I said. "Pull open the curtains in front of the stained glass windows on the sides. They look real different in the sun from the outside when they aren't covered. That way I'll know that you're there."

“Okay,” Mark said.

After we finished talking, I went back downstairs, and Mark went back to his house. As I came around the front of the church building, I didn’t see a soul coming out of the front doors even though it was already past noon. If I hadn’t heard the organ vibrating when I opened the door, I would have sworn that everyone had already gone home. In the foyer, I heard the music and peeked inside one of the long windows in the door leading to the sanctuary. Everywhere I looked, people were out of their pews and down on their knees. The entire church was covered with people nodding their heads and holding hands, their mumbling voices sounding like a swarm of bees.

After a few minutes, Brother Neil went up to the podium and motioned for the organ music to stop. As it finally faded, he said, “I want to thank you all for being such shining examples of God’s love and forgiveness. I could have never hoped that you would show such compassion and commitment to the work that’s happening here in Lost Cain. I’m humbled by your dedication and the sincerity of your faith. As we make our way back to our seats—”

When he said this people started getting up from where they were and settling back into their seats. I saw Macy and her Dad holding hands and walking up the aisle. Macy’s face was wet with tears.

“I hope we all remember,” Brother Neil continued, “that during this time of revival, Satan is ever ready to ensnare us at every turn. Pray a hedge of thorns around your life—”

While people got settled, I opened the door and

slipped down the aisle. Momma Jewel patted me on the shoulder when I sat next to her, probably thinking it was sweet of me to come back and sit with her at the end of the service.

After the closing prayer, everyone chattered, commenting on how the Lord's spirit was with them today and "ain't it something how Brother Neil always knows just what to say."

"I'm behind him one hundred percent," Mrs. Lane said.

"It's only natural for the young to make some foolish mistakes," Mr. Hannon added.

"Let those without sin cast the first stone," I heard from somewhere.

I asked Momma Jewel what they were talking about and she just looked at me funny.

"Wasn't you listening at all today?" she asked.

I didn't want to lie, so I just didn't say anything. She shook her head and said, "It's just as well. Now come on and help me home, I got some white beans and bacon stewing." She leaned on my shoulder and moved out of the aisle. I tried to get a glimpse of Macy somewhere in the crowd of people heading for the door, but couldn't see her anywhere. Mrs. Leggett, in a pink dress the color of Pepto Bismol, pushed her way through the crowd, all elbows, until she got to the door. Then she turned around and looked at everyone with her upper lip buried underneath her bottom teeth in a sour frown.

Chapter Twenty Four

Not Above That

Lola McAllister

Leon had asked me to mind the store, while he was gone. He'd gone down to Memphis for some reason, though he wouldn't tell me what. I figured he was gambling again. If it helped him get through things, I guess I didn't mind. I unlocked the door and let myself inside. I'd almost decided that whatever it took to be happy in this life, you just ought to do it and sort everything out later.

I had avoided coming to the store every chance I could. It reminded me too much of Trudy. It was probably the first time I'd been inside for over two minutes since she'd been gone. It was odd to see her neat, clean handwriting on the little cards that said "Specials" down the aisles. It seemed that everywhere I turned, I saw evidence of her touch. Over the meat slicer she'd written on a little card taped to the wall, "For Employee Use Only (Don't you touch this, Cain McAllister, it'll cut your finger off!)" I smiled when I saw that, but then started to cry.

All those reminders of Trudy had set me off, so I grabbed a cigarette out of my purse and lit it to calm my nerves. My first customer of the day came in and I turned around to see Peggy Leggett, standing at the counter with her back to me, one foot tapping the floor. I set the cigarette on the counter and put my guard up before I went on over. I had no idea why Peggy hated me so. There probably hadn't been more than six words said between us our whole lives. Momma Jewel said that she was awfully in love with Dip before we married. It's hard to believe a grown woman would hold a grudge over a high school sweetheart, but I guess maybe I'd do the same if I had loved someone I never got.

"Hey Peggy, what can I do for you?" I asked.

"Oh, Lola, I didn't expect to see you here this morning. Are you okay?" she asked while she waved her hand back and forth in the air and coughed a little as if she still needed to make the point.

"Yes. Is there a reason I shouldn't be?" I asked.

"Well, I heard that you had a request for prayer on the prayer chain right after church yesterday," she said.

"I didn't ask for any prayer," I said.

That prayer chain had gotten entirely out of hand. Since all the ladies at church had given up soap operas, they spent all day, every day, talking to each other on the prayer chain. They'd sit there and take notes as they went from one to the other until something worked its way around town three times before I bet anyone had gotten around to praying.

Peggy got a dramatically puzzled look on her face and said, "Well, I got a call from Sylvia Ledbetter right after church saying that there was a special request made for you. An unspoken."

The only time anyone used an unspoken on the prayer request was when there was something to hide. It could be something of the "female problems" variety or something involving drinking, drugs or gambling. And of course, sex. Never mind that no person in their right mind would put a sexual prayer request on a Baptist prayer chain, it was still the first thing everyone thought of. Then it dawned on me what had happened. Somebody knew that it was me that Brother Neil was talking about on Sunday and this was their way of getting the word out. I could just see the wheels turning in the minds of women all over town. Brother Neil confessed to kissing a woman other than his wife, but didn't tell who. Lola McAllister, a single woman, asked for an unspoken prayer request immediately after. *They'd hung horse thieves with less evidence.*

"Is there something I can get for you, Peggy?" I asked, trying not to sound as annoyed as I was.

"Well, I just came in to see about—" she said.

I could tell she was just looking for something to say or an excuse to be there. That's when it hit me that she was the one. She wanted to make sure I knew that she knew it was me that kissed Brother Neil. I had thought that same thing when she kept staring at me in church on Sunday. Something about the look in her eye was plain spiteful.

"I just need a new pair of pantyhose," she finally said. I pointed down the first aisle. She smiled and said, "You can just put it on my tab."

Every now and then she looked back as she walked down the aisle. I turned the big metal contraption behind the counter where Leon kept people's accounts. I lifted the one marked L-M and pulled her bill from underneath the metal clip. I noticed that there were several entries for the exact cost of a pack of Virginia Slims. I thumbed through the receipts and every three days like clockwork, there was the same charge.

"Peggy Leggett smokes," I whispered to myself. Something about it struck me funny. Peggy always had an opinion on everything and acted as if she were completely above "the baser desires," as she'd called smoking at a Baptist Young Women's meeting once, looking in my direction. *Miss high and mighty, holier than thou, smokes just like us "lesser" sinners.*

Peggy came back with an egg-shaped Leggs container and set it down on the counter. I smiled bigger than I normally would, then reached over for my cigarette and took a puff.

"Is there anything else I can get for you, Peggy?" I asked, letting the smoke go where it may.

I saw her eyes dart toward the cigarettes but I knew she'd never ask. She just said, "No thanks," and kept waving her hand across her face. I didn't say anything, but when I pulled out the bag, I slipped a pack of Virginia Slims into it along with the pantyhose. She saw but didn't say anything.

"I'll just put all that on your tab," I said.

"Thank you," she said and grabbed the sack. She was out the door in a flash and I just smiled and shook my head. *Who the hell cares what the women in this town think?* I stubbed the cigarette out in the ashtray on the counter and realized I'd still never once cussed out loud in front of anyone in my life. *One of these days I'm liable to really cut loose.*

Mrs. Odell Brinkley

There I was, a married woman, meeting my lover at some seedy motel down in Memphis. I could barely say the word lover and yet I had one. I shook my head, sitting in my car and wondered how I'd come to this. I had the doors all locked, but still felt like I might get mugged at any moment. Finally, I saw Leon's van pull into the parking lot.

He had tried to talk me into meeting him at one of the truck stops over in West Memphis and then coming down together. I told him I'd rather we just do it like we have been. Every Tuesday morning after Odell left for the farm, I got in my car and came down to the Drift Inn off Summer Avenue in Memphis. It was a horrible little place. I think I picked it that first time for just that reason. If I'm going to do such a despicable thing, it ought to be in the worst place possible, I told myself.

I came in each week to get the room and the clerk looked at me winking and smiling as she took my money, like the cat that ate the canary. I could tell exactly what she was thinking. *We're not that different now, are we*? And I guess she was right. I had on a two piece, pleated pantsuit and she had a tattoo of a lightning bolt on her arm, but when it came down to it, there we were in exactly the same dilapidated motel on a Tuesday morning. At least she could say it was an honest living that brought her there.

I could have waited in the room, but I felt more comfortable there in the car where I could see what was coming from all directions. The whole time I waited, though I kept the doors locked, the car running, and my hand on the gearshift.

Leon hopped out of the driver side of his van. It was set up with a knob on the steering wheel so he could turn it, and long handles that worked the gas and brake pedals. I fought the urge to go help him get the wheelchair out of the side door. He preferred to do everything on his own. Once I saw that he was doing okay, I opened the door, pushed the lock back down, and got out of the car. I walked over to room sixteen and used the key to open the thin door that rattled when I shut it.

It had been about three weeks since all this had started. I don't know what had come over me, and quite frankly, I didn't care. For the first time in twenty years I felt happy. Not all the time happy, but sometimes happy. Now and then happy beats always miserable, I can tell you that. I doubt Odell would've even cared if he knew. Well, he'd have cared but it wouldn't have had anything to do with me. He'd have only been mad because Leon was pulling something over on him. It'd be no different than if he found out Leon was using his favorite fishing hole, pardon the pun. *Listen to myself. I've gotten downright vulgar.*

I heard a knock on the door. When I looked out the peephole, I saw nothing, which I always took to mean it was Leon, since he was in his chair. If I ever did look out and saw anyone standing there, I don't know what I'd have done. I opened the door and Leon wheeled himself in.

"Sadie Lynn, I don't like you coming down to this place ahead of me," he said. "You oughta let me find a nice place, somewhere downtown."

"This'll do for me," I said.

I closed the door, sat down on the bed and put my hands to my face. Leon reached over and pulled them down.

"I'm sorry," he said.

"I don't want you to be sorry. I'm not," I said.

"Then what's wrong?" he asked.

"I think I've got to tell Odell that I want a divorce," I said.

I'd thought about this the whole week. I didn't want Leon to feel that I expected anything from him, but I just couldn't live like that—deceiving Odell so.

"If that's what you need to do, I'll do whatever you want," Leon said.

"We don't have to tell him anything about us. I wouldn't want that. I just think I ought to make a clean break. I'm not asking you for anything, Leon," I said.

He moved from his wheelchair to the bed beside me and put his arm around me. "You can ask me for anything in the world, honey," he said.

I was grateful for that and I knew it was true. As I folded into his arms, I thought of Trudy and of Leon's grief and wondered if maybe I was nothing more than a substitute. But then it struck me that the truth was that we were all just putting someone in the place of something else and trying to get a little peace in this life.

I'm not above that, I thought and lost myself in Leon's embrace.

Macy Hollister

They look asleep. In my room I looked through the photo album filled with grandma's dead relatives. Most were just profiles, lying in their coffins, looking not quite human, but more like wax figures you'd see at a museum. In one, there was a young baby, maybe a year old, with a white rattle next to its head on the pillow. I heard a knock at the window and saw Cain standing there, waving.

I was glad to see him, but at the same time I got frustrated with myself that I had left the shade up. He'd come there before, but each time I'd heard him knock, I pretended like I wasn't there. With the shade pulled down it was easy to do. But seeing him looking at me through the windowpane, I couldn't help but want to talk to him. I closed the album and walked over, turned the latch and lifted up the window.

"Macy, where you been?" Cain asked.

"Nowhere," I said.

He reached his hand through and took mine. I didn't try to stop him.

"Is your Dad going to make you go home?" he asked.

The first day Daddy had come down I told him that if he came anywhere near me, I'd scream my head off and tell Grandma everything. He clinched his teeth and told me he was real sorry for everything that had happened. His words said one thing, but I didn't believe him. He said that he'd gone down to the church in Memphis and had a special prayer meeting with the elders there, and now things were going to be different. Toward the end of what he was saying, I started to believe that maybe he was telling the truth. For some reason it made me even madder to think of him really being sorry. I'd almost rather he came right out and say how much he hated me, rather than sit there crying, promising nothing like that would ever happen again.

"He said we're going home after church on Sunday," I told Cain.

"Come see Mark and me tomorrow at the church. We meet there every morning around nine, behind the puppet stage," Cain said.

"I don't think I can," I said. "They won't let me go anywhere and they check on me all the time."

"Macy, I don't want you to leave," he said. "Do you think you could ask to stay here and live with your grandma?"

I shook my head no. "Daddy won't let me. It'd be like saying he didn't know how to raise his kids right."

"You've got to try to come see us at least before you go home," Cain said.

"Cain, I'm not going home with Daddy," I said. "I hate him more than anything this whole world over."

The look in Cain's eyes told me that he knew everything. I didn't want to ever say what had happened to me out loud, but Cain just looking at me like that—like he knew and he was there—it made me love him even more than I already did. Tears started running down my cheeks for the first I could ever remember.

"You could come stay with me and Momma. I know she'd let you."

I pulled my hand away from his.

"Use this if you need it, Macy," he said and put a wad of money in my palm. I looked down and saw that it was a thick stack of tens and twenties rolled up. "It's my life savings. Almost three hundred dollars," Cain said.

When I thought about running away, I got this tired feeling all over me. I didn't want to be by myself. But I knew Daddy wouldn't let me stay there in Lost Cain. I knew that as much as I might like to go live with Cain, that Daddy would stop that too. Even if I could bring myself to tell somebody what had happened and they believed me, I still didn't know what they'd do or where I could go. It seemed to me that I had no other choice.

I didn't try to say no to the money Cain offered. I knew no matter what I said he'd make me take it. And the truth was, that if I were out on my own, I'd have needed it. That wasn't what was going to happen, but I let Cain slip the money into my hand and gave him a hug.

There was nothing else I could do.

"Will you please try to come see us tomorrow?" he asked.

"I will," I said.

"Please try hard. Mark wants to tell you goodbye," Cain said.

"You better go," I said and looked back toward the door to my room. "I'll see you tomorrow," I said.

"Promise?" he asked.

"I think I hear someone," I said and closed the window.

I don't make promises I can't keep.

I wouldn't let myself cry as Cain walked away. Instead, I went over to the tall chest with a fold out flap that pulled down to make a desk. I took an envelope out from one of the drawers, straightened out the folded bills, then put them all inside, licked the seal, and pressed it shut with both my hands. With a felt tip pen I wrote in big letters across the front of the envelope, "Please give to Cain McAllister," and underlined it three times.

Tomorrow is as good a time as any.

Chapter Twenty Five

Jesus on the Cross

Peggy Leggett

I snuck out the side door and ran behind the church bus right after Bible study wrapped up. It'd been almost four hours and I felt like if I didn't have a cigarette soon, I might suffocate. I pulled a match out of the pocket sewn into the waist of my dress. I kept exactly five kitchen matches there to last me through the day. I struck it against the rusty patch above the rear wheel of the bus and breathed in while I lit up.

No, I didn't tell anyone that I smoked, and what of it. It was nobody's business but my own. There's nothing in the scripture that said anything about smoking, no matter what anybody else says to the contrary. Lord knows I needed it. I pulled in a breath deeply and poked out my lower lip to try to let it out slow, so that no one could see it coming up from behind the bus.

Getting ready for Brother Neil's special guest speaker had been almost more than I could handle. He'd put me in charge of the twenty-four hour prayer barrage. I had people signed up in forty-five minute intervals to come to the church and pray for our revival. That was round the clock, mind you, not just total. It wasn't as hard as I thought it would be. Everybody was supposed to come at least ten minutes early so they could seamlessly take over for the previous person—the goal being that for not one minute during the entire time, would someone not be praying for the revival.

Brother Neil had called me his right hand lady in front of the entire Bible study. He was giving a talk on New Age religions and how they all tried to convince everyone that there was no such thing as Hell. It was riveting.

Anyway, afterward, he said he hoped that everyone there would be signing up for a slot on the prayer barrage. I jumped up and told him that I had already filled each and every spot. He was so impressed that he clapped and said what he wouldn't give for a dozen just like me.

Brother Neil and I had been getting closer all the time. Since his confession in front of the church, he seemed like a new man. People had been coming by at all times of the day to offer him some encouragement or pray with him. Thankfully, Lola McAllister had the good sense to keep to herself. I felt a little guilty after I called in her name on the prayer chain like that. It didn't take anyone long to put two and two together.

But after Lola pulled that stunt with the cigarettes at the store, I didn't feel a bit guilty anymore. Stashing those Virginia Slims in my bag, just lording it over me that she knew that I smoked. Like that makes her better than me. *Well, at least I'm not kissing married men in front of Jesus on the cross*. I took another puff. They weren't even the right kind. I always got the unfiltered and these were menthol.

After I finished, I threw the cigarette down on the ground and stamped it out with my foot. Then I kicked the butt under the bus and sprayed a little Charlie out of the bottle I kept in my purse. I walked around the end of the bus and ran straight into Belle, who was wearing a god-awful red jumpsuit that didn't do a thing for her figure, such as it was.

Belle sniffed at the air, waving her hand, and said, "Easy on the Charlie, Peggy. I've been looking everywhere for you. You are never going to believe what I heard!" She grabbed my hands so tight it almost hurt.

"Stop being so dramatic, Belle, what is it?" I asked.

"There's visual confirmation on Leon McAllister and—You. Know. Who," she said.

There had been rumors for weeks that something was going on between the grieving widower and the high and mighty, Mrs. Odell Brinkley. Several of us on the prayer chain had been keeping our eyes open, and had noted that the two seemed nowhere to be found at regular intervals. Usually on the Tuesdays when Lola was minding the store or Sunday afternoons when Mrs. Brinkley used to always be working at the courthouse, but was now otherwise engaged. Of course no one wanted to spread idle gossip, so we'd all kept it under our hats for the moment. At least until we had something more solid.

"So?" I asked.

"At the store this morning, Eupha Lovelady stopped by to pick up a bottle of Breck, and she said she walked right in on the two in a passionate embrace, right there in the store," Belle said.

I just shook my head. Everybody knew Eupha Lovelady exaggerated beyond belief. "Belle, there's a reason why Eupha's called Times Three. You gotta take everything she says and divide it by three," I said.

"I know that Peggy, that's why I asked her, now Eupha, what did you exactly see? Well, sure enough she didn't actually see them, but she said you could tell. Sadie was practically out of breath on the other side of the store, and Leon's hair was all tussled," Belle said.

"Is that it?" I asked.

Belle just stood there, milking out the moment. "There was lipstick, clear as day on Leon's cheek," she said with a flourish. "Mango peach."

That settled it. Everybody in town knew that Sadie Brinkley bought every stick of mango peach in a thirty mile radius, just to keep them all for herself.

"That's just awful," I said, trying hard not to hop. "Poor Odell." Odell Brinkley had more money than God. *But I guess riches don't guarantee happiness.*

"I think we oughta put him on our prayer list," I said to Belle.

Mrs. Odell Brinkley

If I was expecting fireworks from Odell, then I should have known better. He put the napkin down beside his plate just as calm as could be. I could see his lip swell as he fished some corn out of that spot on his eyeteeth where it caught.

"Now Honey, where have you come to get it in your mind that we need a divorce?" he asked. He pronounced the word, "dee-vorce" like someone on Hee Haw and I rolled my eyes at his grammar.

Then all of a sudden I saw it from Odell's perspective

for once. Living for twenty years with a woman constantly correcting you. Who spent all her time fixing everything up just so, and never seemed to be satisfied with who you were, but was forever trying to turn you into someone else. *I wonder how it is he's lasted this long.*

"You can't be happy with how things are," I said.

"Shit. Happy? What the hell's happiness got to do with marriage?" he asked, sincerely. He got up from the table and walked toward the den. On the way, he leaned over and pecked me on the back of my head with his lips. "People's only happy in the movies, Sadie. You're old enough to know that." He walked away and after a moment, I heard the television come on from the other room.

He was right of course. I cleared the dishes, putting each one in the dishwasher before I filled up the little triangle in the door with detergent. After I closed the door, I pulled it out from under the counter and connected the hose to the kitchen faucet. I lifted the handle and turned the knob to heavy wash. When I heard the water kick in, I stopped and looked around the kitchen.

Everything was spotless, as was the entire house. Odell had a chance to start over clean if he wanted. I remembered what Trudy told Leon about me. *I suppose I have left this house better than I found it. It's how I was raised.*

I wiped my hands on the cloth on the counter then folded it square. I walked out through the kitchen door, past the azalea bushes and right past my car sitting in the drive. When I turned to walk down the dirt road that led to Main Street, I didn't look back.

All the way down the street, I did nothing but look straight ahead. For the first time in my life, I really did feel like I was in a movie. When I saw the light from the Pepsi machine on the front porch of V.R.'s and could make out Leon sitting in the swing, I started to run.

Lola McAllister

For the first time in as long as I could remember, I sat still on the sofa in my living room. There was nothing in the oven, no plaster frames setting, no laundry soaking in the sink, no half-finished macramé project or leftover visitation cards to follow up on for Vacation Bible School.

Finally, alone and quiet, I told myself it was time. I reached into the jeweled box and took out Dip's arrowhead for the first time in years. I forced myself to hold it in both my hands in front of me while I rocked gently back and forth. I took a deep breath in and out. In and out. As much as I wanted to stop right then and do something else, I made myself keep breathing. The first few minutes I got a dizzy feeling, like what I had always imagined it would be like to smoke pot. Then I pushed through that and I didn't feel dizzy anymore, I felt solid. For what seemed like forever, my mind kept darting from one project to another, making plans in spite of myself. I couldn't seem to will it to stop working, so I just stopped trying. Then I noticed that I wasn't aware of what I'd been thinking about for a little while. It was like all of a sudden I came to myself and found that I wasn't exactly sure of where I'd been.

I saw Ida during some of those thoughts. She was there correcting, pronouncing and denouncing this that or the other. In my mind, she turned from herself into the little girl I'd seen in her old pictures she kept in the dresser in the guest bedroom. Pigtails and a wool petticoat, still correcting, but with a little girl's voice that sounded sweet and faint. And even though she was bossing and throwing tantrums, I just looked at her the way I did a little girl who didn't know better. I smiled and picked her up. She was light as a feather and every time she started to talk, I pulled her head to me and stroked her hair. When she fought me, I started to sing.

Finally she fell asleep in my arms and I noticed Cain was there too. I reached out and took his hand. I thought to myself, the best thing I can do as a parent is to be a whole person. To not need my child to fill some empty part of me that never seems satisfied. Then I let go of Cain's hand and kept rocking. When I looked down, little Ida was gone as well. For a moment, I swear to God, I felt Dip beside me. I knew he wasn't really there but when I opened up my hands, the arrowhead was gone. I came back to myself and looked at the clock. For three hours I'd been sitting there, doing nothing in particular. I was all alone in the room, but for once, I wasn't afraid.

Chapter 26

Anything To Hold on To

Cain McAllister

Mark and me had been waiting behind the puppet stage for Macy for about an hour. He had snuck out of the house that morning while Brother Neil was doing his morning prayers in his office.

"She promised she'd try to come," I said.

"I wish you'd of come got me when you went to see her," Mark said.

"The only time I could go was in the afternoon," I said.

"I know, don't worry about it," he said. "There's no way I coulda got away from Daddy then anyway. I just don't like the thought of Macy leaving without me seeing her."

"I think she's going to run away from home," I said.

"Did she tell you that?" he asked.

"No, but I gave her some money," I said.

"How much?"

"Three hundred seventeen dollars."

"I don't know if that was too good an idea," he said. "Macy don't need to be out by herself."

"I think things are really bad," I said, fiddling with the hair on one of the puppets with my hand. Then I looked up and said, "with her dad."

He didn't seem to know what I meant. Then I said, "I think. I think maybe he does stuff to her."

"Why do you think that?" Mark asked. I didn't want to tell him, but he grabbed the puppet out of my hand and asked again. "Why do you think that?" When I still didn't answer he said, "Doggonnit, Cain, if something's the matter, we gotta tell each other. That's what friends do. Tell me what she said."

Then the curtain from the puppet stage started to sway and I felt the whole building shake a little.

Brother Neil

In my study that morning, each time I bowed to pray, I found that my thoughts wandered elsewhere to some of the preparations being made for Brother Preston's arrival. It didn't help that it was almost a hundred degrees outside. The little window air unit was trying in vain to cool my office, but the heat was winning the battle, so I decided to cut my time short and go see how the preparations were coming along at the church.

As I walked by Mark's door I thought about knocking and asking him to come next door with me to look things over. He must have been sweltering with the door shut. He'd hardly spoken to me since the day I forbid him to ever talk to those children again. Each time I'd made any effort to include him in the preparations at church, he'd politely declined with nothing more than a no, sir. It was his way of punishing me. I didn't want anything to dampen my enthusiasm, so I decided to let him be and left the house to go over to the church.

When I walked into the sanctuary, I was more than a little impressed with what Mrs. Leggett and the ladies had done with it. In keeping with the Revelations theme, they'd decorated the entire sanctuary like the battlefield of Armageddon. On the right were God's angels prepared for battle and on the left, the forces of Satan. Both walls were covered with butcher paper from top to bottom, on which were drawn scenes taken from scripture.

At the front of the sanctuary was a tall dragon figure made of chicken wire covered in different colored tissues. As I was admiring it, the large head swiveled, causing me to jump.

"It's really something, ain't it?" a voice from inside the dragon said.

I tried to look down the thing's mouth, but could see nothing. "Uh, yes it is," I said.

Then I saw a person backing out of a slit in the side of the fabric covering the dragon's body, as if the creature were having a breach birth. The birthed thing wiggled for a bit causing the entire beast to quake, then the bleached white hair of Peggy Leggett appeared.

"I got my cousin Jimmy to come down and help. He does Christmas floats for Goldsmith's down in Memphis. He did a real good job."

"It looks wonderful, Mrs. Leggett. It all does," I said.

"Please Brother Neil, you know you can call me Peggy," she said while she pushed her hair away from her eyes and over her ears.

When I had confessed to the church about my lapse in judgment, I expected I might be run out of town on a rail. The effect had been quite the opposite. Male members of the congregation with whom I'd always had trouble connecting had taken me aside to explain their understanding of the temptations. The women, instead of shunning me for doing what they all feared their husbands might, had become more friendly, a few even flirtatious, as if my lust somehow reflected on their own personal charm.

"Well, Mrs. Leggett, you know I'm from Mississippi, and we have a hard time calling a lady anything other than Mrs. down there," I said.

Giggling, she patted my arm with her hand. "Always a gentleman," she said, tracing one finger down to my elbow.

I turned back to the dragon, genuinely impressed with its size and appearance. "Now, how will this work?" I asked.

"Well, Jimmy's going to be in here," she said as she guided me over to the side and lifted the fabric. Inside I saw a little space about the size of a barrel.

As if reading my mind, she said, "He's just a little thing, skinny as a stick. It was a tighter fit for me," she said. I looked again at the space inside and thought it surely must have been. She fanned herself. "It's sure gonna be hot enough in here tonight. It really will feel like the end of the world!" she said. "But don't worry, Jimmy was the Injun Runnin' Joe mascot over at Arkansas State for three years. He can handle the heat." As I stepped away to take a broader look, I noticed the cross above the baptistery swaying. Then the room quivered, and Mrs. Leggett grabbed my arm for support.

"Goodness, we must be having a quake," she said,

leaning closer than I'd like.

"Must be," I said. I had felt several tremors that morning during my prayers. After a moment, it subsided and I tried to direct her attention back to our task. "You've all done fine work."

"Whenever you like, he can move the head back and forth, or you mentioned you'd like to be able to put stuff in its mouth or take it out. You can do that, see," she said putting her hand down the dragon's throat and pulling out a puppet with straight black hair and red lips. "For dramatic effect," she said.

"In the scripture, it talks about three unclean spirits springing from the dragon's mouth like frogs," I said.

"Well, I believe we've got some frog puppets up in children's church. You want to go with me to look?" she asked smiling.

"No, you stay here and finish up. I'll go check," I said, hoping to get out while I could.

"You sure you don't need some company?" she asked.

"I need to finish my prayer time, but I'll be back to check the progress," I said and headed quickly toward the door.

Cain McAllister

I didn't want to tell Mark what I thought about Macy because I wasn't one hundred percent sure. But he kept asking until I told him about the time a few weeks ago when Macy and I were walking in the cemetery one Sunday with her grandmother. Mrs. Hollister was off at her husband's grave while Macy and me walked barefoot down the rows. It had rained that morning and the grass was still wet. Macy stopped by a little stone, flush with the ground. It was old concrete, barely raised up in a curve, like the top part of a buried tire. It read "Infant Ross, 1938." Macy ran her hand over the letters that were so worn down you could hardly read them.

"I could tell she was thinking about her baby," I said.

"I know about that," Mark said. "I stayed there that day Daddy caught us in the baptismal pool and he yelled at her about it."

"I stayed too," I said. "Do you think it's wrong, what Macy did?" I asked.

"No, Cain, I don't. It's easy for people like Daddy to say what's right and what's wrong 'cause he's running the show. Least he thinks he is. Truth is that he don't know what God thinks any more than you or me. He's just good at pretending like he does. Did Macy tell you it was her Dad's?" Mark asked.

"No," I said. "But when I asked whose baby it was, all she would say is that she hated its father more than anything else in this whole world over. That the baby was better off in Heaven than here on earth with a father like that."

"She's right about that," Mark said.

Then I told him about the Sunday at church when Macy was there with her dad and how she pulled away from him when they sat down. "Yesterday, when I went to see her, she said the same thing again. That she hated her dad more than anything in this whole world over," I said.

"That don't mean he did that to her," Mark said.

"You didn't hear the way she said it. She had the exact same look." I said. "That's when I knew she wouldn't go home."

Mark put his finger over his mouth and said, "Shh." I heard the door open and then footsteps coming toward us. It was dead quiet for a second and then all of a sudden the puppet stage pulled away, and the white tubing that held it up fell all around us. I looked up and Brother Neil was standing there, the curtain balled up in his hand.

"Get out from behind there right now!" he yelled.

"Daddy, we were just–," Mark started to say.

Brother Neil swung his arm up in the air and slapped Mark's face hard, and yelled, "Shut up!"

Mark fell down beside me and I reached across to put my hand on his shoulder. Brother Neil grabbed my arm and pulled me up off the ground. "Get your hands off him!" I heard something snap and screamed out in pain.

"Stop it, you hurt him," Mark said, but Brother Neil ignored him and dragged me by the arm over to one of the wooden chairs and tossed me into the seat.

"Brother Neil!" a voice yelled from down the hallway. "Brother Neil!" When he turned toward the door, Mark ran over to me and put his hand on my shoulder. I cried out in pain when he touched it.

"Brother Neil!" the voice cried again.

Brother Neil looked back at Mark with his arm

around me and said, "You disgust me."

Mrs. Hollister ran into the room, breathing hard, holding an envelope against her chest. "Brother Neil! Macy has run away," she said in between deep breaths. "She took my car this morning and there's no telling where she's gone. I come to see if the boys know where I can find her." She handed Brother Neil the envelope and looked over at Mark and me. "She left this in her room. It's full of money." Mrs. Hollister started to shake, and said, "Trent's gone out looking for her, but I don't know what I should do!"

Brother Neil asked, "Do either of you boys know where Macy went?"

"No, sir," Mark said.

"Can you explain this?" Brother Neil asked me, holding out a wad of money he took from the envelope. I just shook my head. *I'm not telling you. You'll just send her back to her daddy.*

"Fine." Brother Neil said. He took Mrs. Hollister by the arm and turned toward the door. "Come downstairs Mrs. Hollister, we'll get on the phone to the state police."

After they left, Mark asked me, "Are you okay?"

"Mark, I think I know where Macy went," I said.

He touched my arm and I cried out as a pain shot down it.

"We got to go get your Mom to take us to a doctor," he said.

"No. There ain't no time. I think Macy's gone to the bridge," I said, standing up.

"Why would she go there?"

"To jump," I said.

The bridge was at least twenty miles away, so we ran

to Momma Jewel's house and took the keys from the little hook beside her kitchen door. Even though I was better at driving than Mark, I couldn't seem to move my arm at all, so he drove. I screamed when he swerved the car on the loose gravel and my shoulder hit the passenger side door. It didn't hurt as much as at first, as long as I didn't touch it. I winced again when he made the turn in the old blue Vega onto the road running beside the river picking up speed.

If it was much higher, this would all be covered in water. The idea of it made me dizzy so I tried to think of something else. *Please God, let Macy be okay,* I prayed.

I saw Mrs. Hollister's car as soon as we pulled up to the long arching green beams of the partially built bridge. The Nova was pulled over along the side of the road where all the bulldozers were parked next to a huge barge tied to the shore, covered with pipes and big concrete pillars, poking out into the river like a long black pier.

A hot wind blew off the river like a person's breath in your face. Mark pulled the car up as close as he could. By the time we climbed over the silver gate and ran down the path toward the foundation of the bridge, my shoulder ached, but felt more numb than anything else.

Mark saw Macy first. She was way up the scaffolding that ran along the large beams. They spanned halfway across the river, leading to the highest point in the middle before dropping off. A third of the way up, on one of the beams, Macy sat with her feet dangling over the side. Mark yelled but she didn't seem to hear him. Immediately he started up the rails, climbing ten feet before I even got to the side where he had dropped the keys to the car.

Being that close to the river made my legs feel weak

and heavy, like I was standing in mud. I hollered for Macy as well, but she wouldn't move. It took Mark about five minutes to get close enough for her to turn her head toward him.

"Macy," Mark yelled. "Come to me."

The little waves on the bank started to seep up toward me over the mud and when I looked up at the bridge, I noticed the wooden boards between the beams falling all around Mark. A section of the scaffolding toward the bank gave way, slowly falling off from the side toward the center like a line of tinsel falling from a Christmas tree. Underneath me, I felt the ground move and it knocked me to my knees on the grassy bank. By the time I looked back up, Mark and Macy were both gone.

Macy Hollister

It feels so nice, I thought as I felt a breeze all over my hot body and realized I was falling. I heard a voice calling my name. A rush of cold. And then everything was black and I hoped that I was finally asleep.

Cain McAllister

I got to my feet and searched for them both in the wide river. Mark waved his hand at me and then I saw Macy just before a piece of the steel frame from the bridge fell onto her and she disappeared under the water. I yelled to Mark and pointed to where Macy had been but I didn't think he could hear me. Large pieces of the steel scaffolding were still falling all around him.

He dove under the water and when he came up, he had Macy in his arms. He started swimming toward the bank, trying to keep both their heads above the water. He took short strokes and dragged Macy behind him. After what seemed like forever, they finally seemed to get a little closer. Macy's eyes were shut and her mouth was just under the line of the water.

Then another earthquake came, this one stronger than the last and knocked me back down. I fell onto my shoulder and the pain tore at me again. I could see Mark and Macy getting closer to the bank. Mark switched places and started to push Macy in front of him as he swam behind.

"Cain, help," he yelled. "Come pull her to shore."

I got up off the ground and stepped into the water, not allowing myself to stop. I pretended it was a dare and like Macy I didn't flinch. My feet sank into the thick muddy riverbed. Once I got out past my knees, then past my waist, I replaced my fears with motion and waded out to my chest and reached out for Macy.

My right arm hung useless at my side and I used the other one to grab her by the foot when Mark pushed her toward me. From behind, Mark held her head above the water and pushed us both.

"I can feel ground," Mark said. "Keep pushing."

I hardly noticed the water collecting around my mouth. I still felt my feet in the mud and Macy's foot in my hand. I pulled her toward me and got my arm around her waist, and started pushing her while Mark put his hands against my back and pushed as well. We were all moving slowly toward the shore. One step, then another. Then the next step was nothing.

The water rushed around me all at once and I slipped into it, gasping for breath, as I caught glimpses of Mark pulling Macy on top of him by the shore. I reached out my hand then something pulled me under and away.

Whatever had hold of me seemed to come from every direction. I tasted the gritty water in my mouth and tried not to swallow. The more I fought the river, the more my arm felt like it was torn from my side and floating next to me, unattached. Then I stopped struggling. I let every muscle go limp and kept completely still. Something moved me along so smoothly that I felt weightless. It was like the water flowed through me instead of around.

Suspended, I rocked gently back and forth with the pulsing rush and thought, *I must be drowned.*

Macy Hollister

Is it over? Is it over? Is it over? I kept asking, but there was no answer.

I woke up and felt the water lapping against my legs. Then I felt the hot sun against my face and chest and after a moment, I opened my eyes. It was as quiet as dawn. I sat up in the shallow water on the bank of the river. I didn't recognize anything at first. I saw part of the bridge, towering above me to one side and the old barge off the shore to the other. Between the two was only the river, dark and smooth. Peaceful.

Cain McAllister

I felt air come into my lungs. Something hard scraped against my side, cutting into me and everywhere I reached out with my arms, I felt something hard, then water, then little pockets of air. I tried to breathe again but each time the current pulled me back under. I flailed both my arms trying to get hold of what was all around me, but untouchable. I turned in the water and felt my breath leave my lungs while my hand hit against something so hard and cold and flat. It was so dark. The current pulled my legs until it seemed like they were above me as I tried to find a grip. Something. Anything to hold on to.

Macy Hollister

They need me. I put my hand against my forehead and saw the blood when I brought it down. That was when I remembered everything. I jumped to my feet and called out for Mark and Cain. About thirty feet out in the river, I saw Mark's blonde hair pop up, then down again. Just beyond him, right next to the barge, I spotted Cain's legs in the water, kicking back and forth. Mark surfaced again, this time on the far side of Cain toward the open river. He took a deep breath and disappeared underneath the barge next to Cain.

Cain McAllister

Something pushed against me. I pushed back, then it pushed again. I felt another hand in mine. Fingers between my fingers. A body against mine. Pushing. Pushing again.

I knew Mark was there. I couldn't see him, but I felt him all around me and knew. He pushed me again and I pulled him closer to me. I couldn't think of anything else but pulling whatever was within my reach to myself. But Mark pushed me away. I felt his legs kicking into me and the last of the air leave my body from the blows. The water rushed inside me, and Mark kicked and kicked again. I felt his hands on my chest and his face close to mine. He grabbed my head, pressed his lips against mine and breathed into my mouth. Then he pushed me violently away and I was swept up into the air.

Macy Hollister

Don't give up. I pulled Cain up out of the water and toward me. He coughed and swung his arms as I dragged him through the mud to the bank. I looked for Mark but couldn't see him anywhere. Beside the river, I held Cain close and prayed to God that Mark would come back up.

But God won't hear my prayers. He never has.

Cain McAllister

Once I caught my breath, Macy went back to her grandmother's car to go get help from town. She tried to get me to go with her, but I wouldn't. I stayed there and searched the river's surface for any sign. I told myself that maybe Mark found a space of air underneath the barge. That as soon as help got there, they'd be able to send someone down to get him out. That he was going to be okay. I started hollering so that he could hear me if he was under there. I kept saying, "I'm here, Mark, I'm here. Macy's bringing help. I'm here!"

When Brother Neil got there, he ran past me and straight into the water. I watched him from the banks until Momma came and put her arms around me and led me away to the ambulance. I looked back and saw several men walk into water. I tried to make Momma let me stay, but she kept pulling me away and I was worried Mark would think that I didn't wait for him.

Chapter Twenty Seven

Blasphemy

Brother Neil

It was my first time back in the pulpit since the accident. I stood before the congregation and tried to catch my breath before I began. I could see the sympathetic looks in the eyes of everyone looking back at me. Several said I should have waited a few more weeks before coming back, but I'd always preached that hardships could strengthen your faith if only you let them.

I cleared my throat and said, "Everything I've ever thought has been wrong."

I had almost been pulled into the current a few times when one of the local river rescue squad members came out in a boat and tried to get me to get in. I refused. He finally convinced me to put a rope around my waist that he tied to the end of the barge. By that time, I was joined in the water by several others. I heard one of them say that another crew had been sent to Big Slough Bend down river. I knew this was where the water formed a natural pool that collected most of the floating objects in the river.

It was some time later when one of the men called out, "Over here!"

I was diving on the opposite side of the barge from the voice and tried to swim along the side, but couldn't keep from being pushed into the metal by the strong current, so I had to put hand over fist and work my way around. As I rounded the corner, I saw that one of the men, backing away toward the bank, held my son from behind, just under the arms. The rescuer pulled him toward the bank with slow steady heaves that shook his little body, yet Mark's face was peaceful and still, his arms outstretched. *The last time I had seen my boy, I hit that face,* was all I could think.

I went over as fast as I could and grabbed my son. The man resisted at first. The rescue worker next to him held out his arm and put it on the man's shoulder. "It's his son," he said. At this the man released Mark and I pulled him to my chest, his face leaning into my shoulder. My feet sank in the mud as I worked my way out of the water. They tried to take him from me when I couldn't make it up the side of the bank, but I refused to let go. Finally the two men behind me pushed me up while another pulled the rope that was still tied around my waist and leading back to the water.

With Mark still pressed against me, I managed to get to the top of the bank. I laid him down on the ground. Someone pushed me aside and began to do CPR on his body. I sat down and looked away. I knew that he was gone. I reached out and held his cold hand in mine. Crinkles were what he called them, when he was a little boy. The little indentations on his fingertips when he stayed too long in the tub. The rope still ran from me, into the water and across to the side of the barge. After several minutes the man doing CPR finally gave up and put his hand on my shoulder.

"I'm sorry," he said, then stood up. I took Mark's hand and folded his arms across his chest and lifted him toward me, putting his back in my lap, his head against my shoulder, and rocked him while I kissed the side of his forehead.

Looking out on my congregation, I finally understood the weight those of us bear who called ourselves servants of the Lord. Realizing the love they felt, the guidance they sought and faith they gave, I couldn't help but see my own shortcomings and pride. I had prayed for a revival thinking it would come in the ways I expected. *How arrogant. To think I knew all the answers.* A true revival requires a dying of our old ideas and the allowing of God to breathe life into something new and alive.

"Those few moments with my son were the most beautiful of my life," I said before stopping to wipe my cheeks. I saw many people in the congregation do the same. "I'm not proud of that. I should have understood much sooner. You may ask how something like that can be beautiful. Beauty, I've come to believe, is not something pleasing to the eye. It is something vibrant. And like a brilliant white light, it contains all the colors of the spectrum. Those were the most vivid moments I have ever experienced. There was a beauty inside the pain, and I felt a love from God that I'd never known before that moment. I know now what Paul meant when he said the scales fell from his eyes."

I paused a few moments before I continued. "I would like to thank everyone for their support during this time," I said. I knew what I had to do, but found it difficult all the same.

"I wanted to let you know that today will be my last Sunday in the pulpit."

At this there were a few mumbles in the sanctuary, but I didn't hear much other than my heart beating fast in my chest. "Two weeks ago I stood right here and quoted a scripture about the just punishment of the wicked by a joyful God. That exact scripture is Deuteronomy, chapter twenty-eight, verse sixty-three." I opened my Bible to the page and continued, "It reads, 'And it shall come to pass, that as the Lord rejoiced over you to do you good, and to multiply you; so the Lord will rejoice over you to destroy you, and to bring you nought; and ye shall be plucked from off the land whither thou goest to possess it.'"

The tears welled up in my eyes again before I could speak. *How could I have been so deceived*?

"I want to apologize to you. To all of you who have suffered tragedy in this life. Who have lost people you love. I'm ashamed that I ever spewed those despicable words."

I heard their uncomfortable reaction, but continued anyway, unsure of what I would say next until it came from my mouth. "The God I have come to know these past weeks could never rejoice in this kind of suffering. What this does to my faith and belief, I don't yet know. However, I do know that I reject those particular words. I reject the idea that God ever put them down on paper."

"This is just blasphemy!" Dulan Meacham said, springing to his feet.

"The man's lost his son, Dulan," someone said from behind him.

"Are you saying you don't believe the Bible no

more?" Dulan asked loudly.

"I'm saying that I can't accept that God rejoices in any way in the suffering of anyone," I said. "If, in your opinion, that means I don't believe the Bible, then so be it."

"My opinion?" Dulan said. "My opinion don't mean diddly. It's what the word of God says!"

"God has told me differently, that's all," I said, with no fight in the words.

"Sit down, Dulan. The man is grieving," Bud Leggett said.

His wife Peggy bristled and looked at her husband like she didn't know him. "That's no excuse to blaspheme the word of God," she said, holding up her Bible and waving it back and forth. She stood to her feet and said to everyone, "Without the word of God, there's nothing to separate us from any heathen on the street!"

Lola McAllister stood up in her pew about three rows back and said, "You got a lot of nerve, Peggy Leggett, to stand there and think you're better than any so-called heathen on the street." Peggy's shoulders drew up when she recognized Lola's voice, but she refused to turn around.

Lola went on, "You've never shown anything but spite and contempt for almost every person in this church."

Someone called out, "Amen to that," rather loudly, and then another was murmured. Peggy darted her eyes around the room looking for the source of the 'Amens,' one of which originated remarkably close to her best friend Belle, who, when Peggy eyed her suspiciously, just looked in the opposite direction. Peggy swung around to face Lola like a snake, ready to strike.

"Lola, we *all* know what kind of woman you are," Peggy said, taking a long look straight at Cain and then at myself up in the pulpit. Lola protectively put her arm around Cain's shoulder. Peggy thrust the Bible in her hand in Lola's direction and shook it. "If I weren't a good Christian woman, I'd take this Bible and beat you to death with it!"

Lola said slowly but firm, "You wave that book at me or my child one more time, Peggy Leggett, and I will shove it up your ass." The way she said it reminded me of her sister, Trudy. I couldn't help but laugh, the sound echoing through my microphone across the congregation. Peggy took shallow, hurried breathes and huffed as she turned to face the pulpit and sat back down. She moved her head slightly to the side, and said out of the corner of her mouth, "Harlot!"

"Go to hell, Peggy," Lola said and then sat back down, a slow smile crossing her face.

"What exactly are you saying then, Brother Neil?" another deacon asked.

"I'm saying I have questions," I said. "Before now I had the luxury of believing that everything in this world had a simple answer. Now, that I see things differently, I'm ashamed I spoke before with so much certainty and so little compassion."

"What kind of Christian is it that don't think the Bible answers all those questions?" Dulan asked. Peggy said a loud "Amen to that."

There was an uncomfortable silence for a few moments and I found myself at a loss for what else to say.

Then Momma Jewel stood up from her seat next to

Lola. "I've got something I need to get off my chest," she said with an apologetic look on her face. "I think what the preacher means is that we all got questions about some things. The truth of the matter is that when it comes down to it, I don't even believe in Hell." There were a few gasps from here and there around the room.

She took a deep breath and continued, "I'm sorry, I never have. I was just too afraid to say anything to anybody. It don't make no sense to me. I know how I love my children and there's nothing they could do that would make me let them go to hell. Even if they wanted to. I just flat out don't believe in it. I guess if that means I ain't a good Christian, then so be it."

She sat back down and a few people here and there started to discreetly gather their things, worried, I was sure, about what might come next. Then Hickory Milow, the chairman of the deacons, threw his arm up in the air and blurted out, "I believe in evolution!"

His wife, Belle, yanked at his arm, trying to pull it back down.

"I'm sorry Hon, but I do," he said, standing up and then said to the room, "It's just good science. Does that mean I'm not a good Christian either?"

Peggy Leggett sprung out of her pew and around to the front of the sanctuary, her Bible still clutched in her hand. She pointed her finger back and forth across the room.

"Lies! Lies!" she screamed. "Straight from the pit of hell! Which is exactly where you're all going, whether you believe in it or not, Jewel McAllister," she said giving Momma Jewel a nasty look. "I guess we know now why the McAllisters have suffered such tragedy in their pathetic little lives, don't we? Maybe it's your sin what got Dip killed over there in Vietnam!"

I saw tears streaming down Momma Jewel's face and a shame settled in on me as I realized this was the logical conclusion to the words I'd preached for years. I couldn't even feel anger at Peggy's cruelty, for she was simply giving voice to the message I had so foolishly and arrogantly endorsed for most of my life. Before I knew true loss.

"You leave my family alone," Lola McAllister said, jumping to her feet and walking quickly down the aisle toward Peggy. I watched helplessly from the pulpit as the members in the congregation began to argue among themselves.

Peggy took a deep breath and shouted, "It's just like the Bible says, God is rejoicing in bringing you to nought. Y'all better take back everything you said, lest God strike you down right here!"

Lola grabbed the Bible out of Peggy's hands. "Peggy, I swear if I have to, I'll knock the holy shit right out of you." Peggy put her fists up like a ridiculous boxer in training, ready to take Lola on and the crowd silenced.

Then the sound of ripping filled the room, and Peggy whirled around to see me holding a torn page in my hand, a look of utter horror plastered on her face as she realized what I had done.

"You see this!" I held the paper up to the congregation. "This is what I'm going to do with every page in this book that doesn't speak to my heart as the truth of God's love!"

I said it with more true conviction than I'd ever felt in my life. In my hand I crumpled the paper and threw it into the baptismal pool behind me, feeling something like joy coming over me. Across the sanctuary, I heard first one rip, then several others.

"Don't just listen to me!" I said. "Discern for yourself what God puts on your heart!" I started to pace across the stage, feeling a charge of excitement. "Don't let anyone tell you who God is. You figure it out for yourself. What the world could accomplish if people started thinking for themselves!" Half the room broke out into applause and several others headed for the doors.

Excitedly, I said "Now, turn with me to First Samuel, Chapter two, verses two through three." I heard a flurry of turning pages all around me. The sound had always thrilled me as I preached and that day it was so much sweeter than ever before. I read from the book, "Thus saith the Lord of hosts, I remember that which Amalek did to Israel, how he laid wait for him in the way, when he came up from Egypt. Now go and smite Amalek, and utterly destroy all that they have, and spare them not; but slay both man and woman, infant and suckling, ox and sheep, camel and ass." I let the words sink in.

"Secretly, this verse has always troubled me," I said. I ripped the page out of my Bible and held it up in my fist. "I don't believe God would order the killing of little babies like that no more than I believe in the man in the moon!" Across the sanctuary the pages ripped as several shouted, "Amen, Brother!"

"This book, that I love with all my heart," I said. "I fear has been made into a golden calf of idolatry, relieving us all of the responsibility to seek God for ourselves."

About half the congregation had either run out or was leaving at this point. But a good number was staying put, their faces looking at mine with great enthusiasm. The rest of the service, one by one they stood up and shared their beliefs and doubts. We talked about the Bible verses that troubled us, those that inspired us, and those that had changed our lives for the good. Well into the afternoon, we shared our thoughts on predestination, the rapture, literal versus metaphorical interpretations. All kinds of things. We talked, argued, laughed and cried together—as God's people, telling the truth.

None was more surprised than myself by the events of that day. Some called it blasphemy, but all I can say in my defense is that where the Spirit leads, I must follow. There was real love in that room as we all searched our hearts and fearlessly lay our hopes and doubts before the Lord. Being a true follower of God is a tough responsibility with many unanswered questions. Anyone who says differently is selling something. The Lord knows my heart.

Every single night for the rest of my life as I lay in bed, I will remember the words I said to young Macy that day I found them all together in the baptistery. The words my heart fears led her to that bridge the day my son died.

"Nothing but heartache will follow you the rest of your life," I had told her with complete self-assurance and righteousness over what I believed she had done. How those words must have sounded to a wounded young girl, abused by a parent charged to love her, condemned by the society meant to nurture her, and abandoned by a faith called to embrace her.

"I'll not get my son back in this life," I told the congregation that day from the pulpit. "But I'll be damned if I send anyone else's out into this world with anything other than God's overwhelming love and acceptance."

Cain McAllister

About fifty or so other people stayed into the afternoon having a discussion about what everyone believed. A few of the men had some words here and there, but they all laughed about it too. When it finally wound down, Brother Neil asked me if I would lead us in a closing prayer.

I hadn't seen or talked to Brother Neil in the weeks since Mark died. I figured he hated me still, but when he asked me to lead the prayer, he smiled at me when he said it. I'd never led a prayer in front of adults like that before. Momma squeezed my hand and stood up beside me with her arm around my shoulder. I looked around the room, a little hesitant, but saw that everyone had their heads bowed and eyes closed. Momma smiled and bowed her head too.

"Dear God," I said, kinda quiet at first. "Could you please watch over us all and help us when we need it? Could you let us know how we can help other people when they need it? Will you please bless Macy, God, and keep her safe. We thank you for this church, God, and we thank you for our food, and our friends. We ask that you be with Brother Neil and Mrs. McElroy because I know they miss Mark a lot."

I couldn't help but cry when I thought about Mark. Momma Jewel reached out and put a tissue into my hand.

"He's a great best friend," I said. "I know you and him are going to have a lot of fun together. Show us how we can all be that kind of a friend to each other. In Jesus' name, Amen."

EPILOGUE

Greater Love

Cain McAllister

After that Bible-ripping Sunday sermon of Brother Neil's made the state news, the congregation divided into two factions and the Southern Baptist Convention put the church on probation until a victor was declared. Once Brother Neil's followers succeeded in gaining control of the deacons and the building, the Baptists made it official and kicked them out of the convention. In a press release they stated, "It is with great sorrow that we part ways with our brothers and sisters in Lost Cain, Arkansas. However, the integrity and absolute infallibility of God's Word remains, to our congregations, the bedrock of our faith and beyond questioning."

Brother Neil took the news in stride, naming his new church, "God's Amazing Grace Fellowship," and filling the pews practically every Sunday for years. Some folks said that Brother Neil didn't preach the Bible there, but they were wrong. He covered all the important parts, at least.

When he learned from me what was going on in Macy's home, Brother Neil confronted her father and told Trent Hollister that he'd move heaven and earth to make sure he never saw his daughter again. Macy moved in with her grandmother until Mrs. Hollister had a stroke in 1983. Then Brother Neil and Mrs. McElroy asked her if she'd come stay with them, which she did. One of the proudest days in my life was when my best friend Macy called me from college one day and asked me to meet her at a little Chapel over in Eureka Springs so I could walk her down the aisle and give her away to a man who loved her even more than I did. They live down in Memphis, but visit the McElroys regularly. Macy is an oncology nurse and her husband, a computer programmer. The last time I saw them we all picnicked together at the park in Jonesboro where Brother Neil had founded a free medical clinic, all three of Macy's kids ran up and jumped into Brother Neil's arms, calling him Papaw.

After I left for college in 1986, Momma moved to Blytheville. She had married a man she met one summer when the air-conditioner went out and she went to work at the credit union to get the money to buy a new one. He was good to her, and she said that after he survived the first year, she started breathing a lot easier. Mammy Pico thoroughly approves of the match, him being a banker and all. At ninety-eight, she runs a tight ship at the assisted living home where she lives in Memphis.

Momma Jewel lived in her home until the night she passed away in 1994, surrounded by all the people who loved her and on whom she had lavished all the love a person could stand. She's buried between her husband and my father's remains at the old cemetery in Calumet.

Just a few years ago, they discovered the remains of six soldiers in a field in Vietnam. Among them were my father's wallet and a chain with his dog tags and Momma's class ring. After DNA testing, they flew Momma and me to Honolulu to reclaim the items. At the ceremony, Momma clutched the ring in her hand, putting the dog tags in mine. In his wallet there were bits of a torn picture, though you couldn't tell who it might have been. After the publicity surrounding the discovery, a man who served with Daddy called us up one afternoon. He told us that Daddy had just heard about the pregnancy in a letter from Momma Jewel before they were overrun by a North Vietnamese unit in 1967. Until then, we weren't ever sure if he had gotten word of me or not. It meant a lot to us both that he knew.

Uncle Leon and Miss B closed down the store in 1981. They bought a Winnebago, and started traveling around the country. They kept the trailer in Lost Cain for a year or two but came back less and less, so they reluctantly decided to sell. Once they finished with the United States, they traveled across the world seeing all the places Uncle Leon knew Aunt Trudy would have wanted to go. Uncle Leon passed away in 1992 from a heart attack on the Champs Elysees in Paris, France. "It wasn't a scary thing at all, not like you'd think," Miss B told me. "Leon simply said, 'Ain't that something, Sadie Lynn,' clutched his hand to his chest and was gone."

He had lived about sixty years longer than expected. As he wished, his ashes were spread over Aunt Trudy's grave. Miss B lives in Blytheville now and works at a little bookstore and volunteers at the library. I visit about twice a year when my work allows.

Miss B gave me the desire to set down in ink, the good and the bad in this world. My little attempt to preserve a moment in time so that it could be documented, remembered, regretted or cherished. I'd always wondered if I was meant to die that day on the river. An earthquake had brought me into this world, and perhaps one was meant to take me away, until Mark stepped in.

After college I wandered around, working as a newspaper reporter, a photographer, a teacher, an activist and finally a writer. The truth was that I'd always felt a little lost in all that extra time. The sacrifice Mark made for me that day took a toll on me at first. It made me feel that I had to do the good we both might have done in the world. When I was younger it drove me from one cause to another, but now that I was older, the thought brought me comfort.

"Greater love hath no man than this, that a man lay down his life for his friends." That's John 15:13, my favorite verse.

I'd been loved greatly in this life and that made me more fortunate than many. God doesn't require anything of us in this life, I believe. He simply gives each person the choice whether to love each other as we have been loved or not. The free will to choose love. It saddens me that more people don't see it that way.

And Lost Cain? Well, I guess you could say the Mississippi began to slowly take back over the day Mark McElroy drowned in its waters back in 1979. The earthquake that caused the bridge to collapse also sent a torrent of river water down Big Slough Ditch on the west side of town. For a day or two, the ditch rose back to its former glory when it was known as Devil's Spur. Eventually, they repaired the road leading to Lost Cain, but it was susceptible to frequent flooding thereafter, which helped seal its fate. The changes were gradual, but in the end, it was much cheaper to relocate everyone than to maintain the roads.

In 2008 a special River Commission decided that the land around and under Island Thirty Seven should be reflooded and returned to its natural state. A few protested at first. With neither real leadership nor a true desire to stay, they halfheartedly put up a fight. Eventually, given the fair compensation the government offered and the decaying state of the town, one by one, each family sold their property, and settled into the surrounding towns. Just as families have done in communities throughout time, they moved on.

As I walked through town one last time, the memories flooded over me as strong as any current in the river ever could. I've come to refer to what Brother Neil preached about, that Sunday after Mark's death, as the beautiful pain. Things that hurt a fraction less than they uplift, yet are somehow more vivid than any moment of pure joy. A beautiful pain was what I felt when I stood on the steps of the store and looked out at what remained of the church, Momma Jewel's house, the old gin, the empty playground, and beyond them all, the remnants of our little town.

"There's nothing left but the bones," I said quietly.

Everything of value had been stripped away and like an old Indian that the farmers used to uncover now and then while plowing the fields out by Barfield Point—all that was left were the hardened remains of something long since gone. A protrusion here, a ridge there—only a faint remembrance of the life and people that gave this place flesh and blood.

Like I had done so many times as a child, I hopped

onto the oval concrete ring around the stripped gasoline pumps and walked it like a tightrope once more before heading down Main Street for the last time.

In the eyes of the world, Lost Cain never was much to look at, and never would be. I walked back to my car and my life beyond.

But to me, it will always be the most beautiful place on earth.

The author would like to acknowledge the following people:

Allen Crowe – the novel's kind first reader whose encouragement has been unending and ever appreciated.

Molly Giles – the novel's first editor whose patience has been tested and whose insight proved true.

Ellen Gilchrist – whose guidance and humor always helped.

Victoria Pryor Gould – whose hours have been noted and with whom he'd liked to have crossed the finish line.

Regina Riney-Williams – whose indulgence for italics has been appreciated and with whom good things are hopefully to come.

Author Page

T. Daniel Wright lives and teaches in Kansas City, Missouri. His previous works have been in Theater, Film and Elvis. His plays, screenplays, and essays have attracted Oscar, Tony, and Emmy award-winning actors. *Lost Cain* is his first novel. He proudly lists 'rejected by Paul Newman' as a literary accomplishment. He hopes to complete a book of essays the fall about random celebrity encounters of a naïve country boy making a movie. He is also a strong advocate for LGBT acceptance in today's church and is always happy to speak to congregations willing to listen. You can learn more about him at tdanielwright.com

CPSIA information can be obtained at www.ICGtesting.com
Printed in the USA
BVOW08*0431130815

412947BV00002B/26/P